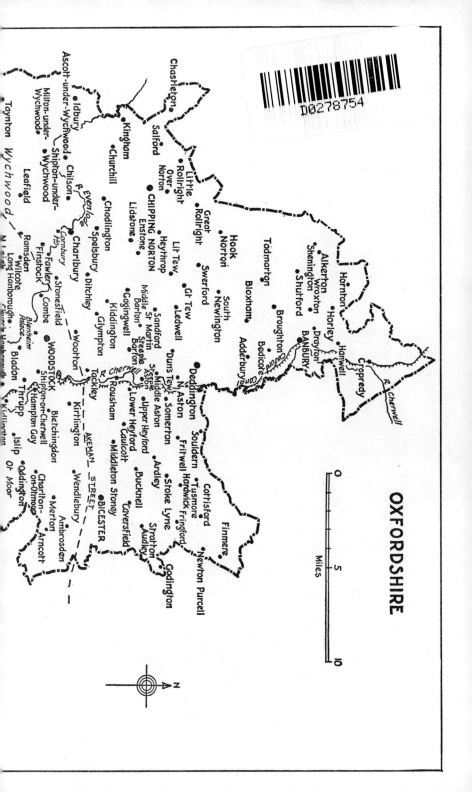

OXFORDSHIRE

Miles

0 — 5 — 10

N

THE NEW
OXFORDSHIRE
(1974)

THE MAKING OF THE ENGLISH LANDSCAPE

THE OXFORDSHIRE LANDSCAPE

THE MAKING OF THE ENGLISH LANDSCAPE
Edited by W. G. Hoskins

The Oxfordshire Landscape

by

FRANK EMERY

HODDER AND STOUGHTON
LONDON   SYDNEY   AUCKLAND   TORONTO

DR

942·572T

22 JUN 1974

FOR PAT
without whose criticism and help
this book would have been completed
sooner, but less happily

Author's Preface

In *Uncle Vanya* the country doctor, Astrov, tells Yelena about his passion for preserving Russia's forests and the old rural order:

"Now, look here. This is a picture of our district as it was fifty years ago. The dark and light green show the forests; half of the whole area was covered with forest... Besides the villages and hamlets, as you can see, little settlements were dotted about here and there, small farms, hermitages of Old Believers, water mills... Now look lower down. That's what the district was like twenty-five years ago. There was only a third of the area under timber... Now let's have a look at the map of the district as it is now... It is, as a matter of fact, a picture of gradual and unmistakable degeneration, which, I suppose, will be complete in another ten or fifteen years."[1]

Chekhov completed the play in 1896, when the Russian forests were being cut down drastically to meet demands for timber and fuel. Astrov's set of three 'period maps'— drawn by him to show the changes over fifty years—are familiar stuff to the historical geographer of landscape, whether in the context of Russia or the Thames Valley.

My intention in writing this book (probably the last to be written before the old county gives way, after a thousand years, to a new administrative unit in 1974) is to explain the making of the Oxfordshire landscape as we now see it. 'Landscape' in this context means much more than scenery, because a full landscape is constituted, directly or indirectly, by the actions of the people who live and work within it.

[1] *Chekhov: Four Plays,* translated by David Magarshack (London, 1969), pp. 94–5.

We know only too well how a new power station here or an airfield there can revolutionise in detail the appearance of a piece of countryside. If therefore we accept that in a more basic, persistent and integrated way the living landscape of Oxfordshire always had this quality of reflecting the actions of its people, then we may grasp the scope of this kind of analysis. We can ask how, when and why the land was first brought into use; which succession of man-made environments was created; why particular patterns of farms, villages, fields, roads or towns came into being; how long they lasted; and whether or not they influenced the patterns that came later.

But there is more to the historical geography of landscape than explaining the origins of things that survive. The chief lesson it tells is the constantly changing character of landscape. As new features or patterns make their appearance, sometimes rapidly and drastically, sometimes slowly and surreptitiously, older features may disappear from the landscape. Countless prehistoric sites and structures lie hidden beneath the Thames-side fields from Dorchester to Bampton; the Roman town of Alchester has vanished virtually without trace; scores of villages have been deserted, because of plague at Tusmore, conversion of arable fields to pasture at Shifford, the creation of a park at Nuneham Courtenay; great country houses have been destroyed by fire or by mere whim, Ambrosden in 1776, Rycote in 1785, Ledwell in 1790.

Because of this flux and reflux of detail in the landscape at all scales, it would be unwise to think that we can call a halt or make a standstill in the continuing progression, and there decide to explain all we happen to see at that time. We should be willing to discuss any feature we know to have had its significant place in the landscape, because it may have had an influence beyond itself on other features, past or present. In this sense the complete landscape amounts to more than the sum of its ingredients at any given point in time. If it succeeds, the book should add an extra dimension, a sense of historical origins, to even the most casual viewing of the Oxfordshire scene, so that we realise how its component parts were evolved. This reconstruction of *Altlandschaften* is particularly favoured by the German geographers, who consciously and purposely call it 'landscape history', seeing it as a legitimate and rightful part of the historical geographer's business.[2]

I have adopted the approach of isolating the main formative phases that we can trace in the making of the Oxfordshire landscape. Each phase was sufficiently distinct to emerge in its own right from the sequence of four or five thousand years during which man has moulded the natural scene, and each phase on its own or in conjunction with others has added something of itself to the texture of the landscape. They show, too, the indisputable truth that the landscape itself, its physical form and content, may be handled as a valid source of historical information. Indeed the answers to matters on which the documents or commentators are silent may be found only 'in the field', where ecologists, geographers, archaeologists, economic and social historians can all study their common questions. A Clanfield farmer has reconstructed the opening up of the arable land in the Saxon period, mapping the *balks* in his fields as the headland boundaries of old furlongs. He thinks Longlands, nearly 1,200 yards long and with the largest balks, was the nucleus of West Field, the earliest common field: "What the records and the archaeologists fail to tell us may still be found in the land and in a common-sense approach to the evidence it preserves."[3]

The first consideration we must face is that the county contains within its boundaries a number of quite distinct

---

[2] Helmut Jäger, *Progress in Historical Geography* (ed. Alan R. H. Baker, 1972), p. 61.

[3] Ernest A. Pocock, 'The First Fields in an Oxfordshire Parish', *Ag. Hist. Rev.* Vol. 16 (1968), p. 100.

landscapes. As it stands now, before the changes which will alter its shape and size after 1974, Oxfordshire (including the city of Oxford) has an area of just under 750 square miles. We can also say that it was the home of 380,800 people in 1971, growing by twenty-three per cent over the 1961 population; but fifty-one per cent of them live in what are (administratively, at any rate) rural areas, giving them the barest of holding interests over the forty-nine per cent of townspeople. But generalisations of this sort about area and population are soon overridden when we come to realise how landscape-making ran a different course in one part of the county from that in another. Due to its varying resources, attitudes and the relative placing of its districts, Oxfordshire has a fair range of natural and historical environments. The astringent open slopes beyond Banbury, after all, seem to be a world away from the languid riverside country round Henley, with its metropolitan overtones. Let us look first, then, at the natural foundations upon which the Oxfordshire scene has materialised.

Thanksgiving Day, 1972 FRANK EMERY
St Peter's College,
Oxford

Acknowledgments
I wish to record my sincere thanks for help freely given by many friends, in advice and materials, especially by David Sturdy, Ronald Lloyd, Mrs Mavis Batey, John Walton, Trevor Rowley, Mrs Penelope Lively, John Patten, the late E. W. Gilbert, Phillip Beckett, Mrs Joan Thirsk, T. H. Lloyd, R. W. Burchfield, and the late Mrs V. Wickham Steed. The editorial encouragement and patience of Professor W. G. Hoskins claim a special word of thanks. The collecting of my maps and photographs was made easier by the generosity of Mick Aston, Don Benson, H. M. Colvin, Alan Crossley, Malcolm Graham, David Hinton, and Ald. P. S. Spokes.

Contents

List of plates

ACKNOWLEDGMENTS

The author wishes to thank the following for permission
to use their photographs:
Thomas-Photos Oxford: Plates 1, 9
The Ashmolean Museum, Oxford, for the late Major
    Geo. Allen: Plates 3, 5, 15, 21, 23, 24, 25, 29, 30, 31, 32, 35
Ministry of Defence (Air Force Department): Plates 4, 10,
    11, 18 22, 26 (Crown Copyright Reserved)
The late Mrs Violet Wickham Steed: Plates 6, 7
P. S. Spokes: Plate 8
The Bodleian Library, Oxford: Plate 12

The Ordnance Survey: Plates 14, 28 (Crown Copyright
    Reserved)
Mrs Mavis Batey: Plates 16, 17
Hugh McKnight: Plate 19
Central Library, Oxford: Plate 20
A. R. Edney: Plate 27
Science Studio (Oxford) Ltd: Plate 33
St John's College, Oxford: Plate 34
Oxford Mail & Times Ltd: Plate 36
Miss Ann Keyser: Plate 13

Plate 2 is by the author

List of maps and plans

Editor's Introduction

SOME SIXTEEN YEARS ago I wrote: "Despite the multitude of books about English landscape and scenery, and the flood of topographical books in general, there is not one book which deals with the historical evolution of the landscape as we know it. At the most we may be told that the English landscape is the man-made creation of the seventeenth and eighteenth centuries, which is not even a quarter-truth, for it refers only to country houses and their parks and to the parliamentary enclosures that gave us a good deal of our modern pattern of fields, hedges, and by-roads. It ignores the fact that more than a half of England never underwent this kind of enclosure, but evolved in an entirely different way, and that in some regions the landscape had been virtually completed by the eve of the Black Death. No book exists to describe the manner in which the various landscapes of this country came to assume the shape and appearance they now have, why the hedgebanks and lanes of Devon should be so totally different from those of the Midlands, why there are so many ruined churches in Norfolk or so many lost villages in Lincolnshire, or what history lies behind the winding ditches of the Somerset marshlands, the remote granite farmsteads of Cornwall, and the lonely pastures of upland Northamptonshire.

"There are indeed some good books on the geology that lies behind the English landscape, and these represent perhaps the best kind of writing on the subject we have yet had, for they deal with facts and are not given to the sentimental and formless slush which afflicts so many books concerned only with superficial appearances. But the geologist, good though he may be, is concerned with only one aspect of the subject, and beyond a certain point he is obliged to leave the historian and geographer to continue and complete it. He explains to us the bones of the landscape, the fundamental structure that gives form and colour to the scene and produces a certain kind of topography and natural vegetation. But the flesh that covers the bones, and the details of the features, are the concern of the historical geographer, whose task it is to show how man has clothed the geological skeleton during the comparatively recent past—mostly within the last fifteen centuries, though in some regions much longer than this."

In 1955 I published *The Making of the English Landscape*. There I claimed that it was a pioneer study, and if only for that reason it could not supply the answer to every question. Four books, in a series published between 1954 and 1957, filled in more detail for the counties of Cornwall, Lancashire, Gloucestershire, and Leicestershire.

Much has been achieved since I wrote the words I have quoted. Landscape-history is now taught in some universities, and has been studied for many parts of England and Wales in university theses. Numerous articles have been written and a few books published, such as Alan Harris's *The Rural Landscape of the East Riding 1700–1850* (1961) and more recently Dorothy Sylvester's *The Rural Landscape of the Welsh Borderland* (1969).

Special mention should perhaps be made of a number of landscape-studies in the series of Occasional Papers published by the Department of English Local History at the University of Leicester. Above all in this series one might draw attention to *Laughton: a study in the Evolution of the Wealden Landscape* (1965) as a good example of a microscopic scrutiny of a single parish, and Margaret Spufford's *A Cambridgeshire Community* (*Chippenham*) published in the same year. Another masterly study of a single parish which should be cited particularly is Harry Thorpe's monograph entitled *The Lord and the Landscape,* dealing with the War-wickshire parish of Wormleighton, which also appeared in 1965.[1] Geographers were quicker off the mark than historians in this new field, for it lies on the frontiers of both disciplines. And now botany has been recruited into the field, with the recent development of theories about the dating of hedges from an analysis of their vegetation.

But a vast amount still remains to be discovered about the man-made landscape. Some questions are answered, but new questions continually arise which can only be answered by a microscopic examination of small areas even within a county. My own perspective has enlarged greatly since I published my first book on the subject. I now believe that some features in our landscape today owe their origin to a much more distant past than I had formerly thought possible. I think it highly likely that in some favoured parts of England farming has gone on in an unbroken continuity since the Iron Age, perhaps even since the Bronze Age; and that many of our villages were first settled at the same time. In other words, that underneath our old villages, and underneath the older parts of these villages, there may well be evidence of habitation going back for some two or three thousand years. Conquests only meant in most places a change of landlord for better or for worse, but the farming life went on unbroken, for even conquerors would have starved without its continuous activity. We have so far failed to find this continuity of habitation because sites have been built upon over and over again, and have never been wholly cleared and examined by trained archaeologists.

At the other end of the time-scale the field of industrial archaeology has come into being in the last few years, though I touched upon it years ago under the heading of Industrial Landscapes. Still, a vast amount more could now be said about this kind of landscape.

Purists might say that the county is not the proper unit

[1] *Transactions of the Birmingham Archaeological Society,* Vol. 80 (1965).

for the study of landscape-history. They would say perhaps that we ought to choose individual and unified regions for such an exercise; but since all counties, however small, contain a wonderful diversity of landscape, each with its own special history, we get, I am sure, a far more appealing book than if we adopted the geographical region as our basis.

The authors of these books are concerned with the ways in which men have cleared the natural woodlands, reclaimed marshland, fen, and moor, created fields out of a wilderness, made lanes, roads, and footpaths, laid out towns, built villages, hamlets, farmhouses and cottages, created country houses and their parks, dug mines and made canals and railways, in short with everything that has altered the natural landscape. One cannot understand the English landscape and enjoy it to the full, apprehend all its wonderful variety from region to region (often within the space of a few miles), without going back to the history that lies behind it. A commonplace ditch may be the thousand-year-old boundary of a royal manor; a certain hedge-bank may be even more ancient, the boundary of a Celtic estate; a certain deep and winding lane may be the work of twelfth-century peasants, some of whose names may be made known to us if we search diligently enough. To discover these things, we have to go to the documents that are the historian's raw material, and find out what happened to produce these results and when, and precisely how they came about.

But it is not only the documents that are the historian's guide. One cannot write books like these by reading someone else's books, or even by studying records in a muniment room. The English landscape itself, to those who know how to read it aright, is the richest historical record we possess. There are discoveries to be made in it for which no written documents exist, or have ever existed. To write the history of the English landscape requires a combination of documentary research and of fieldwork, of laborious scrambling on foot wherever the trail may lead. The result is a new kind of history which it is hoped will appeal to all those who like to travel intelligently, to get away from the guide-book show-pieces now and then, and to know the reasons behind what they are looking at. There is no part of England, however unpromising it may appear at first sight, that is not full of questions for those who have a sense of the past. So much of England is still unknown and unexplored. Fuller enjoined us nearly three centuries ago:

"Know most of the rooms of thy native country
before thou goest over the threshold thereof.
Especially seeing England presents thee with
so many observables."

These books on The Making of the English Landscape are concerned with the observables of England, and the secret history that lies behind them.

Exeter, 1970   W. G. HOSKINS

I. The earliest landscapes

The bearing of natural features on landscape history. The initial phase: prehistoric settlement. The Roman landscape

The bearing of natural features on landscape history

OXFORDSHIRE SPANS THE central scarplands of England in a more complete measure than any other county. Between the Cotswold limestones and the Chiltern chalk the landscape is ribbed by three lines of hills with their intervening vales, giving in all five major belts of terrain in succession from north to south: Cotswolds, Oxford Clay vale, the Oxford Heights, the Gault Clay vale, and the Chilterns. Although a simple framework in outline, this pattern must be elaborated a little more in detail to give a true idea of the natural divisions of Oxfordshire. In the first place the scarpland succession of rock-types should not be compressed into simply clays and limestones, because the various sandstones which separate them are of great importance both to the mechanism of ground water and water supplies and to the characteristics of certain soils. A second amendment is that in parts of Oxfordshire the solid geology of clays, sandstones and limestones is overridden by superficial deposits which conceal or modify the nature of the solid rocks beneath them. Outstandingly important here are the oolitic gravels smothering the clay of the Thames valley upstream of Oxford; the plateau gravels lying on some of the limestone ridges, with related gravel patches here and there on the clays; and the distinctive clay-with-flints that obscures so much of the Chiltern chalk (Fig. 1).

So the five-fold geological graining of Oxfordshire, while it accounts for the main differences of kind (for instance, the facts of height and slope) nevertheless has to be multiplied to include a series of differences of degree. The relationship between water supply and land settlement, for example, is totally different on the gravel-covered clays to the west of Oxford and on the more open clays to the east, even though they are basically alike in height and slope.

Such fundamental distinctions in the physique of the county were well known to its earliest authors. The first to adopt what may be termed a scientific approach was Robert Plot, who carried out his field scrutiny in the fine, dry summers of 1674 and 1675. His notebooks show that he ranged through the whole county on a systematic plan. He studied the countryside between the rivers Evenlode and Cherwell in June and July 1674, completing the season's work by travelling between the Cherwell and the river Thame in August and September. In the following year Plot spent the early summer in the westernmost sector beyond the Evenlode, and then finished his survey by going across the Thame to see things for himself in the Chilterns in July–September 1675. The gain from all this first-hand observation and a concern with the natural elements of land, water and air were evident in Plot's book, published as *The Natural History of Oxfordshire* in 1677, and a well-known, much-cited source it is. As we might suppose, he could and did record the natural contrasts he had seen in the landscape, principally those of varying soils and their relative usefulness for the farmers of his time.

These soils were eight in number and reflected remarkably closely the solid and superficial geology outlined above. Plot should be given plenty of credit for treating them so fully, especially as many subsequent writers on Oxfordshire have been quick to criticise other aspects of his book. He described the Stonebrash, the Redland and the Chiltern country based on the limestones; on sandstones there were

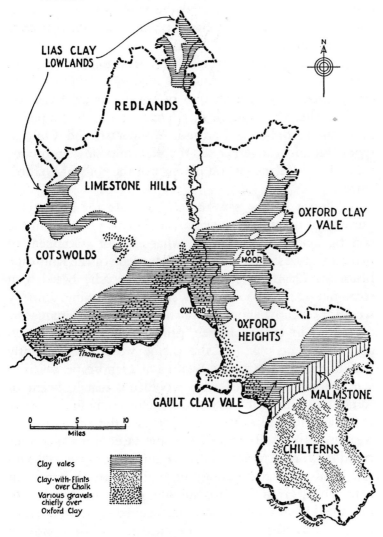

NATURAL DIVISIONS OF OXFORDSHIRE

LIAS CLAY LOWLANDS

REDLANDS

LIMESTONE HILLS

OXFORD CLAY VALE

River Cherwell

COTSWOLDS

OT MOOR

OXFORD +

'OXFORD HEIGHTS'

River Thames

GAULT CLAY VALE

MALMSTONE

CHILTERNS

River Thames

N

0 5 10
Miles

Clay vales

Clay-with-flints
  over Chalk
Various gravels
  chiefly over
  Oxford Clay

Fig. 1. This summarises the geology and physiography underlying the
different kinds of terrain upon which the Oxfordshire landscapes have
materialised. Recurrent landscape patterns of a more detailed nature
(extending from river valleys on clay; scarplands; and chalk) may be
found in P. H. T. Beckett and R. Webster, *A classification system of
terrain* (M.E.X.E. No. 87a, 1965).

Maumy and Sandy lands; Clay was widespread; Sourground and Gravelly lands completed the range of soils as agricultural resources. It is a further tribute to Plot that over a century later, when the Board of Agriculture's reporters were compiling their unique surveys of farming in England, Arthur Young in his *View of the Agriculture of Oxfordshire* (1809) incorporated a scheme of natural tracts based on Plot's earlier division. In fact Young radically simplified it, retaining only the Redland, Stonebrash and Chiltern types, lumping together all the rest into an amorphous class of 'Miscellaneous' on his map of the soils of Oxfordshire.

No doubt Young saw this as adequate for his specific purpose of describing the agrarian systems practised in the county, but it is right to ask what kind of assessment of natural features is best suited to the needs of the landscape historian. Clearly it should be more broadly based than something devised solely for a survey of farming. Initially we want to know about the relative value of different sorts of terrain in terms of their primary colonisation by an agricultural people. For the theme we must constantly bear in mind is the taming by men of a landscape which to start with was covered with woodland, marsh, heath or scrub, only gradually giving way before a mounting wave of reclamation. First we must consider the strengths and weaknesses of soils in terms of the ease with which they could be worked with primitive equipment or managed with few hands; soil texture and soil drainage are all-important here. Then, given their workability, come the rewards to be gained from soils that were well suited to various crops or grass, whether or not they yielded well or poorly in proportion to the effort and capital put into them. This leads in one direction to their potential for improvement and in the other to their liability to lapse to a less intensive form of land use, as wood or heath.

Thirdly, an adequate supply of water for men and animals

had to be guaranteed, either from pre-existing streams and springs, or from wells and pools contrived by those who needed them. Finally, we have to remember that the slope and height of the ground was one determinant of the trend taken by land use at various scales. We find it in the ample flat spaces for laying out the common fields; again in the taking advantage of slight but better-drained elevations for settlement in damp surroundings; in the selection of steep-sided hills for defensive sites; and in the avoidance of bare open heights as too exposed for settlement or cultivation.

These four considerations or 'natural' properties are singled out only for the ease of explaining them separately. It would be exceedingly hard to place them in some constant order of priorities. Indeed, we shall see in the succeeding chapters of landscape history in Oxfordshire that it is the juxtaposition of some or all of them in a given locality which helps us understand what happened there; even then we shall appreciate it fully only if we accept that there were many juxtapositions relative one to the other in time or space.

But if we go to the trouble of arming ourselves with knowledge of the natural regions in this or any English county we stand to acquire even more. Admittedly the chief gain is to be better able to grasp the natural factors bearing on the differing origins of elements in the landscape, especially those of settlement. Yet it is hard to draw a line between such implicit questions and their actual showing in the landscape as we see it now. Geology not only provides a pointer to the parent material from which soils are formed, but also furnishes through the medium of rocks and the streams dissecting them the bones and foundations of the landscape. Hence its gently dipping strata and many rivers account for the somewhat tame appearance of much of Oxfordshire's surface, robbing it of extremes of height, of rocky crags, steep-tilted plateaux or (apart from the

Chiltern scarp face) anything the slightest bit dramatic as natural landmarks (Plate 1). In *The Living Village* we read of the impression made on Paul Jennings when entering Oxfordshire: "the landscape becomes dominated by horizontals; marching lines of light . . . echo the hedge trees on ridge after ridge".

Instead in Oxfordshire physical controls are exercised, and exercised very forcibly, in a minor key and very subtly, as where the lift of twenty feet from land liable to river floods to land usually safe from them will bring a change from water and grass to houses and ploughland. Geology can also colour the landscape. Most directly it happens where the bared soil in cultivated fields reflects the rocks beneath, the best example in Oxfordshire being the Redlands or Marlstone plateaux, where around Banbury the iron-rich limestones of the Middle Lias yield rustily under the plough. Again the use of native materials for building houses in the countryside, as well as for barns, bridges and field boundaries, adds its own touch of colour and fitness to the scene in different localities.

For many centuries before about 1800, when cheap mass-produced materials began to reach Oxfordshire by canal and then by rail, it was generally the rule that building was done in local stone or flint on the limestones, brick, timber, thatch and tile on the clays. In the Chiltern countryside we find that flint is the commonest material in dwellings of early and Victorian age alike. Flints were easily obtained from the outcrop of the Upper Chalk, at its broadest here in the much-dissected dipslope from which most of the clay-with-flints and other superficial deposits have been stripped, exposing the flint resources.[1] Brick is the other common building material in the Chilterns, as we should expect in a district where brick-making was an early industry, at Nettlebed, for example, from the fifteenth century. Around Woodcote,

[1] J. W. R. Whitehand, 'Traditional Building Materials in the Chilterns', *Oxoniensia*, Vol. XXXII (1967), pp. 1–9.

brick may account for three-quarters of the pre-Victorian buildings, and appears in all those built after 1850. If not of brick, then the old houses were timber-framed in oak; plain tiles were the rule on the larger roofs, with thatch on the cottages, but slate became the stand-by of the Victorian builder. Nowadays most new roofs are tiled once more.

The many consequences of rural living on a particular natural formation in Victorian times were interpreted by John Jordan in his splendid account of Enstone, published in 1857. This bald farming landscape on the stonebrash was almost entirely in arable fields, and Jordan summed up the strength and weakness of the well-used soil as "somewhat light and friable", and easy of cultivation; it was "very suitable for wheat, barley and oats, and forming also good turnip lands for sheep, but liable to have its artificial grass crops dried up with too much heat, or excessive drought". The rocks influenced more than the soils, however: in Jordan's view they were responsible for the rounded configuration of the hills, and for their stoniness. "There is very little variety except in the texture of the stones, some of them being very excellent, durable, and dry, and valuable for all building purposes, while others are poor and friable, and scarcely fitted for the roads." Further, the rocks gave a localised natural supply of water: "in some places they afford us very admirable springs of water, while in others there is a considerable dearth".

Here then, from one spot in Oxfordshire, we pick up a hint of the need for a whole and down-to-earth view of its natural features, as J. Meade Falkner referred to them in his *History of Oxfordshire* (1899). Treating them in general terms, Falkner stressed two aspects above all others—the abundance of rivers large and small in the county, and the wide extent of its woodlands. He saw it as having been one continuous sea of woods in pre-Roman times, "out of which a barrow-studded down or camp-crowned hilltop rose here and there like an island". It is easy to appreciate the meaning of these features for landscape history. A dense network of rivers suggests hazards like flooding or assets like water-power, as well as the roads making their way along the river valleys, or more usually on the ridgeways between them. Woods are more difficult to accept in Falkner's terms because men have not only allowed stretches of primeval and secondary woodland to persist in the landscape but have also planted woods themselves, devising a series of institutional forms of forest, chase and park. Thus not only are they less 'natural' than rivers, but their incidence in Oxfordshire is more concentrated and localised, so we are brought back to the need to delineate the county into those tracts or land-types where the nature of the place has had a characteristic and pervasive bearing on the making of landscapes. Such a scheme is set out in Figure 1, and it will be used where necessary in the course of the book.

The initial phase: prehistoric settlement

Compared with the chalk downlands of Berkshire and Wiltshire, not far away to the south, the Oxfordshire landscape is poorly provided with the physical traces of prehistoric man. We do not find anything like Avebury and the other great monumental sites, nor densities like the Lambourn barrows, but before we take stock of what we can see it would be fair to point out that the visual impact of such prehistoric sites has weakened steadily over the years. As the most ancient and least comprehensible of our landscape structures, they have been very vulnerable to destruction or concealment. Thus we may find it hard to imagine why Enstone should have got its Saxon name from the Neolithic burial chamber known as the Hoar Stone. But until 1844 and the enclosure of Enstone by Act of Parliament "it stood like a beacon on the hills"; thereafter it has been hidden by trees in Enstone Plantation.[2] Another Hoar

[2] John Jordan, *History of Enstone* (1857), p. 5.

Stone at Langley was the relic of a chambered cairn, but its disappearance had been predicted by Akerman in 1858 when he found it "cracked in several places"; like one of Wychwood's boundary marks, the *Frethelestone*, it was probably broken up and used for making new roads. Even a scheduled ancient monument like the Roman villa at Fawler can have a pumping station put in its midst as part of a local authority's sewerage scheme (1970).

There is a clear connection between such traces left by prehistoric inhabitants and those well-drained, light and therefore easily cultivated soils, which are more characteristic of western Oxfordshire, but which also appear in the belt of country running below the Chiltern scarp. We have to admit, of course, that the picture may be distorted by chance factors like the concentration of modern gravel-pits and quarries (from which many complete discoveries have come) in some localities and not in others; or by the more detailed surveying of certain districts by early air-photographers or field-archaeologists working from Oxford. The record is in a critical state of flux just now. Prehistoric sites are being obliterated by powerful agents of change in the landscape: commercial gravel-quarrying (eating up the land to the tune of one and a half million cubic yards each year), the spread of buildings of all kinds, road improvement schemes, the remorseless ploughing on mechanised farms.

Sometimes these sites can be examined, however briefly, before they pass into oblivion. The degree to which existing ideas about early settlement can be thus confronted with fresh evidence of this kind is nowhere better shown than by recent discoveries along the line of the M40. As the machines moved in to start making the new motorway, the M40 Research Group continued their rescue operations in 'sudden death archaeology'. During 1970–72 they explored along the nine miles of motorway between Stokenchurch and the Waterstock crossroads. In effect this line makes an arbitrary but ideal transect of the different kinds of terrain

c

and settlement sites found in south Oxfordshire. It begins on the wooded Chilterns, drops down the chalk scarp to the belt of loamy soils and plentiful springs at its foot; crossing the Icknield Way it then traverses the clay lowlands where they are overlain by scattered spreads of drier gravels.

Previously the distribution maps of early occupation did not have much to show from this countryside, which seemed to be archaeologically barren. But the M40 excavations have revealed a different picture in which men had cleared the land, farmed it and built their houses on it throughout a period of 2500 years. First of all, a large Iron Age village came to light (on gravel) at Milton Common; not far away from this site there were Romano-British settlements, and again at Lewknor they found evidence of more omano-British occupation, in particular a rich farmstead just below the Chiltern scarp, in the sort of location favoured by the grander villas (p. 42). Close by at Beacon Hill there was a cemetery dating from the fourth century A.D., while a smaller Saxon burial-place of the seventh century was found at Postcombe. Then, in a later and more properly historical context it is clear that the houses of Tetsworth (not recorded in documents until about 1146) were in fact grouped to the south of its church in the twelfth century, but later this 'creeping village' shifted itself towards the London road, in the opposite direction. Finally, one of the best discoveries was a large farmstead at Sadler's Wood on the Chiltern summit, an assarted settlement (see p. 86) that thrived from about 1250 to 1400 when the woodlands were being gradually cleared, and previously unknown from the documentary sources.

Given the incompleteness and continuing fluctuation of the material evidence, however, it is clear that prehistoric settlers had a distinct preference for sites on the Thames-side terraced gravels; the limestones of the Cotswolds and Redlands lying west of the Cherwell; the open Chiltern chalklands; and the Corallian limestones and sands of the

Oxford Heights. By contrast, the various clay lowlands and Chiltern clay-with-flints were less attractive, not necessarily because they were thickly covered with woodland and undergrowth but because their soils were too heavy and wet for primitive people whose means of cultivation were weak. See, too, how the lines of two prehistoric thorough-fares, used for perhaps 5000 years, follow the outcrops of dry, permeable rocks. The Icknield Way running along the chalky Chilterns and the Jurassic Way striking with the Cotswold limestones provided a natural framework to which the earliest Oxfordshire landscapes were fastened.

The deeper (or, at least, better known) imprint made by prehistoric settlers to the west of the Cherwell and along the upper Thames was due to more than just the greater inci-dence there of limestones, sands and gravels. That whole western district was intersected by transverse ridgeways trending roughly from north to south. They provided a means of travel and trade from distant sources like Wales or between one local centre of population and another, say on the iron-bearing Jurassic hills and on the chalklands of the Berkshire Downs. With fords or ferries over the Thames, and summer pastures along the river, the district was accessible and frequented in a way denied to eastern Oxfordshire.

Among the most tangible of the earliest relics of human settlement is the group of Neolithic tombs, long barrows and stones in the Cotswolds. About a dozen in all, they are scattered over the limestone dipslope from the Whispering Knights long barrow at Little Rollright, on the highest and bleakest summits at 700 feet (Plate 2), to the Crawley mound at only 300 feet in the Windrush valley. They were built by the first farmer-colonists known in Oxfordshire, probably no later than about 2000 B.C., people who could cultivate the land with digging-sticks in order to grow cereals, covering the ground extensively with a 'slash-and-burn' or shifting occupance of the kind we still meet today in certain forest environments. But the Neolithic settlers also liked to graze their cattle, pigs and sheep in the woods and clearings; together with this strong pastoralism they retained a high degree of skill in hunting and snaring wild animals. Ignorant of metal though they were, it is to these versatile Neolithic immigrants from the west that we must attribute the initial momentum in landscape-making at the hands of men. Besides their burial vaults, they, or their close followers the Beaker people, also built circles of standing stones, such as the seventy-seven King's Men at Rollright, and orthostats like the Hawk Stone near Chadlington.[3]

From about 1700 B.C. there were distinct advances in technology by the Bronze Age population. They had metal sickles for reaping their barley and wheat, and they practised mixed farming with a wide range of domesticated livestock. Their handiwork survives in many of their burial mounds, too, more plentiful than the older stone tombs but found in the same localities. Where a commanding Bronze Age site has been planted with trees, it is all the more noticeable in our eyes: Asthall Barrow alongside the A40, or Leafield Barrow (641 feet) with its prospect over Wychwood and the Cotswolds.

More acceptable to us as proof of prehistoric *settlement*, as distinct from burial sites, are the ditched and embanked enclosures of the hill forts constructed by an Iron Age population, running in time from about 500–300 B.C. down to the Roman conquest and the start of written history.[4] Naturally in an iron-using society the Cotswold and Redland

[3] T. G. E. Powell (ed.), *Megalithic Enquiries in the West of Britain* (1969); Chapters 2 and 3 are on 'The Cotswold-Severn Group', by J. X. W. A. Corcoran, with the Oxfordshire sites listed on pp. 289–90.

[4] The earliest phase of the Iron Age in the upper Thames valley was first thought to date from the late fifth to early fourth centuries B.C.; recent studies have argued for taking it farther back in time, to the sixth to fifth centuries B.C. (Don Benson and D. W. Harding, 'An Iron Age Site at Kirtlington, Oxon.', *Oxoniensia*, Vol. XXXI (1966), pp. 157–62). The most recent discussion is found in D. W. Harding, *The Iron Age in the Upper Thames Basin* (1972).

districts, with their resources in ironstone, were thickly occupied. Of ten hill forts whose defensive enclosures are clearly visible above ground, and which usually command good views all round, six are grouped together on these limestone slopes. And if we increase the total by adding another dozen earthworks probably or possibly of the Iron Age, we still find sixty per cent of them in the same area. As a group, however, the Oxfordshire hill forts are puny, minor works by comparison with those at Uffington or Segsbury on the Berkshire Downs, and do not make much impact on the landscape. Most have been ploughed over, others are covered with bushes, they are small in area and show only single univallate defences. The most impressive is the bivallate hill fort at Tadmarton Heath (640 feet), now bisected by a road and absorbed by a golf-course. Standing in the middle of a fair-sized plateau, it does not occupy a strong defensive site, so proving 'fort' (and perhaps 'hill', too) as something of a misnomer for these enclosures into which people and livestock were packed as places of refuge only in time of exceptional danger.[5]

But it is not enough merely to point out the visible relict features—megaliths, round barrows, hill forts—that survive to us from the prehistoric landscapes. A second step we must take is to evaluate those earliest traces no longer before our eyes, to place them alongside those which are, and regard them all collectively as evidence of the initial phase of landscape-making. Otherwise we are in danger of being misled by the better survival rate of barrows and hill forts on the limestone hills. The other light soils on the gravels were at least as fully settled by prehistoric populations, but their remains have been thoroughly hidden and smoothed out. They lie beneath the surface of the ample, flat fields that are still such productive farmlands, cropped for generation after generation. We know of them only from

[5] J. E. G. Sutton, 'Iron Age Hill-forts and Some Other Earthworks in Oxfordshire', *Oxoniensia*, Vol. XXXI (1966), pp. 28–43.

their appearance on air-photographs in the form of crop-marks or variations in grass and soil, which archaeologists have come to interpret with much accuracy. Thus there were Neolithic settlers at Dorchester and on other gravel sites downstream along the Thames. The Neolithic henge monument of the Devil's Quoits at Stanton Harcourt is currently being excavated, before gravel-working destroys it. In this locality a close pattern of settlements by Beaker people came into being on the terraces between Yarnton and Standlake, persisting there into the Bronze Age, as we see from the clusters of ploughed-out sites of many round barrows. They are overlain and augmented by the outlines of Iron Age farmhouses, enclosure ditches, tracks, storage pits and fields, although Oxfordshire is deficient in prehistoric field systems, above or below ground (Plate 3).

We are faced at the outset, then, with a persistent settlement of the limestone hills and river gravels by a succession of prehistoric cultures. The populations involved may have been small, but they were well able to clear the wooded ground by means of controlled burning and by felling trees with their polished stone, bronze and iron axes. Their farm animals grazed the clearings and could check the regeneration of a tree-cover. These actions persisted through a time-span of more than 2000 years from the Neolithic colonisations to the advent of the Romans, and we cannot escape the recognition of an initial phase in the making of the landscape whereby prehistoric farmers and graziers brought about radical changes in the natural scene. From the dense broad-leaved woodlands which they first encountered they hacked and burned a succession of footholds, always on the lightest soils, later expanding them into patches of farmland. Thus the buried soil profile at a Neolithic long barrow shows the change from a closed woodland to an open grassland environment.[6] However interrupted the ecological

[6] The site is L.B.1, Coldwell Bridge, Ascott-under-Wychwood, excavated by Don Benson: *Oxoniensia*, Vol. XXXII (1967), p. 71.

sequence may have been, when we view the wind-riven summits of the Cotswolds, the open country above the Chiltern loams, or the spreading fields of the Thames terraces, we must acknowledge them as the successors of primeval landscapes that existed before recorded history.

A few conclusions on persistent early settlement may be illustrated from the excavation of sites at City Farm, Hanborough, a typical location on terraced gravels. Digging exposed six Bronze Age ring-ditches with adjoining burial pits; farmsteads of the Early Iron Age; and a small Anglo-Saxon cemetery. All the sites, despite their differing chronology, shared a linear layout along a prehistoric trackway. This trended southwards from the limestone hills, threading a dry course over the Thames-side gravels to cross the river and then heading for the western chalklands. Along such a natural route for wheeled and foot traffic, possibly as old as the Neolithic period, goods of flint, stone, copper and bronze would have entered the Thames Valley.[7]

Prehistoric settlement in the upper Thames Valley was comparatively late, intermittent and sparse. At the City Farm site it began in about 1700 B.C. with Beaker people, but their first occupation was nevertheless made in an open grassy environment, not in woodland. They may have taken advantage of clearings in the forest cover at the margins of an area of older Neolithic settlement. This Early Bronze Age use of the land, down to about 1450 B.C., was for grazing by the flocks and herds of stockmen who practised seasonal migration or *transhumance*. They may have used the north–south tracking for moving from winter folds and permanent cornfields in the Cotswolds or Oxford Heights to summer pastures by the Thames, when the riverine lands were drying out. Then comes a break in settlement of perhaps 500 years in the Late Bronze Age, a period that seems to have brought depopulation to much of the Oxford

[7] Humphrey Case (*et al.*), 'Excavations at City Farm, Hanborough, Oxfordshire', *Oxoniensia*, Vols. XXIX/XXX (1964–5), pp. 1–98.

region. The vacuum was filled by a good deal of Early Iron Age settlement: settlers brought farmsteads and ploughed fields into the landscape of the third and second centuries B.C., or even earlier, and they made iron from what could have been local ore. Unlike the gravels at Cassington, Eynsham and Stanton Harcourt, these Hanborough occupations did not continue into the Belgic and early Roman periods.[8]

The Roman landscape

Reading through the multitude of archaeological journals and newsletters being circulated nowadays, one would be forgiven for thinking that, wherever the Oxfordshire soil is disturbed by digging, Romano-British remains will come to light. At Middleton Stoney in 1970, for example, what began as the excavation of a medieval motte-and-bailey castle then proceeded to unearth instead a large building with Roman pottery of second- and third-century date. Few parts of the region seem not to have shared in the developments that followed the Roman occupation after A.D. 43, and for at least three centuries the Oxfordshire landscape responded to innovation on a scale it had not experienced before. The changes were also more intensive than in the past, bringing an integrated pattern of new towns, planned roads, farming estates and many kilns for manufacturing pottery.

Already in the century before the conquest a new influence had intruded from the east, in the form of Belgic settlers whose territory reached substantially as far as the Cherwell. As the result of this incursion there may have emerged the forerunners of the two main Roman roads—Akeman Street from east to west (Plate 4), and another running north–south

[8] Ann Hamlin, 'Excavation of Ring-ditches and Other Sites at Stanton Harcourt', *Oxoniensia*, Vol. XXVIII (1963), pp. 1–9; Humphrey Case, 'Notes on the Finds and on Ring-ditches in the Oxford Region', *ibid.*, pp. 19–52.

Plate 1 An Oxfordshire landscape, looking over flooded Otmoor and the Oxford Clay vale. Beckley village is at the left, perched on a low limestone ridge; in the foreground a Romano-British villa stood by the Roman road that drops here to the Otmoor fenland—one of the last pieces of primeval landscape to be tamed in the 1830s.

Plate 2 The Whispering Knights, Rollright: the remains of a Neolithic burial chamber.

Plate 3 Prehistoric sites showing as crop-marks, Southfield Barn, near Eynsham. The view is towards the Thames, over gravel terraces on which have been found traces of Bronze Age burials and beakers, in conjunction with the round barrows and ring-ditches; an extensive Iron Age settlement, with pit-clusters and enclosure ditches; also Belgicised and Romano-British habitations, block-like fields and a system of tracks.

Plate 4   The line of Akeman Street near Finstock. The Roman highway cut diagonally cross-country in the direction of the arrow (bottom left). Its alignment may be picked out as it strikes through Wilcote Park, close to the house on the north side. All that survives of the medieval village of Wilcote is the Park, Wilcote Grange and the Manor House, surrounded by the woods and permanent pasture that show dark grey against the lighter arable fields of Finstock. Another line, bolder than Akeman Street, is made by the railway (formerly the Oxford, Worcester and Wolverhampton) as it follows the Evenlode valley upper right of the picture). Scale *c.* 1:10,000.

across the Thames at the site of Dorchester. A further sign of Belgic penetration may be seen in the Grim's Dyke near Ditchley, where a system of linear earthworks enclosed an area of several square miles. It lies where the proto-Akeman Street would have cut across the prehistoric thoroughfare mentioned earlier (p. 39), and this locality was to become the most thoroughly Romanised part of Oxfordshire. The other Grim's Ditch running into the Chilterns from Mongewell, while also pre-Roman, is thought to be a boundary between two adjacent and yet mutually exclusive settlement patterns: on the one hand, the light soils cleared first for cultivation and sheep-rearing, on the other the later forest clearings whose farmers were concerned with pigs and cattle.[9]

Thus the two principal metalled roads set out by the Romans ran through a countryside that was in many respects a frontier region between the Belgic Catuvellauni to the east of the Cherwell and the Dobunni people to the west. Essentially, therefore, the two Roman towns established here served as frontier posts rather than as regional capitals or large markets for a populous farming district. Dorchester was minute, sited at the river crossing and succeeding an Iron Age village that lay at the confluence of the Thame and Thames. Its ramparts dated from the early second century A.D., and it functioned until well into the fifth century, probably surviving into the Saxon period when Dorchester became the see of a seventh-century bishopric. The other town, Alchester, was a posting station and store depot on the north–south Roman road, close to its junction with Akeman Street. The wet ground needed draining and building up with gravel before the first timber buildings could be constructed. It was twice the size of Dorchester, and was carefully planned with two main streets intersecting at right-angles in the town centre. Alchester probably

9 R. Bradley, 'The South Oxfordshire Grim's Ditch and its Significance', *Oxoniensia*, Vol. XXXIII (1968), pp. 1–12.

fell into decay by the early fifth century when the Roman roads that nourished it became less used. It dwindled to extinction and was superseded by the Saxon settlement of Bicester.

Throughout the Roman era a thickening pattern of native farmsteads, some standing singly, others grouped in villages, persisted on the gravel terraces of the Thames and its tributaries. They were very numerous between Cassington and Standlake, Northmoor and Eynsham. Small in their scale of agricultural working, rather poor, and frequently rebuilt, they gave rise to an intricate landscape of ditched and stockaded farmhouses, sometimes rounded, sometimes straight-sided. The ground about them was peppered with storage pits, chiefly for grain, and covered with a jigsaw pattern of cropped fields and enclosures for farm stock. Field tracks and droveways seamed their way through this countryside, decipherable now only indirectly through the crop-marks they created. Later methods of working the land have obliterated most of the rather flimsy handiwork of the Romano-British farmers.

There was a sharp contrast under the *pax Romana* between these simple valley communities and the more sophisticated, intensive farming of the uplands. In the Redlands, at least ten big farms are known, but nowhere was the scale of Romanisation more impressive than on each side of Akeman Street where it crossed the valleys of the Windrush, Evenlode and Glyme, in the neighbourhood of Grim's Dyke (Fig. 2). Here the free-draining stonebrash land was brought into a high pitch of productivity for barley, wheat and wool which could be marketed at great towns like Cirencester. Some of these farms were unpretentious, partly timber-built, sheltering inside rectangular ditches. But the keystones of this commercial agriculture were the magnificent country houses which appeared from late in the first century A.D. We can glimpse something of their splendour at the North Leigh villa, a courtyard house

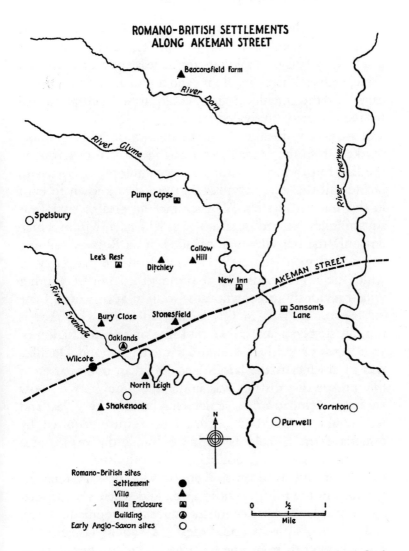

ROMANO-BRITISH SETTLEMENTS
ALONG AKEMAN STREET

Beaconsfield Farm

River Dorn

River Glyme

River Cherwell

Pump Copse

Spelsbury

Lee's Rest

Callow Hill

Ditchley

New Inn

AKEMAN STREET

River Evenlode

Bury Close

Stonesfield

Sansom's Lane

Oaklands

Wilcote

North Leigh

Shakenoak

Yarnton

Purwell

N

Romano-British sites
Settlement ●
Villa ▲
Villa Enclosure ▣
Building ◉
Early Anglo-Saxon sites ○

0   ½   1
Mile

Fig. 2. The distributions are based on 'Roman sites in north Oxford-shire', Fig. 1 in *Excavations at Shakenoak Farm, near Wilcote, Oxfordshire*, by A. C. C. Brodribb, A. R. Hands and D. R. Walker, Part 1 (1968); and 'Early Anglo-Saxon sites in north Oxfordshire', Fig. 1 in *ibid.*, Part 3 (1972), where their dating is given (p. 133) as probably from the early or middle sixth century to the eighth century A.D. This map should be compared with Fig. 2 in W. G. Hoskins, *The Making of the English Landscape* (1955).

sited in a sheltered bowl by the Evenlode, whose owners did not lack comfort or decoration. The colonnaded villa at Ditchley had outbuildings for at least part of its labour force, stables, threshing floors and a granary (Plate 5). It is calculated the Ditchley granary could store the crops yielded by 1000 acres of cultivated land.

If we accept this figure for the amount of cultivated land worked from the Ditchley estate at its most prosperous in the late fourth century A.D., we can multiply it by ten to include all the villa or villa-enclosure sites known to exist in this nuclear district. We then take an area of sixty-four square miles centred on the Stonesfield villa, within which not only the ten villas are included but a Roman building and a settlement site at Wilcote, and on the periphery of which lie other villas. What promises to be yet another villa, previously unknown, came to light at Sansom's Lane (or Sansom's Platt) in this locality in 1972. This area is roughly 40,000 acres, so we find that on the calculation of 1000 acres of cultivated land for each villa (and Ditchley was by no means the largest) no less than one quarter of this prosperous district was under the plough. We know we have excluded other settlements besides the villas, and we should also add the acreage of pasture required by essential farm animals. Even if we double the farmed area to 20,000 acres we are not being too optimistic.

Half of this landscape, then, was in field systems or grazings in the fourth century A.D., and when we find that much of it lay in later centuries under the woodland, heath and scrub of Wychwood Forest we should visualise the forest having to re-invade what had been an open, farmed landscape in the Romano-British period. Despite the obvious intensity of Romanisation in this part of Oxfordshire, with so many architectural and other finds made over the years, it is curious there have been no traces of the associated field systems within which the wealth of the villas was generated. We may be wrong to assume that their lands would be set out in great geometrical blocks, and certainly field archaeologists have been prone to find such systems of *centuriation* all too readily, where none may have existed. But in this villa country west of the Cherwell we could expect the dominant line of Akeman Street to serve as an unrivalled base line; and we do find in fact, on the maps and even more clearly on the air-photographs, that another line runs parallel with Akeman Street, about a mile south of it, running for twelve miles from Asthall on the Windrush to Enslow on the Cherwell. The two lines are often joined by short connecting links, making up a series of squarish blocks of land: this ribbon of country is much interrupted, for instance by Blenheim Park, but it would bear further investigation.

SELECT BIBLIOGRAPHY

Arkell, W. J., 'Place-names and Topography in the Upper Thames Country: A Regional Essay', *Oxoniensia*, Vol. VII (1942), pp. 1–23.

Brodribb, A. C. C., Hands, A. R., Walker, D. R., *Excavations at Shakenoak Farm, near Wilcote, Oxfordshire,* Part 1 (1968); Part 2 (1970); Part 3 (1972).

Emery, F. V. and Scargill, D. I., 'The Central English Scarplands and Oxford', Ch. 8 in J. A. Steers (ed.), *Field Studies in the British Isles* (1964).

Martin, A. F. and Steel, R. W. (eds.), *The Oxford Region* (1954), especially Chs. 1–6.

Riley, D. N., 'Archaeology from the Air in the Upper Thames Valley', *Oxoniensia*, Vols. VIII & IX, (1943–4), pp. 64–101.

Rowley, Trevor and Davies, Max., *Archaeology and the M40 Motorway* (1973). Summaries of current work on, and discoveries of, prehistoric sites may be found in the *Newsletter* of Group 9 of the Council for British Archaeology, the first of which was published in 1971.

Wood, P. D., *The Oxford and Newbury area* (British landscapes in maps), published by the Geographical Association, 1968.

2. The English settlement

Continuity or persistence? Primary settlements. Saxon survivals and reconstructions

Continuity or persistence?

BY 'THE ENGLISH SETTLEMENT' is meant the invasion and colonisation of much of Britain by groups of Germanic immigrants, from the early fifth century A.D. onwards. They sailed over the narrow seas and established themselves in various threshold regions; from these they expanded tenaciously in succeeding centuries, and the sum of their actions as the agents of landscape-making through 600 years may be assessed conveniently in Domesday Book in 1086. Traditionally the Saxon or Old English settlers are acknowledged as having been very influential in the making of the landscape, superimposing their own patterns on whatever Romano-British systems they found in being when they arrived, and, in short, laying the foundations of the English countryside. They are credited with taming the woodlands, heaths and marshes in order to clear the ground for their fields, to gain the best pastures for their cattle and sheep, to build their villages and other farming settlements.

We see how their pioneering prowess has been accepted as an article of faith for many years in the words of a down-to-earth topographer, who regarded "the early English village as a centre of life and work in the midst of a surrounding wilderness. The poorest and most distant part of the estate," he thought, "was left in its native wildness, affording timber for fuel and fencing, mast and acorns for swine, and rough pasture for the ordinary livestock."[1] But nowadays it is not accepted so readily that the genesis of an expanding man-made landscape lies to such an exclusive degree with the English settlement. There has been some re-thinking about the relationship between what the Saxons discovered already in being, their inheritance from the developed countryside of the Romano-British population and their own actions.

It was assumed originally that the newcomers shunned the old towns, villas and fields as they came across them, and instead followed a course of choosing virgin sites for their settlements. In opposition to this interpretation it has been argued in recent years that it was more likely the English settled themselves in close association with villas and other places already present in the landscape: Withington, in the Gloucestershire Cotswolds, is the type-study of this argument.[2] In other words, instead of a clean break between the Romano-British (and perhaps even the pre-Roman Iron Age) and the Saxon landscapes, we should presume an element of continuity between them. The idea of a complex of Roman buildings at Caistor near Peterborough in 1971 was hailed as revealing "a superb example of a site where human settlement has been virtually uninterrupted for the past 2000 years". Others are more cautious. Archaeologists see a possibility that Celtic rural life based on the villas continued in the Cotswolds for at least two centuries after A.D. 400, but they also say that the Withington thesis "is ingenious, but lacks real proof".[3]

The full implications of the idea of continuity are difficult to determine. On the face of it there is more common sense in picturing the English taking advantage of lands already

[1] J. C. Blomfield, *History of Upper and Lower Heyford* (London, 1892), p. 2.
[2] H. P. R. Finberg, *Roman and Saxon Withington. A Study in Continuity* (Leicester, 1955).
[3] Graham Webster, in *The Roman Villa in Britain*, ed. A. L. F. Rivet (London, 1969), pp. 235–6.

cleared and productive, rather than turning their backs on them and striking out into the apparently untouched waste. But on the other side it is hard to imagine even the majority of the early Saxon villages—all those plain, honest Waltons and Kingstons—as standing by the sites of Romano-British settlements. Questions are raised at once. Was the village always typical of the earliest English presence? Which were the earliest villages, and how early did they have to be in order to occupy an existing foothold? What were the proportions between the continuing settlements and those generated later as the Saxon population multiplied and filled out the countryside? Perhaps these questions are prompted because of the confusion of two separable ideas, continuity and persistence. The persistence of prehistoric and later settlement is quite common in Oxfordshire. We need think only of the overlap of cultures evident at the important focus of Dorchester or at some of the desirable valley sites, such as Purwell near Cassington. On this gently swelling ridge, capped with gravel, there are signs of a Bronze Age burial; an Early Iron Age farming settlement that grew cereals and kept cattle and pigs; together with many remains of an early pagan Saxon village and cemetery. Here we have persistence but not continuity, because there is a break in the sequence for the crucial Romano-British phase. Neither do we know what happened after the village ended its life, because Purwell Farm (the sole habitation there now) does not appear in the records until 1551.

A variant is the early Saxon settlement in localities known for their general degree of persistence from prehistoric times, but whose site was virgin and whose life was cut short. Such is the site at New Wintles Farm, just half a mile from the City Farm complex mentioned earlier (p. 39), occupying the same gravel bench, and just across the Evenlode from Purwell. Here an early English settlement, small and rather loose-knit, was made in two stages over a period of about 100 years in the sixth and seventh centuries. It was at least partially protected by a ditch and strong fence. A track ran through the inhabited area, and alongside it, naturally enough on the highest and best-drained site, stood two post-built houses, one long, the other square in plan, accompanied by what was probably a sheep-fold. Around them were scattered eleven dug-out huts sunk into the gravel, their roofs supported by posts and completed with wattle-and-daub walls. Some of these were weaving sheds rather than dwellings.

It is also possible to find cases where there was continuity from Romano-British to sub-Roman settlement on the same site, but with no trace of continuing use afterwards. The best instance is the large villa near Shakenoak Farm at North Leigh, where occupation from the first to the eighth centuries A.D. has been established. Even here the record is irregular. One set of buildings was used from about A.D. 100 but had been completely abandoned by the late fifth century, and its ruins were used subsequently as a Saxon burial ground. The main dwelling of the corridor villa began its life earlier and was occupied until about 430; thereafter signs of Saxon settlement appear and lasted from the fifth to the mid-eighth century, linked to agriculture, weaving and iron-working. Certainly we have continuity from Roman to English cultures at Shakenoak, but it was cut short to such an extent that the villa site did not show itself even to the probing eye of the aerial camera.

Despite this, Shakenoak may figure in a fresh possibility to do with continuity. From a study of early place-names in England that derive from the Old English word *wīchām* it has been noticed that almost all of them are located near a Roman road, and in many cases near a Romano-British settlement. Oxfordshire has two *wīchāms* in the Redlands near Banbury, but a third lay close to Shakenoak. Clearly they raise the question of possible co-existence between the native British people and Saxons, "in a type of settlement called a *wīchām*, which occurred close to Roman roads and usually near small Romano-British settlements", deriving its name from a general connexion with these *vici* or villages of Roman Britain.[4] It is a further possibility that they were settled by Germanic *laeti*, mercenary soldiers employed by the British as a protection against the general invader, who were rewarded by land-grants from the village or group of villas that they guarded. At the Shakenoak site, with its *wīchām* nearby, there is archaeological evidence of the presence of these *laeti*.

The idea is strengthened by a recent study that recognises a phase of transition in sub-Roman Britain between about 410 and 450. During this phase the local native regimes were able to maintain themselves against barbarian pressure, with or without the help of federate settlers. In the Oxford region they did so with the help of *laeti*, whose inhumation (rather than cremation) cemeteries are found along the south bank of the Thames below Oxford, and at places like Cassington and Brighthampton upstream, where so many small farming settlements flourished in Roman times. We can visualise, therefore, a series of Saxon foundations beginning as "groups of barbarian soldier-settlers planted out among the existing villages on the riverside gravels, and dependent perhaps in the first instance on the fortified bridgehead at Dorchester".[5] The pottery evidence also suggests that the upper Thames, partly under Saxon control at least since the phase of transition early in the fifth century, then received a further influx of Germanic population in the phase of uncontrolled settlement that followed.

A final word: on grounds of accessibility of the evidence one would expect to find proof of continuity through the excavation of villages deserted in medieval times. Such places could have continued as settlements beyond the

---

[4] Margaret Gelling, 'English Place-names derived from the Compound *Wīchām*', *Medieval Archaeology*, Vol. XI (1967), pp. 87–104.

[5] J. N. L. Myres, *Anglo-Saxon Pottery and the Settlement of England* (Oxford, 1969), p. 89.

critical period of the fifth or sixth centuries, without interruption down to the time of their abandonment. They could hold the material key to the question, and the key would be in easy reach, not sealed under the houses of a living village. Unfortunately, none of the hundred or so deserted villages in Oxfordshire has been fully excavated (p. 98), but a stone's throw away we do have the full examination of Seacourt and we must make the most of that. Traces of Romano-British occupation were found on the site, although it was nothing more than a native single farmstead. There was then a complete break in the archaeological evidence of settlement until the tenth century, when the village may have originated (it was mentioned in a land charter of 957). All the buildings found, however, were of late-twelfth-century origin. Seacourt thus offers little to encourage the champion of continuity, but we should hope for further excavations of the sort in Oxfordshire.

Primary settlements

On *a priori* reasoning one would expect there to be a greater likelihood of continuity in those parts of Oxfordshire known to have experienced the earliest waves of English settlement. A pointer to where these lay is given by the pattern of pagan cemeteries and other burials, dating from the fifth and sixth centuries when the English were still to become Christians. The map (Fig. 3) revives some distributions already familiar to us from the prehistoric and Roman periods, fortifying the theme of persistent occupation of certain kinds of terrain, particularly the light and intermediate soils found in the valleys and on the gravel terraces. We see again the clustering along the Thames, very noticeable in respect of the known Saxon villages and houses; around the stonebrash margins of Wychwood to the west of the Cherwell; on the Oxford Heights, and along the Icknield loams below the Chiltern crest. But there is no

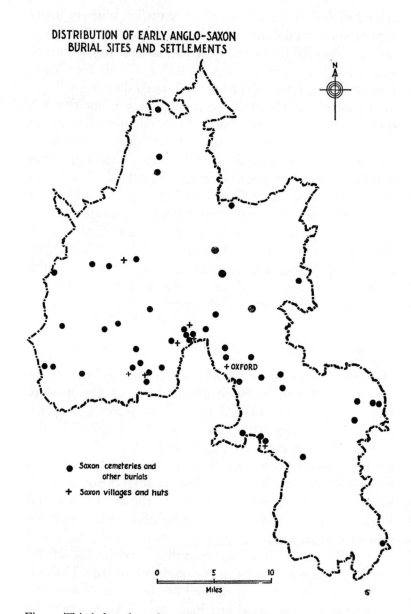

DISTRIBUTION OF EARLY ANGLO-SAXON BURIAL SITES AND SETTLEMENTS

● Saxon cemeteries and
other burials

+ Saxon villages and huts

+ OXFORD

0   5   10
Miles

Fig. 3. This is based on data in *Britain in the Dark Ages*, published by the Ordnance Survey (2nd edition, revised, 1966).

simple contrast between upland and valley in the disposition of the pagan sites. Neither the Chilterns nor (departing from the prehistoric precedent here) the Cotswold hill-country show us anything in the way of pagan traces, and neither does the stonebrash-clay lowland that lies eastwards of the Cherwell. It is on the light soils of the valleys, in other words, that we meet with persistence of settlement.

We can therefore accept the penetration of this country-side by Saxon settlers in growing numbers from the early fifth century onwards. They may have come mainly from earlier-settled regions to the north-east through Bedford-shire and Northamptonshire, moving overland in a direction parallel with (or even along) the Icknield Way. Some may also have come by boat and portage upstream along the river Thames, near to which so many of the earliest English settlements lay. Here we should be prepared to take to the water and travel upstream, looking at the landscape with the eyes of newcomers seeking choice places in which to settle. The point is made for us by Chimney, now a tiny remote corner in the flat river country above Eynsham. Not only was it a larger, more prosperous place in medieval times, but its boundaries were set out in a land charter of 1069. The village stood very close to the Thames and was notor-iously apt to be cut off by floods in winter; its Old English name meant *Ceomma's island*. According to the geological map Chimney was sited on the alluvium of the flood plain and therefore contradicted the usual rule of old villages always perching themselves on terraces. But from the river, and only from the river, it is easy to see the low ledge of gravel which in fact Chimney occupies, just as its first settler (*Ceomma*, perhaps) would have appreciated its merits from his boat.

It is along the Thames valley and the Icknield Way, too, that we find a high proportion of places whose names are understood by their form to be relatively early, of the late sixth or early seventh century. These include (coming upstream) Mapledurham, Goring, Newnham Murren, Shillingford and Nuneham Courtenay, with Watlington, Ingham and others below the Chilterns. At the other extreme a few early place-names occur in the far west, but there is "no picture of a heavy early Saxon colonisation of the Cotswolds".[6] The long-settled lowlands of the Thames valley, particularly where they were traversed by ancient routes like the Icknield Way or others above Oxford, were more attractive to the early English.

The continuing development of the riverside landscapes progressed so well that by the late sixth century the upper Thames valley had become the heartland of the English kingdom of Wessex. Subsequently, however, it was debatable land between Wessex and the midland Mercians, the river acting not as an axis of natural cohesion but rather as a frontier between the kingdoms. Despite the political fluctuations it is possible to identify some of the primary English settlements in the royal villages (*villae regales*) that served as focal points for the earliest administrative units, long before the emergence of Oxfordshire as a county. Three of them stand in close association with groups of pagan cemeteries and may be the oldest villages of all— Bampton in the uppermost Thames valley, Headington, on the Oxford Heights, and Bensington (now Benson) in the Icknield scarp-foot of the Chilterns. Shipton-under-Wychwood in the Evenlode valley may be similarly associated with later burials of the seventh century, while Bloxham, Kirtlington and Wootton may be later still; all of them are key-points in the unfolding pattern of English settlement and the making of its landscape.

Alongside the primary villages there also grew up a series of early ecclesiastical settlements sited close to the Thames. Dorchester became the seat of the West Saxon

---

[6] A. H. Smith, *The Place-Names of Gloucestershire* (Cambridge, 1965), Part IV, p. 41; compare Margaret Gelling, *The Place-Names of Oxfordshire* (Cambridge, 1953), p. xviii.

bishopric after the bringing of Christianity by St Birinus in 634, and later retained an important function if only as a minster church. Other monasteries were founded, on the site of Oxford by St Frideswide in the eighth century, and possibly at Eynsham by the end of the tenth century. Political events then also led to the building of strongholds along the Thames to protect the frontiers of Wessex against the Danes. The chief of these *burhs* was Oxford, first mentioned by name in 912 when assuming its status as the centre of an embryonic Oxfordshire. In this setting of the expanding English settlement, before the close of the tenth century we again find the recording in documentary sources of many other places in favoured districts: Thame, Lewknor, Pyrton and Watlington ("at least as old as the 6th century")[7] below the Chilterns; Cuddesdon and Holton on the Oxford Heights; Witney, Woodstock, Heyford, Chastleton and Tadmarton on the Cotswold stonebrash.

One speculation about the earliest stages of the Saxon colonisation would see it as having an economy that was pastoral and nomadic. As such it would have differed sharply from the Romano-British system, reverting instead to the older prehistoric practices we have met in the Late Neolithic and Bronze Ages at sites like City Farm (p. 39). It is suggested that the ancient estates belonging to St Frideswide's, the mother-church of Oxford, may have thus originated as the grazing rights of such a nomadic economy early on in the English settlement: its upland sheep pastures were located at Tackley, summer grazing for cattle and woodland feeding for pigs were found on lowland estates at Binsey, Cowley and Cutteslow. This idea would weigh against the argument for continuity in a majority of permanent settlements, and we may subject it to gentle criticism on two grounds. The first is that it omits to think out the ecological circumstances of the fifth and sixth centuries. Admittedly this is very difficult to do, but we should be prepared at least

7 Victoria County History, *Oxfordshire*, Vol. VIII (1964), p. 268.

to frame the questions to which we would like the answers: was it likely that the farm animals wintered in the fields, or did they have to be stall-fed on hay and other winter fodder? If the latter was the case, did it place a premium on riverside meadows for this purpose of hay-cutting, rather than for grazing?

Secondly, nomadism is surely too strong a term, with its implications of transitory, impermanent settlement. A modified kind of *transhumance*, such as was followed in the Welsh and Scottish uplands until the nineteenth century, may indeed have been practised in Oxfordshire when its landscape was less cleared, lightly settled and offered free movement of livestock. But it is as likely that the St Frideswide's lands were an 'open', dispersed variant of the Saxon ideal of having together, side by side, a range of differing kinds of land, whether merely grazing for all kinds of livestock or with arable fields as well. Instead of nomadism we can visualise the maximum use of well-watered river meadows wherever they occur, even at a distance from the main settlement. After all, the Old English word for meadow appears in two of the earliest place-names, Eynsham and Culham, and we can also recall the right of freeholders from places standing high and dry on the limestone hills to mow hay in richly-yielding meadows miles away by the Cherwell. Down to 1863 they went from Duns Tew to riverside hay-cuttings at North Aston, and from Wootton to Steeple Aston, making a rustic July holiday of it.

This alternative view of a search for the right blend of land meeting all the needs of the farmer in due season, even if the lands were well separated, may be nearer the mark for the early English motivation and intelligence. It does not require a wholesale dependence on pastoralism, let alone nomadism. It must have been an early working principle in the curious situation that locates Charlbury within the hundred of Banbury although they lie fifteen miles apart. The reason behind their association is that the Saxon farmers living in the Bishop of Dorchester's villages around Banbury had to walk to the nearest portions of Wychwood Forest (where Charlbury came into being) for their timber and swine pasture. Incidentally, this implies the shortage of woodland and the openness of the Banbury Redlands as early as the seventh and eighth centuries. Another case of the same kind of thing may be seen from the thirteenth-century records of Merton College, in sending herds of pigs from its Cuxham estate to another college property at Ipsden, where they could be grazed in the Chiltern beech woods, while the Cuxham farmers had to find all their timber at Ipsden.

Saxon survivals and reconstructions

Given that the documentary pointers to what the early English landscape was like are few and fragmentary before the unrolling of Domesday Book in 1086, we are led to remedy this deficiency by fieldwork taken in conjunction with the patterns revealed by maps of various kinds. It is still possible, for instance, to recognise and piece together the relic outlines of pre-Conquest estates and their boundaries. We see some of the possibilities and problems of this type of exercise by reviewing the reconstruction by W. G. Hoskins of Fritwell, on the borders of Oxfordshire and Northamptonshire.[8] His proposition is that the three settlements (now separate parishes) of Fritwell, Somerton and Souldern were originally a single unit centred on Fritwell as the primary and oldest place. Somerton was where its summer pastures were, or, remembering the arguments against 'nomadism', perhaps it was more likely to have been Fritwell's hay ground lying close by the Cherwell. Souldern, completing the triumvirate, was a small nameless place in 1086, when all three manors were held by the same man. But it was sufficiently developed by about

[8] W. G. Hoskins, *Local History in England* (London, 1959), p. 44.

1150 to merit a name of its own, and its church has Norman work of that period, indicating that it became a separate parish and the newest of the three villages to appear in this corner of the Oxfordshire landscape. On the map (Fig. 4) it is not difficult to see how the three parishes conform together, giving the coherent outline of an ancient estate.

We can now add some further pieces of tangible evidence. The first would weaken Hoskins's reconstruction of the sequence of settlement, because at Souldern a pagan Saxon burial was found close to the village. If it is taken to denote an early dwelling-place, then Souldern could be the oldest rather than the youngest of the three settlements, dislodging Fritwell as the centre from which the estate was brought into a productive state. Another piece of evidence confirms the antiquity of the estate itself, because the most easterly section of Somerton's boundaries runs along the linear earthwork known variously as Ash Bank, Wattle Bank or Aves Ditch. Much of this intriguing embankment has been levelled: in Upper Heyford (where it was called Soldier's Bank) it was pulled down after the enclosure of 1842. Archaeologically it is an enigma, combining the two functions of a pre-Roman boundary dyke, ditched on the western side, and of an embanked road used in the Romano-British period. At any rate it was old enough to furnish a good, clean line for Saxon boundaries and was so used by several early settlements. Fritwell village is built astride Aves Ditch, and that section of it followed by the Somerton boundary is still a high, tree-crowned stretch of roadway. More important, this same boundary is shared by the neighbouring parish of Ardley, and is included in the Saxon limits of Ardley (*Eardwulf's wood or clearing*) in a land charter of 995, when it was called the Great Dyke. It thus helps to confirm the antiquity of the threefold Fritwell estate.

Pioneering studies of such reconstructions of Old English boundaries were published by G. B. Grundy for several counties. While his linguistic interpretations often need

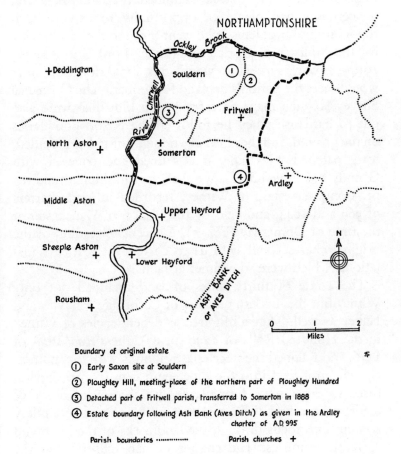

RECONSTRUCTION OF A PRE-CONQUEST
ESTATE IN THE CHERWELL VALLEY

NORTHAMPTONSHIRE

+Deddington

Souldern ① ②

Fritwell +

③

North Aston +

Somerton +

④ Ardley +

Middle Aston

Upper Heyford +

Steeple Aston +

Lower Heyford +

Rousham +

ASH BANK OR AVES DITCH

N

0 1 2
Miles

Boundary of original estate ━ ━ ━

① Early Saxon site at Souldern

② Ploughley Hill, meeting-place of the northern part of Ploughley Hundred

③ Detached part of Fritwell parish, transferred to Somerton in 1888

④ Estate boundary following Ash Bank (Aves Ditch) as given in the Ardley
charter of A.D. 995

Parish boundaries ·············   Parish churches +

Fig. 4. Two other pieces of field evidence that put a premium on
Souldern as the early focus of settlement within the estate are (i) the
location near to it of a meeting-place for the hundred of Ploughley,
and (ii) the 135 acres of land belonging to Fritwell that lay detached
from the parish until 1888, being river meadow alongside the Cherwell:
it seems to have lain within the run of Souldern's boundaries.

correcting, it is easy to refute those who have criticised him for making his identifications of landmarks from the comfort of his armchair rather than in the field. Grundy says in his autobiography that he examined 'the actual sites' and he certainly had plenty of opportunity to explore such topographical problems as he went through the countryside for the Ministry of Agriculture (under Lord Ernle) in the 1914–18 war, surveying woodlands in Oxfordshire that would meet the nation's demand for timber.[9] The Ordnance Survey six-inch maps he carried with him then were also put to hard use when he followed the Saxon boundaries on the ground, and they bear all the signs of it, being folded, torn, patched with tape, mud-stained and covered with Grundy's scribbled notes. We shall go with him around the pre-Conquest estate of Witney, recorded in land charters of 969 and 1044, and held by the Bishop of Winchester at the time of Domesday (Fig. 5). A recent re-reading of the original charters will help us to correct his textual translations, which were sometimes at fault.[10]

The estate of thirty hides of land included not only Witney but the modern parishes of Curbridge, Crawley and Hailey as well. They all figured as dependencies of Witney in the Hundred Rolls of 1279 (p. 87), the *Feudal Aids* of 1316, and retained their ecclesiastical links with the mother-church until well into the nineteenth century. So, having fused together these four places into a compact block of territory, we find their common outer or ring boundary coming into focus through the landmarks of the tenth and eleventh centuries. The charter of 969 tells us that the countryside lying north of the Windrush was distinctly different in character from that to the south of the river, so the whole estate was composed of two contrasting but

[9] G. B. Grundy, *Fifty-five Years at Oxford* (London, 1945), pp. 132, 156–8.
[10] Margaret Gelling, *art. cit.* (1967), pp. 99–103 (Appendix II, '*Wicham* between Ramsden and Wilcote, Oxfordshire'); Grundy discusses the Witney charters on pp. 76–85 of his *Saxon Oxfordshire*.

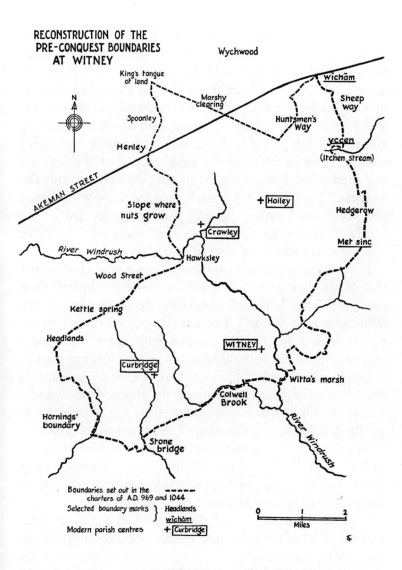

RECONSTRUCTION OF THE
PRE-CONQUEST BOUNDARIES
AT WITNEY

Wychwood

King's tongue
of land

Marshy
clearing

Spoonley

Henley

wichām

Sheep
way

Huntsmen's
Way

yccen
(Itchen stream)

AKEMAN STREET

N

Slope where
nuts grow

+ Hailey

+ Crawley

River Windrush

Hawksley

Hedgerow

Met sinc

Wood Street

Kettle spring

Headlands

WITNEY +

Curbridge
+

Witta's marsh

Colwell
Brook

Hornings'
boundary

Stone
bridge

River Windrush

Boundaries set out in the
charters of A.D. 969 and 1044

Selected boundary marks } Headlands
wichām

Modern parish centres + Curbridge

0   1   2
Miles

Fig. 5. These are based on the sketch-maps by Margaret Gelling in
Medieval Archaeology, Vol. XI (1967), p. 103, and in Part 3 of *Excavations
at Shakenoak Farm, near Wilcote, Oxfordshire* (1972), p. 137. The territory
enclosed by the boundaries now comprises the four parishes of Witney,
Curbridge, Hailey and Crawley; not all the boundary marks are
included, and the original boundary is not certain in places, as in the
Windrush valley below Witney.

complementary sections. Northwards the boundary cut immediately into a landscape still dominated by woodland, thinned out here and there by clearings with their *-ley* place-names (derived from the O.E. *leah*, a wood or clearing in woodland). We read of thickets of hazel and willow, we find Nutley, Henley (high clearing) and Spoonley (clearing where wooden shingles were cut), we follow the sharp angle of land jutting into the king's forest of Wychwood, and then swing back along the marshy clearing towards the *huntsmen's way* (obviously a track used by those who chased the Wychwood game), passing the *wīchām* (p. 49) before finally emerging by the edge of the wood into the more open country along the eastern boundary.

Here the *green way* ran on through open land close to the site of the Romano-British villa at Shakenoak, and then gave way to a lane and hedgerow trending towards the Windrush near Witney. The valley floor of the river was clearly in a natural state, braided with many backwaters and brooks, some of the landmarks being 'quaking marsh', 'slippery place' and 'foul island'. It is easy to imagine in this riverine setting the value of the dry cornbrash inlier on which Witney stood, surrounded by the alluvial levels of the Windrush: the meaning of the place-name is *Witta's island*. Yet some of the river land was used as watermeadows, part of which belonged to Shilton, a village six miles away from Witney in dry limestone country—another case of long-distance appropriation of meadow (p. 56).

The southern section of the estate had evidently been cleared of woodland, because in this open countryside the boundaries were usually the headlands of cultivated fields, the *ealdan dic* or old ditch (probably preserved for us in the continuous, curving boundary hedges, the oldest of their kind in this landscape); a stone bridge, a pit or a spring—no suggestion here of woods, clearings and the maze of tracks we found to the north of the Windrush. This contrast was clear again two or three generations later when the other land charter was composed in 1044. For good measure it referred to the *wood street* running down from the cultivated lands towards the Windrush, as if it was the accepted way for travelling from the open country into the woodlands for timber and grazing. A new feature was the presence of some tillage in the tongue of land closest to Wychwood, suggesting the active progress of clearing and cropping the forest margins in the early eleventh century. The re-naming of *old way* as *sheep way* in this same extremity of the estate points also to the lines of seasonal movement of farm animals to forest pastures. It should draw our attention to the fact that the *wīchām* was situated hereabouts, and from the map it is obvious that the boundaries take their most complex course around the block of land jutting out towards a property now called The Hayes. Here we may have the outline of a Romano-British estate that was adopted and absorbed into a more ambitiously demarcated tract of Saxon land. It is very carefully delineated by a good number of boundary marks, including three trackways running around its margins (*huntsmen's way, old* or *sheep way,* and *green way*), and it takes the Witney estate to the verge of Akeman Street.

Turning to the undulating countryside east of Oxford we can find a land charter for Cuddesdon (*Cuthewine's hill*) dating from 956, when the king granted an estate of twenty hides of land to Abingdon Abbey. It throws light on the settlement history of Wheatley, which was included within its boundaries. There was no reference to Wheatley in Domesday Book, but it had appeared before 1135 and was a manor held separately from Cuddesdon. Thus on the face of it Wheatley was a creation of the early twelfth century. In fact it was much more ancient, because the original settlement lay well to the south of the village as we know it: Old Wheatley was perched on the highish open country of the Portland limestones where (*pace* the idea of continuity) a Roman villa and Saxon burials have been found in juxtaposition to the east of Coombe Wood.[11] The charter boundaries ran at one juncture along Hollow Brook, and it was in this valley that another settlement appeared by 1135, first as an offshoot of the primary village on the hill and later superseding its parent. The boundaries of 956 also clearly demarcate the parent parish of Cuddesdon which survived until Wheatley was taken from it and made a separate parish in 1852. Grundy did not interpret them accurately, and when the charter referred to the Garsington–Wheatley road as 'the Street' he mistakenly took it to be the Roman road and tried to force Horspath into the estate as well. There is indeed something of a link here, because the original Horspath settlement was sited like Old Wheatley, Cuddesdon and Garsington villages by a spring at about 400 feet on the limestone hill. The present village is the result of migration to, or better survival at, Lower (Church) Horspath.

We look finally at another piece of landscape that experienced early English settlement, lying below the Chilterns where the scarp-foot countryside is traversed by the Icknield Way. The village of Pyrton is one of many set at regular intervals from Chinnor to Goring along this favoured shelf of loamy land, and it reveals another facet of how the English settlement proceeded. The most striking of its characteristics is the way Pyrton was sited precisely at the crossing of two ancient trackways—Lower Icknield Way running with the natural grain of the land, and Knightsbridge Lane (or *Ruggeway*) going transversely across it. These pre-Saxon roads intersected each other close to Pyrton church in the original nucleus of the village. Knightsbridge Lane was a thoroughfare from the direction of London via Henley, leading over the Chiltern hills, continuing through Pyrton to cross the clay lowlands to

[11] W. O. Hassall (ed.), *Wheatley Records, 956–1956* (Oxford Record Series, 1956), pp. 5, 27–30; V.C.H. *Oxfordshire*, Vol. V (London, 1957), pp. 96 *et seq.*

the west. It still has the appearance of an old routeway. On leaving the B4009 road it makes for Pyrton as a hollow-way; beyond the village it is arched over with elms as it humps and bends to cross the stream that is fed by the Lewknor spring or *townpool*, which flows strongly even in the driest summer; the Lane then climbs a ridge, still devoid of the wide grass verges found along most of the minor (and much later) roads in this locality.

Where Knightsbridge Lane ran between two streams it formed part of the boundaries of forty hides of land from the royal estate at Pyrton, granted to the Bishop of Worcester. Reputedly this was done by King Offa in 774, but in fact the boundaries were listed in the early eleventh century, when they outlined two separate and adjacent portions of the estate. The main portion survives in outline as the parish of Pyrton, the other (originally an area of woodland attached to the estate) may be taken to be the parish of Pishill-with-Stonor. It is important they be taken together as a single Saxon property, because in Grundy's view Pyrton alone ran as far into the Chilterns as the two portions combined. As he therefore found no woodland boundaries he concluded, falsely, that the Chiltern woods have been 'artificially created' since the Saxon period.[12] Rather, should we reconstruct the estate and its woodlands together, the single unit stretching for twelve miles from the farthest reaches of Pyrton at Standhill to wooded Stonor not far from Henley; it was only about one mile wide, on average. This long, narrow layout is found time and again in the estates based on villages at the foot of the Chilterns, for instance the great royal manor of Bensington ran from Benson to Henley. We also know they all probably originated between 571 and the eighth century. But can we explain why these

---

[12] *Saxon Oxfordshire*, pp. 46–7; for the corrected version of Pyrton's boundaries see W. O. Hassall, 'Pyrton Papers and Saxon Woodlands on the Chilterns', *Oxoniensia*, Vol. XIV (1949), p. 89; Gelling, *op. cit.* (1953) Vol. I, pp. 86–9; V.C.H. *Oxfordshire*, Vol. VIII (1964), pp. 138–9.

E

strip parishes (the usual term for them, as common features of the English scarplands) were given their peculiar shape in the first place?

Here the relationship between Knightsbridge Lane and the Pyrton estate can help us find an explanation. First we must disagree with the usual suggestion that because the long layout cut across the natural succession of land-types it was designed to give each place its own spectrum of land best suited to crops, hay, grazing and timber—with an unfailing supply of water from springs added for good measure. In the Chilterns, at any rate, this theory is ruled out because Pyrton and the rest were subdivided in practice into a multiplicity of properties that failed to fit in with the succession of land-types. Furthermore, the whole range of resources included in a long layout estate was not exploited through its length from the chief settlements. A case in point is Aston Rowant, which originally stretched from scarp-foot villages like Kingston Blount into the Chilterns via Stokenchurch, and so on to the slopes overlooking West Wycombe. But the Kingston villagers' right to cut timber for firing and fencing was in woods which, although at some distance were at least on their side of the Chiltern crest-line and not as far away as Stokenchurch. There is in fact no mention of these cutting rights, known as *hillwork*, in the copious records of Stokenchurch, nor in those of Pyrton and Shirburn. They appear once more in Chinnor as a piece of woodland called *Le Helwerk* in 1388, but here again it was on the near side of the watershed.[13]

We should not be surprised, after all, if such timber-cutting was unknown in the Chiltern prolongations of the scarp-foot estates, because if timber was cut there it would have to be brought back by a long haul up the dipslope. By contrast the loads of timber could easily be carted homewards, downhill all the way, from the *hillworks*. The presence of plenty of trackways along which this could be done points

[13] W. O. Hassall, 'Hillwork', *Oxoniensia*, Vol. XVI (1951), pp. 89–90.

to the explanation that might account for the long layout
of estates—namely, they were first marked out by boundaries that either followed or ran parallel with ancient trackways already in being. Knightsbridge Lane, for instance,
served as the axis around which Pyrton was delineated,
and this plan would need to be followed only once or
twice sufficiently early in the estates to set a pattern that
other properties would be obliged to fit in with later. Such
roads had to go transversely (south-east to north-west) to
the natural run of the hills (north-east to south-west) if
they were to serve as through routeways, and the long
layout harmonized with them as clear, indisputable lines
along which boundaries could be set out. Nor should we
overlook the other physical delineations that were already
in the Chiltern landscape when the Saxons arrived: the
prehistoric earthwork of Grim's Ditch in its surviving
form trends south-east to north-west for several miles at
Nuffield, and would have reinforced the precedent of
trackways running parallel with it.

If this was the reason for the choice of long layout it was
not entirely arbitrary, because it was making use of guide-
lines already in the landscape. Incidentally, of course, it also
had the useful result of giving each estate a cross-section of
resources for farming, and even if the farthest Chiltern
woodlands were not used for timber-cutting (as we saw in
the *hillwork*) they could still have been used as forest pasture
by the villages lying below the scarp, with the farm animals
being driven along the routeways. Finally, the whole
countryside below the Chilterns is patterned in a most
distinctive way by the intersection of transverse roads like
Knightsbridge Lane and many others paralleling it on the
one hand, with the Icknield Way and its companions on the
other. Among these trending in harmony with the natural
grain from north-east to south-west was the *Tuddingway*
which linked Goring with the Wallingford to Henley road
a mile or so farther into the plain from the Icknield Way.

Within the latticework formed by such roads there are dozens of green lanes, bridleways and footpaths, some going north-east to south-west, others at right-angles to them, giving a remarkable set of ladder-like patterns on the ground. It shows itself to anyone travelling towards Oxford on the A40, with a sequence of six minor roads going off to the south-west at intervals of about half a mile—the modern expression of factors that contributed to the laying-out of their lands by the Saxon English colonists.

SELECT BIBLIOGRAPHY

Gelling, Margaret, 'English Place-names derived from the Compound *Wīchām*', *Medieval Archaeology*, Vol. XI (1967), pp. 87–104.

Gelling, Margaret, *The Place-Names of Oxfordshire* (1953).

Grundy, G. B., *Saxon Oxfordshire. Charters and Ancient Highways*, Oxfordshire Record Society, No. 15 (1933).

Jope, E. M., 'Saxon Oxford and its Region', in *Dark-Age Britain*, ed. D. B. Harden (1956).

Martin, A. F. and Steel, R. W. (eds.), *The Oxford Region* (1954), Ch. 10, 'The Anglo-Saxon Period'.

Myres, J. N. L., *Anglo-Saxon Pottery and the Settlement of England* (1969).

Sturdy, David. 'Saxon Nomadism Near Oxford', *Oxoniensia*, Vol. XXVIII (1963), pp. 95–8.

3. The medieval expansion

The Domesday landscape. Colonisation of the waste. The forest landscapes. Medieval buildings and parks

The Domesday landscape

DOMESDAY BOOK IS a detailed inquest of resources and population throughout England, from woods to ploughlands, watermills to fisheries, and so should throw into relief the distribution and structure of economic life in 1086. So welcome is this standardised survey, through which the contemporary landscape might be reasonably expected to show itself, that we are all the more frustrated by the uncertainty of some of its evidence. Problems appear at all geographical scales, nationally, as between one county and the next, or in a particular locality. In Oxfordshire the record seems to have more than its due share of them, mainly because the Norman clerks were summarising property on the basis of its ownership rather than its location, so it is a quite separate task to rearrange the facts geographically. As we shall see in discussing Nethercote (p. 104) the Domesday folios are so intricate that places have remained hidden in them despite years of careful study.

We must begin by posing an apparently simple question: how many villages and hamlets were there in Oxfordshire by the close of the eleventh century? In trying to answer it we are hampered because settlements known to have been founded in the pre-Conquest period are not so much as mentioned in Domesday Book, simply because of the 'blanket' entries for the largest estates like the royal manor of Bensington or the Bishop of Lincoln's sprawling manors of Dorchester, Thame and Banbury. These were recorded in summary, not in detail for the individual settlements they undoubtedly included. On a more local scale it is not clear if all the partners in a twin or triplet settlement were founded by 1086. We are told that Great and Little Rollright were there, also Upper and Lower Arncott, but Great, Little and Duns Tew were merged together and appeared under the single entry *Tewam*. Nor was this merging confined to places with the same name. The entry for Beckley made no mention of Horton, known to be of pre-Conquest origin, while from archaeological evidence it is clear that the single reference to Yarnton must have covered more than one settlement. Given this margin of uncertainty and a little arbitrary arithmetic, it can be said that about 250 separate places in Oxfordshire were mentioned in Domesday Book. They were distributed with remarkable evenness throughout the county, the only relatively empty districts being on the Chilterns and around Wychwood. On such a uniform basis, then, we can interpret the Domesday data to make an approximate picture of regional variations in prosperity, which reflected the varying pitch of progress in making the landscape.

The backbone of rural life lay in the arable fields that yielded corn for bread and drink. A total of some 2860 plough-lands can be amassed for Oxfordshire, seeming to indicate the number of plough-teams at work twenty years earlier in 1066. The further listing of plough-teams actually at work on the demesne and those held by the peasantry, however, is a better means of seeing where the Domesday arable was distributed. We should really supplement the plough-team information with that of the recorded population, only some 40,000 strong in the whole county, to get a more complete idea of variations in wealth and prosperity. The highest densities of teams and people were found in the Redland–Cotswold uplands on the one hand, and again on the Gault Clay lowlands between Oxford and the Chilterns, where affluent villages followed the spring-line foot of the chalk scarp (p. 64). The Redland countryside was the most cultivated of all, with densities of five plough-teams and over ten persons to the square mile, plenty of mills and meadows, bare of timber, its villages strung along the small but numerous river valleys. Groups of villages were also well spaced along both margins of the Cherwell valley. Elsewhere the densities were pretty moderate, even on the gravel terraces of the upper Thames, although it may simply appear so because of deficiencies in the data. The same districts that were seen to be so thinly settled—around Wychwood and on the high Chilterns—also show in terms of sparse population and low densities (Fig. 6).

The corollary of these relatively high densities of arable fields, pastures and meadows, the negative as opposed to the positive, would be a broad remnant of the woodland, heath and marsh from which they had been created. After all, given a total community of 40,000 persons in town and country there must have been more or less untouched land in a rough state, as we infer from the known facts of expansion that came when population grew in the following two centuries. The Domesday references to woodland, in particular, can be mapped to reveal a belt of wood, coppice, underwood and spinney stretching through the countryside from Wychwood southwards to Stowood and Shotover on the Oxford Heights. The demesne forests of the king also lay there, set aside for the royal hunt. The oldest was Woodstock Park, known as 'the inclosure' in a charter of 1005 when the Saxon kings had a hunting lodge there, and as *Der Fald* (deer park) in the twelfth century. A separate tract of woodland covered much of the Chiltern hills, where beechmast and acorns, foliage and grass furnished

DISTRIBUTION MAP OF MEDIEVAL
CASTLES AND MONASTERIES

Clattercote

Hanwell

Wroxton
Priory

Banbury

Broughton

Swerford

Deddington

Mixbury

Coldnorton
St John's Priory

Somerton

Chipping Norton

Ardley

Stratton
Audley

Middleton
Stoney

Bicester
Priory

Bruern
Abbey

Ascott D'Oyley

Ascott Earl

Langley

Woodstock

Studley
Priory

Minster Lovell
Priory

Eynsham
Abbey

Godstow
Abbey

Beckley

Cogges

Cogges
Priory

Rewley Abbey

Oseney
Abbey

Oxford

St Fridewide's

Clanfield
Preceptory

Bampton

Littlemore Priory

Sandford Preceptory

Thame
Abbey

Radcot

Shirburn

Dorchester

Dorchester
Abbey

Watlington

Britwell

Benson

Castles   ▲

Monasteries +

Stephens
Mount

Greys Court

Goring
Priory

0   5   10
          Miles

Fig. 6. Only a minority of nine castles were built of stone, the remainder being earth and timber structures of the motte-and-bailey type. Together, however, they show the disposition of the prosperous holders of land in populous and well-developed districts, e.g. the Cotswolds–Redlands and below the Chilterns.

The monasteries are more indicative of the extension of land settlement in the medieval period. Bruern Abbey, for instance, was endowed with the manor of *Treton* in 1147, renamed it *Bruaria* from the Old French word for heathland, and founded Sandbrook Grange, from which the estate was managed.

plenty of forest pasture for pigs and cattle. In this respect the wooded Chilterns were at the other end of an ecological scale from the Cotswolds whose tree-cover, while surviving in pockets, was exceeded by the open grazings for large flocks of sheep. Although the Domesday survey does not itemise the farming livestock, there is no doubting the steady advance of sheep-farming on the stonebrash, with the peasantry's interest in using these animals as a vital element in their sheep-corn husbandry. In turn it sponsored the weaving of woollen cloth in the Cotswolds, with early fulling-mills on record at Cleveley (near Enstone) in 1185, Brightwell (1208) and Witney (1223), also the wealthy wool merchants whose mark is still visible in the town buildings of Burford, Witney and Chipping Norton.

Because Domesday is so approximate in its summary of the facts it is difficult to reconstruct a detailed, clear picture of how much waste and woodland was present in the land-scape of 1086. It is scarcely enough to say the region was fairly fully colonised by then: we have met the same problem in the pre-Conquest phases of settlement, so perhaps we should note at this point a brave attempt at quantification for the whole of that earlier period. As an archaeologist, R. J. C. Atkinson expressed the problem fully in its three stages—the need to determine the primitive physical basis in the region; to demarcate the areas of primary settlement which would be most attractive to early colonists; to isolate the more difficult terrain which would be avoided at first and then gradually penetrated and cleared later on, as organisation and technology gained strength. Subject to a number of caveats and provisos, Atkinson then suggested that the maps of land utilisation published in *The Land of Britain* could be used to show three categories of occupation: (i) by 1940 arable land was confined to easily tilled soils where primary settlement was most likely to have started; (ii) areas of permanent grass would formerly have been forested and sparsely settled; (iii) intermediate areas of mixed arable and pasture could be interpreted as the scene of secondary, expanding settlement.[1]

To test the hypothesis 400 archaeological sites were plotted on the land-use maps of Oxfordshire and Berkshire, distinguished according to their cultural origin as Neolithic, Bronze and Iron Ages, Roman and Saxon. One result was that the arable 'islands' cut off by permanent grassland from the main spreads of arable showed early settlement only of the Iron and Roman ages, not of any earlier period; they were predominantly on the Oxford Heights and marked a new trend of land settlement on these hills (p. 63). Turning to the Saxon data, Atkinson was surprised to find forty-seven per cent of the sites on arable-primary land, thirty-six per cent on secondary-arable/grass, and seventeen per cent on forest-permanent grass. Compared with pre-Saxon cultures, this thirty-six per cent was the highest of all, but the seventeen per cent was the lowest proportion of any. We can imagine the Saxons filling out into the accessible intermediate land, but it is curious that their onslaught on the waste is not more pronounced in the figures. Did they really have to clear as much ground *de novo* as we generally assume they did, or would most of Atkinson's sites have been restricted to the pagan Saxon (and therefore earliest) remains? If so, it would still have been possible for the English settlement to have gone farther into the forest-permanent grasslands after the seventh century, but it might not show in his statistics. This is where the deficiencies of Domesday's record of the contemporary woodlands fail to meet the question fully.

On this score one is inclined to regard Domesday Book not so much as a definitive survey in itself but rather as a springboard from which to make comparisons beyond 1086. It is especially useful as a kind of datum line for

[1] *Oxoniensia*, Vols. VIII and IX (1943–4), pp. 209–13, where R. J. C. Atkinson reviews Parts 56 (Oxfordshire) and 78 (Berkshire) of *The Land of Britain*, ed. L. D. Stamp (London, 1940).

estimating the agrarian expansion that was evident by the time of the Hundred Rolls in 1279. But we may be tempted, nevertheless, to make local reconstructions of places as they were in 1086, and apply ourselves to the intricacies of sorting out for a particular place the hidages, numbers of villeins, bordars or serfs, and all the various arithmetical puzzles stored in the folios. This is a legitimate aspect of historical-geographical research, but it is doubtful if it can throw much light on the understanding of landscape. To illustrate the possibilities we shall anatomise the Baldons, well-known villages in the margins of the Oxford Heights. It is easy to see from the one-inch maps, first of all, that the twin parishes of Toot and Marsh Baldon really stitch together to give a single coherent block of Baldon territory, more or less rectangular in outline. Within it we find four principal settlements in the landscape today, and by name in the historical records, all of which are Domesday or later in date; there is no charter evidence as at Wheatley (p. 64).

To the Domesday clerks they were all simply *Baldedone*, and as this meant *Bealda's hill* we can see Toot Baldon as the primary site where Bealda settled, for this village stands on a low hill. It is one of several in this countryside, in plain sight of Garsington, Cuddesdon and the Miltons, a constellation of old English settlements perched on the outer edges of slopes where the sands and limestones above give way to the clays below. By 1213 it had the degree of *Baldon Major*, presuming the existence of other, lesser places of the same name; these come to light as Little Baldon (1240), Baldon St Lawrence (1242), and Marsh Baldon (1279). Despite their first clear denomination in the thirteenth century, however, it can be assumed that all four were already in existence by 1086, so the question we must ask ourselves is whether or not the landscape shows anything to support or demolish this assumption. Domesday does not help: although *Baldedone* was entered en bloc it constituted no fewer than seven separate estates belonging to five different lords, and assessed at thirty hides in all. One estate was rated at ten hides and another at five hides, but it is clear that Baldon fitted the usual (and somewhat artificial) mode of assessment by five-hide units of land. By careful study in following the descent of the seven estates to other landowners after 1086 it is possible to allocate them either to the parish of Toot Baldon or that of Marsh Baldon, but not to locate them in order on the ground.

As a pointer to the fresh probabilities revealed by field-work it is also clear from the one-inch map that the block of territory comprising 'Greater Baldon' is neatly sub-divided into two almost equal parts by a north–south axis formed by linked stretches of lanes and field boundaries. This alignment, which we can call *Flitway* from the name it carried in its southern reaches by 1713, runs parallel with and just to the east of the presumed course of the Roman road from Dorchester to Alchester. So adjacent are they, in fact, that it would be possible to argue a case that they are identical. The Roman road was traced by Hussey in 1840, but when he reached the Baldons he admitted that he lost the field evidence for it, and again "there is some uncertainty about the exact course of our road as it leaves Baldon".[2] He was honest enough to mark its 'supposed line' on his map, but he ran it into lower Flitway, in contrast to the ruler-like precision of the Ordnance Survey map. However, the important point here is not to champion Flitway as the more likely course of the Roman road, but to demonstrate its crucial part in the laying-out of land in Domesday Baldon.

Two out of several pieces of topographical evidence may be cited in support of its importance. On walking along it northwards in August 1969 a distinct earthwork, bank and

[2] Robert Hussey, 'An Account of the Roman Road from Alchester to Dorchester' (lecture read to the Ashmolean Society, Oxford, 9th November 1840).

ditch, was found going consistently alongside on the west, starting at a stream and then, after half a mile, at the intersection of four lanes symmetrically in the centre of 'Greater Baldon' the bank bends round towards Marsh Baldon green. It has the look of an early boundary, its course respects the focal crossing-point of lanes, and its bank is crowned now with the line of tall trees that strikes a bold crest through the landscape. Secondly, the line of Flitway continues as a green lane from that intersection northwards and heads directly to the isolated church of St Lawrence, which is built practically astride its course. This church stands 'lonely in a field',[3] curiously aloof from its village of Toot Baldon (which also lies on the continuation of the Flitway line); but it was the *capella de Baldendone* mentioned in 1146 when the canons of Dorchester had their old liberties in it confirmed. It has a twelfth-century north door and there could well have been a church on the site at the time of Domesday, accessible to all who used the Flitway.

The oldest detailed plan of the Baldons marks out not only the axis of Flitway itself but a well-developed pattern of other lanes running parallel with it through the fields, then mostly unenclosed.[4] Other tracks ran at right-angles to it, completing an overall network of north–south, east–west thoroughfares and boundaries, giving the appearance of an orderly, deliberate scheme of laying out the land. Furthermore, to a large degree the three principal estates marked on the plan were inclined to respect and fit in with the network. Reverting to Domesday in this problem, it is

[3] John Brookes, *Mid-Oxfordshire Churches* (Thame, 1970), Section 20.

[4] They are in the muniments of Queen's College; 4B:30 is a coloured field map, probably a first draft made before the completion of 4B:29, which is clearer to read; there are photocopies (uncoloured) in the Bodleian Library. As to their date, the Queen's College calendar puts them at *c*. 1680, and the V.C.H. *Oxfordshire*, Vol. V, thinks they were drawn between 1730 and 1740. They could also date from 1713, when the manor of Marsh Baldon was surveyed (Oxon. Record Office, Willoughby Deeds, X/34). The name *Flitway* is used in Queen's Coll. Mun. 4B:25, a terrier of the lands of Dr John Lane "as they lie in the Common Fields", compiled on 2nd July 1713.

not difficult to group the seven estates of 1086 in such a way that three of them lay grouped to the west of Flitway, amounting in all to seventeen and a half hides, and four of them (making the remainder of twelve and a half hides) lay to the east of it. Remembering the existence of four villages it also seems reasonable that the Baldon territory was subdivided at an early stage into quadrants, separated by Flitway as a major axis and the east–west lane intersecting it at a central point, which itself is confirmed by the trend of the boundary earthwork. Thus Toot Baldon and Baldon St Lawrence (now Baldon Row) could have had their lands in the north-east and south-east, while those of Marsh Baldon and Little Baldon may have run to the north-west and south-west quadrants.

Colonisation of the waste

The Domesday Inquest was held at a time of gathering change in the landscape. A recent study has shown what this signified at Watlington, below the Chilterns. Much of its plough-land was cultivable ground that had been abandoned before 1086, due to the transition from a random field-grass economy to the two-field system, whereby the arable in common fields was cropped in alternate years. This system was dominant by 1086 but it left a reserve of former arable. The arable farmland at Watlington was to be enlarged by fifty per cent between Domesday and 1279, partly by cultivating this reserve, partly by clearing virgin land. As all this work went on, by about 1200 a three-field system was emerging and farming was further intensified (p. 110).

To imagine a static scene, then, would be misleading; rather should we go beyond it to look for signs of change. In particular it is not fully realised how many new villages were appearing for the first time. Among those few usually cited as 'minor extensions of colonisation'[5] were Souldern (1173) and Newton Purcell (1198), but they can be supplemented very easily from their immediate locale in Ploughley hundred, sited mostly on the lower stonebrash and partly on the clay vale running north-east from Oxford, with its occasional uncleared woodlands. A broader pattern emerges here if we test the relationships between its ancient villages and their hamlets, no fewer than six of them appearing between Domesday, which was silent about them, and the end of the twelfth century.

We find a typical case of the growth of a satellite settlement in the parish of Lower Heyford. The main village of Heyford has been occupied continuously since the sixth century, there is pagan Saxon evidence from Harborough Bank (a site later absorbed by the common fields and now vanished), and as 'the ford used at hay-making' the place clearly belonged to the pioneer phase of English settlement when the Cherwell meadows had a prime value (p. 56). By Domesday it had grown into two estates of five hides apiece, but not all the available land was under cultivation. It stood on the marlstone brink of the Cherwell valley, with Lower Lias clays beneath, which supplied it with water from wells that were in use until 1954. Like most of the old villages spaced regularly along the Cherwell, its lands were a blend of riverside meadow and stonebrash ground that did well as arable or pasture.

The intermediate settlement had been founded at Caulcott by 1199, a mile away from Heyford on the dry plateau and towards the boundary of Aves Ditch. As its name suggests (*cold place*) it was an altogether bleaker location than the parent village, but it had water from wells sunk in a depression leading down to the Gallows Brook. It is more likely that Caulcott appeared in the twelfth-century landscape for the first time, rather than being an older place omitted

[5] E. M. Jope, 'Saxon Oxford and its Region', in D. B. Harden (ed.), *Dark Age Britain* (London, 1956), p. 247.

from Domesday, because by 1279 the cultivated area of Heyford and Caulcott had increased to about 850 acres, nearly thirty per cent of which had been added since 1086. Caulcott had the lion's share of this land by roughly two to one, and it had to support a larger population, having thirty-three peasant families to the mother village's nineteen; it seems to have been populated by men from neighbouring villages like Souldern, Middleton Stoney and Rousham, who must have been encouraged to settle there by its founder, one of the lords of the Heyford manors to whom most of its lands belonged. It was a successful venture, as Caulcott remained the more populous and wealthier of the settlements in the fourteenth century. The villages still differ physically as much as they did on the plan of 1606. Lower Heyford is a sprawling but essentially nucleated place, always apt (as we shall see later) to respond to forces that evoke new forms in building and layout, whereas Caulcott's houses fall in line along an unusually narrow village street, notched by the spring-fed pond that commended the site to its twelfth-century pioneers.

We find elsewhere in Ploughley hundred the steady progress of reclaiming waste land outwards from old settlements, some of it woodland or scrub, some of it marsh and heath. It was the acceleration of a traditional process, due to sharp increases in population during the twelfth and thirteenth centuries. One of its pre-Conquest villages was called Hethe, meaning 'uncultivated ground', so what we have in Caulcott, Fewcott, Murcott, Fencott and possibly Willaston were also new foundations among fresh fields. Little Chesterton grew between 1130 and 1180 on lands already in use but made more profitable as an estate of the abbots of Thame and Oseney. The village of Newton Purcell was there by the late twelfth century, reclaimed from furze and heathland where the solid geology of Oxfordshire begins to be smothered beneath a glacial drift of sands and gravels; in its turn it generated its own hamlet of Newton Morrell. So, including Souldern (p. 58), we find eight or nine new additions to the landscape to set against the thirty established vills named in Domesday Book. Their fields had characteristic names that survived for centuries, especially the variants of *breche*, meaning land freshly broken for cultivation: Caulcott had its large New Breach, as did Charlton-on-Otmoor, while the *breches* at Fewcott were interspersed with heathland used for sheep grazings in the early thirteenth century.

These new places should be seen as a group because in revealing colonisation of the land they act as a corrective to the assumption that only where the Domesday woodland was thickest did they come into being. Not much woodland was recorded in Ploughley, so its new fields came at the expense of heath and marsh. Elsewhere the labour of reclamation was concentrated on a narrower front, as in the drainage of flood-plain flats along the upper Thames. Thus the new marshland village of Northmoor was founded in the twelfth century as an outlying dependency of Taynton. By 1164 Standlake appeared between the old settlement of Brighthampton and the river, taking its name from 'a stony stream'; much later it was still said to be "situate upon a damned standing Puddle, long, deep and dirty". From the A415 we can still see old Standlake stretched out like a Dutch village along the line of its dyke, making a reclamation frontier at the leading edge of the lowest gravel terrace, beyond it the empty alluvial flats reaching to the Thames at Newbridge. "As the meadows are always overflowed in winter, and subject to inundations in a rainy summer," wrote a later observer of this landscape, "the villages to which they belong are situated at a distance that renders them invisible from the river."[6] Not far away Hardwick did not appear until 1199, and hints of similar expansion in a different environment come from the

[6] W. Combe, *An History of the Principal Rivers of Great Britain* (London, 1794), Vol. I, p. 64.

Cotswolds: Upton was first recorded in 1200 and Signet ('place cleared by burning') in 1285.

The forest landscapes

The purpose of Figure 7 is to show the value of place-names in demarcating areas where medieval colonisation of land was at its peak. In terms of the four elements selected in making the map, describing woodland and the clearing of waste, it refutes the view that because name-elements are so evenly distributed in Oxfordshire they do not merit mapping. Essentially this pattern of a total of eighty-five names, sixteen of them recorded before 1100, conforms very closely to that of the Domesday woodlands but carries the implication of settlement and clearance continuing after 1100. Of the three main concentrations of woods we may look first of all at the central one pivoting on the Oxford Heights. Here ran the royal forests of Stowood and Shotover, centred on the hills that carried over to Bernwood in Buckinghamshire. 'Forest' was primarily a legal status for that portion of the country where forest law replaced the usual legal system because of the priority given to the king's hunting. Naturally the forests usually had plenty of woods, coppices, thickets and scrub to give cover to the beasts of the chase and to supply timber for building, fuel and charcoal-burning, but these were interspersed with open heath, pasture or even ploughed land, as and when the circuit of the forest contracted or expanded by royal decree, or as grazing and cutting made their inroads. Let us look at one of them at a time when the medieval expansion for fresh land to support a quickly growing population had passed its maximum, chiefly to see the degree of woodland it still contained but which is now much reduced, and to point to some of its surviving landmarks.

By the thirteenth century Shotover Forest included the parish of Headington as well as the modern Stowood and

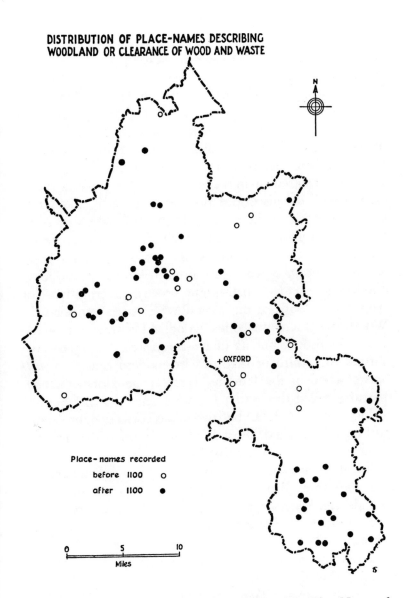

**DISTRIBUTION OF PLACE-NAMES DESCRIBING
WOODLAND OR CLEARANCE OF WOOD AND WASTE**

+ OXFORD

Place - names recorded

before 1100   ○

after   1100   ●

0   5   10
Miles

Fig. 7. Based on data from Margaret Gelling, *The Place-Names of
Oxfordshire* (1956). The elements shown are: Old English *wudu*, wood;
le(a)h, wood, open place in woodlands; *graf(f)a*, grove, copse; Middle
English *assart*, clearing where the land had formerly been waste.

Shotover. A perambulation of its boundaries made in 1298 helps us to locate various woods then in dispute, some lying within the forest and others in adjoining parishes like Stanton St John, where two woods known as Horley and Sidley now have their descendants in Holly Wood and Great Wood. Their full extent is astonishing, as they stretched from Islip to Cuddesdon across the whole expanse of the Oxford Heights. In all, the disputed woodlands of 1298 amounted to about 1300 acres, whereas today only 300 acres or so remain in the landscape, the rest having been cleared with the disafforestation of Shotover in 1660. The forest sprawled in the angle between the old roads from London to Oxford across Shotover Hill and to Worcester via Islip. At its northernmost limit was *Cowaliz*, a great wood of over 700 acres (measured in Domesday as being one league long by a half-league broad), covering most of Islip parish south of the river Ray; this has vanished. In Woodeaton there was thick woodland to the east of the Stowood Brook, but its ninety-seven acres in 1366 have shrunk to a third of that area by modern times. *Peryhale* was a wood of the Knights Templars in Horspath, now pastures called the Perils; *Lynhale* formed part of Studley Priory's woodland, but by 1670 it was converted into arable furlongs (Long and Short Lynehill) close to the turnpike road now superseded by the A40.

For its boundaries Shotover Forest followed streams like the Bayswater Brook, the margins of named fields and woods (e.g. *boscum de Ellesfield*), or man-made features. These are most easily traceable on its southern limits below Shotover Hill. Beyond Wheatley the boundary crossed the old London road by following *Kyngeswodebroke*. From the head of this brook it went with the lower edge of *Akermere*, a wood held by the Templars in Horspath. Next it ran along the *Redediche*, which must have been artificial because it climbed and descended a spur of high ground from Shotover Plain. The 'red ditch' can still be traced in the landscape where it followed *Akermerebroke* as it flows steeply from the summit. Finally the forest boundary went along the *Mereweye*: this is now partly a footpath between Brasenose Wood and the fields of Westhill Farm, partly the service road for a scattering of modern houses under Shotover Edge. In this section the *Mereweye* is now called the Riding, and is as narrow, twisting and deeply ditched on each side as it must have been in 1298.

The largest spread of woodland we may infer from Figure 7 is in the area of Wychwood Forest, surviving stubbornly until its disafforestation by Act of Parliament in 1857, and still one of Oxfordshire's leafiest countrysides. Despite its prehistoric and Roman settlements, or perhaps because of them (p. 44) Wychwood was regarded as secondbest land for farming after the easier gravels, stonebrash and clays. One drawback was its exposure and bleakness: look at it from Cumnor, and Wychwood stands out as a dark wooded ridge between the Evenlode and Windrush valleys; it shows a similar profile from the A40 at Witney, with the spire of Leafield church pointing above the trees. Settlements ran the risk of a summer shortage of water, as in Leafield where carts went round selling water until a reliable piped supply came in 1927: the water-storage is as noticeable a landmark as Leafield Barrow, which it flanks. Neither were its soils thought to be good. There is much plateau gravel and Oxford Clay on the stonebrash, souring it, so that Morison could describe the forest soil as "cold and late country of bad reputation".[7] It made poor grassland unsuited for sheep, and its crop yields were low, facing its farmers with many of the difficulties of a clay, without its compensations. No wonder it was left to the forester and the common grazing enjoyed by the forest villages. The complex attrition that was affecting even Wychwood during the period of expanding population is made evident by the

[7] John Orr, *Agriculture in Oxfordshire* (Oxford, 1916), p. 185; G. T. Morison's chapter is the first modern account of Oxfordshire's soils.

Carta Forestae of 1217, which pardoned the encroachments and *assarts* (clearings enclosed by ditch and hedge) already made. Further assarting continued through the thirteenth century, before the covert of the forest (i.e. unbroken woodland with trees meeting overhead) was defined in 1279. By a new perambulation of 1300 only the royal woods were left inside the forest, and the king followed a policy of granting wastes to those who wished to assart them. Even so, Wychwood covered some 50,000 acres from Woodstock to Taynton, and from Ditchley to Witney.

The new villages carved from Wychwood are the most tangible legacy of medieval expansion in the Oxfordshire landscape (Plate 6). Leafield is chief among them, first recorded as *la Felde* (probably an old clearing or *lawn* of pasture) in 1213, and later known as Field Town; its western lands were assarted by 1298 and three fields to the south of the village (Long Sart, Broad Sart, Purrans) soon after 1300. It grew into "a large primitive village in the very heart of the forest", its people "noted for their uncouth dialect". Rightly or wrongly the forest-dwellers were regarded as a race apart by those living around them, just as they are to the present day in the Forest of Dean. They were absorbed by the forest as their old-settled villages became overcrowded, and we see here an intensification of the clearance already implicit in the pre-Domesday charters of Witney (p. 63). In order of their first appearance in the records the other Wychwood villages most intimately linked to the forest were Finstock (1135), Ramsden (1146), Fawler (1205), Crawley (1214) and Hailey (1240). They were nourished by a century of patient assarting, and they show it today in their straggling form as settlements, their irregular and varying patterns of fields and copses, their chaotic system of many winding lanes and trackways. They had to wait until Victorian times to achieve the status of separate parishes with their own newly-built churches, and still stood apart in many respects from the more ancient places.

For instance, Hailey was a tripartite village, each section having its farms and cottages: at Middle Town stood the church built in 1868, but the manor house, green and pond were at Delly End, while the parish pound stood on another green at Poffley End. Its lands were part of the Bishop of Winchester's manor of Witney in 1279, when thirty-two out of thirty-six freehold farms in Hailey were assarts, i.e. recently cleared land reckoned in acres (rather than yard-lands like the old freeholds) and let at the uniform rent of sixpence an acre. They were located around Delly, Poffley and *Chardesle*, another *leah* clearance name. In addition a third of those holding messuages in the bishop's borough of Witney had arable assarts in Hailey, paying their entry fines in the manor court. Another five assarts were in Crawley with its setting of Bishopswood.

As we might predict from their activity elsewhere in England the monastic landowners were prominent in developing the forest landscape. The great Benedictine abbey of Eynsham had enlarged its demesne by assarts from three ploughs working in 1086 to a dozen or more by 1350, when it had ten plough-lands of good soil and four of poor quality. From 1094 the abbey held estates at Charlbury and were first permitted to assart land in Wych-wood by Henry II sixty years later. The monks were reluc-tant to record their income from this source, but assarting was certainly in progress by 1190, when they were pardoned for it, and in 1230 when the foresters were so disturbed by wasting of oakwoods and underwood at Finstock, Stones-field and Spelsbury that they took them back into their custody. They had to do so again in 1270, as the abbey was still selling off woodland and getting a rent from those who cleared it for farming. At least some of this was aimed at growing crops, for in 1332 (by which time the woods had returned to the abbey) men were paid eight pounds and ten quarters of seed wheat for agreeing that the monks should enclose and assart Charlbury woods, which had long been separated from the Wychwood covert (Plate 7). The men reserved their right of common grazing when the land was fallow; similar encroachments were made on the Heath (*brueria*) at Eynsham.

Assarted lands brought a total of twenty-six pounds in rents to the abbey in 1348. The later and better-recorded clearings of the thirteenth and fourteenth centuries were probably held for money rents only, as it was the twelfth-century onslaught that generated the new villages such as Finstock and Fawler, where the monks held tenant lands divided into virgates and coupled with customary services. From their appearance on eighteenth-century plans these village fields were scarcely distinguishable in pattern from the open fields worked in common around much older settlements (compare Plates 6 and 7). They shared the same layout of sets of furlongs and strips, which (given the uniformity imposed by parliamentary enclosure in the eighteenth and nineteenth centuries) makes them somewhat difficult to detect in the modern landscape. What sets them apart is their conjunction with woods and the smaller assarts undertaken both pre-Conquest and in the later medieval centuries, usually block fields, piecemeal and marked out by massive hedges and ditches. We see this clearly around Hailey, or again at South Leigh, a place created by colonisation between Domesday and 1190: although it had fields with names like *Eefurlong* it also has a different texture in field pattern from the true enclosed champion lands around Eynsham nearby.

Medieval buildings and parks

English church architecture, as to its history and aesthetics, is a well-worn path and need be included in landscape studies not for its own sake but because it can throw light on the age and sequence of the communities by whom churches were built. We have already had hints of its usefulness at

Plate 5 The Romano-British villa at Ditchley, showing as crop-marks. It now seems likely that Ditchley was a small second-century villa, abandoned as an independent dwelling from about A.D. 200 to 370, but then occupied intensively once more until well into the fifth century.

Plate 6 Leafield, in a plan of 1764. At this time Leafield was still the main clearing within the core of Wychwood Forest. It was first recorded in 1213, and here we see its constituent parts (since joined together), one by the green and the other a simple linear settlement like Caulcott and Chilson. Around the green lie the roundish clearances, farther away the more formalised kind of *assarts*.

ISCOAT

A Map of the Manner of Chilson in the Parish of Charlbury Com: Oxon. Survey'd in the Year 1735 by William Frearson Immediatly after the Ivry had Fixed Land Marks Throughout the Said Common Fields

Wakestone Furlong

Pibley Furlong

Wading Furlong

Cannons Grave Furlong

Furlong Shooting on the Town

HICHWOOD

Easev Furlong

Buron Ash dross Furlong

Buron Ash Furlong

Colls Copse

FOREST

Old horse hitching Furlong

Butt Furlong

Plate 7 Chilson, in the Evenlode valley. This plan of 1735 shows the common fields; the process of parliamentary enclosure has given fields that now largely retain the pattern of these furlongs. Chilson is a simple linear village like Caulcott (p. 79), not recorded until about 1200, when it appeared as a dependency of Charlbury, during the medieval expansion.

Plate 8 Wroxton Abbey. Sir William Pope built this house about 1620, on the site of an Augustinian priory. The north front, which we see here, is symmetrical and finely proportioned.

Plate 9 Beckley Park. The house stands centrally within the circuit of a deer park which was enclosed with a stone wall by 1200. A hunting lodge stood on the site by 1347, and it came to be surrounded by three moats. As it stands, the house is of the finest and untouched Tudor style: a Grade I scheduled building.

Souldern (p. 58), Toot Baldon (p. 77) and Hailey. This is not to say we must close our eyes to the visual appeal of such medieval splendours as the churches at Bampton or Deddington, landmarks in their different sectors of the Oxfordshire countryside, but simply that we should apply to them a scale of relevance to other questions. With the Eynsham assarting fresh in mind we can take as illustration the parish church of St Peter at Cassington, which (apart from its Gothic spire) is remarkable for its purely Norman tower, unspoilt Norman doorways, windows, chancel arches and vaulted sanctuary. In this old village the church was built in 1123 as a private place of worship for the manor house, but with the profitable expansion of assarting its rector received more and more from tithes on the newly productive land. This increasing revenue must have persuaded the Eynsham canons, who were close at hand to see it, to secure the appropriation of the church by 1197, to establish a perpetual vicarage and make Cassington a parish in its own right. They were to follow a similar course of action at Charlbury, appropriating the church in 1296.

Later on we find architectural evidence of a different kind of change from Combe, a sub-manor of royal Woodstock. As its name implies (compare the Welsh *cwm*) this village originally stood in the valley close to the Evenlode, its site reminiscent of that of the Romano-British villa nearby at North Leigh. Between 1086 and 1279 the arable fields were expanded from about 500 to 800 acres through colonisation of the furze, underwood and trees growing to the north. Because of this development, by about 1350 the old settlement was abandoned and a new Combe appeared on the hill above, centrally placed for the farmers to have better access to their land. The old Norman church continued in use for another generation, but in 1395 it was succeeded by a new building uphill near the spacious green. Combe church is beautiful "largely due to the uniformity

of its architecture"[8]—which in turn reflects the circum-
stance of its creation on a new site; it is all of a piece in the
Perpendicular style, of impressive proportion, and one of
the earliest of its kind among village churches.

Not infrequently, as at Bletchingdon, Middleton Stoney
and Shirburn, the parish church stands on its own inside
the park of a great house, and (although it was quite
customary for the lord, if he built the first parish church,
to put it close to his own house, whether he had a park or
not), this suggests the medieval origin of some parklands.
The Oxfordshire countryside has plenty of what may be
termed 'demesne landscape', usually signalised to the passer-
by as stretches of high, blank stone walling that shuts out
the roadside world, more often than not shrouded by the
overhanging plantations of massive trees. On its grandest
scale the parkland sequence is met at Blenheim. Its progeni-
tor was Woodstock Park, a hunting place of the Saxon kings
before it was surrounded by a stone wall in the twelfth
century.[9] This amenity, reputedly the handiwork of
Henry I, confirmed the popularity of Woodstock Park with
his royal successors, and eventually in the sixteenth century
the Great Park was extended northwards, overriding the
old fields and possibly some of the houses of Old Woodstock (Plate 10). The Blenheim park wall as we see it was
rebuilt by the Duke of Marlborough in 1727 so as to keep
the deer inside. Thus (as an observer of that time put it)
parks had proliferated because they were places of recreation, nurseries for game, and were "part of the dignity of
domain, an appendage of magnificence to our kings and
great men".[10]

Oxfordshire has much parkland that grew from a medieval nucleus, and the evolution of Blenheim raises two of
its general characteristics. We would expect firstly to find

[8] C. S. Emden, *Combe, Church and Village* (Oxford, 1951), p. 8.
[9] H. M. Colvin, *The History of the King's Works* (1963), Vol. II, p. 1016.
[10] W. Combe, *op. cit.*, p. 81.

most of them where the forests and woods were thickest on the ground at the time of Domesday. This is borne out to a certain extent as in the creation of Blenheim, Cornbury, Ditchley and other parks around Wychwood, which itself had to bear the constraint of a late forest wall (started by Charles I in 1631 and completed by Oliver Cromwell in 1655), "for better preservation and increase of the deer". Thus the Minster Lovell woods were taken out of Wychwood in 1442 and became a free chase for the Lovell family, i.e. offenders were tried under common law rather than in the forest courts. In the second place, however, as the Elizabethan enlargement of Woodstock showed, parks could be brought into being at the expense of existing farmland as and when the lord deemed fit. So their presence in the landscape may be understood by nothing more than the ambition of a prosperous resident lord in his moated manor house (Fig. 8). There is a cluster of parks great and small to the east of the Cherwell, and a trio of them will show the variations in how demesne landscapes came about (Plate 9).

The oldest and most feudal is Middleton Stoney, where Gerard de Camville was authorised by King John to make a park in 1201, close to his motte-and-bailey castle. He was given royal bucks and does from Woodstock to start a deer herd; by 1328 the park was surrounded by a stone wall, surviving as the bank and ditch around Home Wood, which is now ensconced inside the vast new park made in 1825 and covering half the parish. Neither Kirtlington nor Bletchingdon parks had the deer-stocking tradition, but both were in old villages lying close to the medieval highway from London to Worcester. There was 'a new park' at Kirtlington in 1279, probably enclosed from the East Field (*campus versus boscum*) and covering about seventy-five acres. This in turn was absorbed and dwarfed by Sir James Dashwood's park carved out in 1750, again from the East Field. At Bletchingdon we find a more modest and plainly functional park, first recorded in 1322 near to Roger

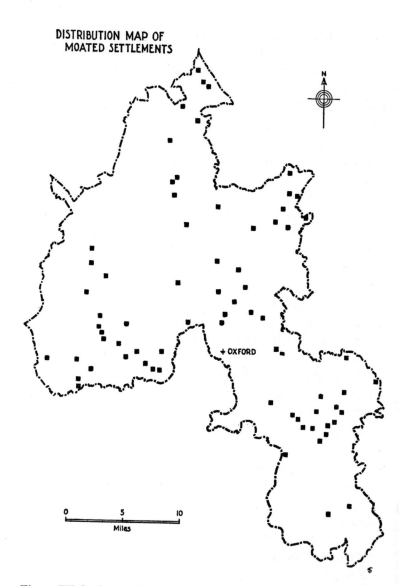

DISTRIBUTION MAP OF
MOATED SETTLEMENTS

+ OXFORD

0   5   10
Miles

Fig. 8. While eleven of these moated sites were castles (and appear on Fig. 6) the great majority were simply manor houses whose medieval owners preferred to surround themselves with a water-filled moat. They are most common on the claylands, for constructional reasons, and especially in the more developed districts. Many moats no longer have houses within them (see Plate 11).

Damory's manor house. It was fashioned to its present size by 1552, thanks to the agrarian policies of Vincent Poure, a great converter of arable land to grass, who extended his park pasture at the expense of farmhouses, gardens and closes which were thrown into it. Bletchingdon Park was walled round by 1623.

Collectively, then, the Oxfordshire parklands are more likely to be reflective of broad issues in the making of the landscape than the individual buildings that survive from the period. We can regard Shirburn Castle as integrated with its park, for instance, not simply as a castellated building of the late fourteenth century. This is not to diminish the value of fine things like the fifteenth-century grouping of church, almshouses and school at Ewelme; the question of how much vernacular architecture adds to the landscape will be asked in the context of a later chapter, as will that of the vigorous forms of urban life that also appeared in medieval Oxfordshire.

SELECTED BIBLIOGRAPHY

Chambers, E. K., *Eynsham under the Monks,* Oxfordshire Record Series, No. 18 (1936).

Darby, H. C. and Campbell, Eila M. J., *The Domesday Geography of South-East England* (1962). Ch. 5, 'Oxfordshire', by E. M. Jope and I. B. Terrett.

Gelling, Margaret, *The Place-Names of Oxfordshire* (1953).

Roberts, Edward, 'The Boundary and Woodlands of Shotover Forest *circa* 1298', *Oxoniensia,* Vol. XXVIII (1963), pp. 68–73. *Oxfordshire Hundred Rolls of 1279,* Oxfordshire Record Series, No. 46 (1968): 1 'The Hundred of Bampton', ed. E. Stone; 2 'The Borough of Witney', ed. Patricia Hyde.

Wickham Steed, V., *Notes on an Exhibition of Maps illustrating the Historical Development of Wychwood Forest,* Ashmolean Museum (1968).

4. Landscapes in transition

The desertion of medieval villages. The discovery of Nether-cote. The texture of early enclosure. New buildings in the countryside

THE KIND OF medieval expansion we have just traced in the forest landscapes was also seen in the wooded Chilterns, although on a less formal basis because they were not *forest* in the legal sense. Rather was it a piecemeal penetration from old villages on the Chiltern fringes, especially from the thickly-settled scarp-foot along the Icknield Way. This was a natural linkage because of the many ancient tracks that ran south-east to north-west across the hills, making available to villages like Chinnor and Kingston Blount the purely woodland resources of the dipslope. The character-istic outcome was not so much new nucleations of settle-ment, as in the Ploughley and Wychwood districts (pp. 79–88), but instead the founding of small clusters of loosely grouped farmsteads, scattered alongside clearings cut from the broad spread of beech, oak and whitebeam, gorse and heath.

Nuffield shows this to advantage, its constituent farms being "the very stuff from which the village has been formed".[1] All we find in Domesday Book is one hide of land, including pasture, at Gangsdown; this lies where a wide embayment breaks the Chiltern scarp, and is followed by the A423 road as it now climbs Gangsdown Hill. The Domesday land was held in conjunction with a chief estate at Chalgrove on the plain, and in view of the common

[1] P. M. Briers, *The History of Nuffield* (Oxford, 1939), p. 86.

94

rights over Nuffield Common later enjoyed by Chalgrove farmers it reveals the direction along which the Gangsdown clearing was made before 1086. It formed the nucleus of Nuffield, although the name under which it usually went was Huntercombe, first mentioned in 1183 as an outlying part of the great royal manor of Benson. Nuffield was sufficiently established to become a distinct parish before 1184, when its church was used for burials by the people of Mongewell, who did not yet have a church of their own. The fabric of Nuffield church still has some Norman work; and close to it are the essentials of village life, the school, post office, rectory and the pool that formerly supplied it with water, together with most of the houses. They are far from centrally placed, being separated by the Common from the new elements (inn, garage) that relate more to the main road beside which they have grown.

The original clearing at Nuffield is probably represented by the Mays estate, even though the name did not appear until 1440: it always enjoyed capital status and stretched east–west along the axis of Green Lane, very similar in miniature to the Chiltern manors (p. 65). At its zenith it appeared on a plan drawn in 1635 and epitomises the Chiltern landscape.[2] 'Mayes Farm' then covered the large area of 667 acres by customary measure, of which 171 acres was 'Wood Land' (twenty-five per cent), the rest arable and pasture. The woodland lay in ten parcels, ranging in size from *Gaynsden* (fifty-two acres, the name a version of Gangsdown) and *Ambrous* (twenty-eight acres, now part of Ambrose Farm), to *Whitbeam Shaws* and *Maple Coppice* at an acre or less. Significantly a number of these largest enclosures of woodland were marked 'Now Arable' on the plan, and from a study of the areas given (by the sixteen-and-a-half-foot perch for land and eighteen-foot perch for woods) it is clear that fields with *Wood* names and the 'Wood Land' were cleared or semi-cleared ground, not parcels of

2 Bodleian Library, MS. Maps Oxon. a.2(4).

standing timber—although these persisted alongside and in association with them. The arable and pasture fields, closes or pieces were also variable in size, from *The Great Field* at 141 acres to *Briary Shaw* at one acre; fringed with belts of trees they were irregular in shape, although it is possible to detect a nuclear grouping of fields. It is again significant how this pivotal (and possibly original) part of Mays spread itself across both Nuffield and Benson parishes, not just in one or the other.

The colonising of wooded and heathy Chiltern from external bases sometimes stretched over a considerable distance, like the five miles between Chalgrove and Nuffield, in which case it was more likely that the Chiltern end of things would grow into a place of independence and status in its own right. In other cases the process went on within a smaller and more compact unit of land, so that the Chiltern side remained in a minor key. South Stoke is typical of these: 'Below Hill' we find the parent village with its former common fields surrounding it, still an open, hedgeless and treeless landscape; 'Above Hill' lies the dependent settlement of Woodcote (first recorded in 1109) and other hamlets at Exlade Street (1241, on a medieval road from Wallingford to Reading) and at Greenmoor (1366). The woodland element in the medieval economy is made plain in the accounts of Eynsham Abbey, whose property it became in 1094. The tenurial pattern in 1279 was such that in a total of seventy-seven holdings Stoke had only three freeholders as against fourteen at Woodcote, with forty as against twenty customary tenants. Such figures suggest the difference in size of the two communities, and the greater emphasis on freeholders' activity in clearing the waste for themselves at Woodcote. The abbey's woods ran to 348 acres in 1366, compared with 334 acres of demesne arable, and the timber from them was sold as an article of commerce as well as being used for the day-to-day needs of the farmers.

Such an environment was specially favourable to the building up of small estates, as commodity–money relations became strong in the thirteenth century, and as plenty of usable land was being taken up through grants or by sub-infeudation (i.e. the creation of new sub-manors). The Stonor family, for instance, increased its estate eight-fold between Domesday and 1279, solely by purchasing one free tenement after another. Theirs grew as a *patchwork* manor, very complex and dispersed in its structure: by 1300 it comprised at least a dozen separate tenements, varying from ten to forty acres apiece, and scattered through the neighbouring parishes of Watlington, Pyrton, Pishill and Bix. In itself it was symptomatic of how the disparate Chiltern landscape had emerged. As the social status of these small landowners advanced and flourished—Sir John de Stonor was Chief Justice of Common Pleas in the fourteenth century—they were all the more likely to make their own tangible impression on the Chiltern scene: witness the mansion and park at Stonor (p. 124).

Agrarian life in the Chilterns, then, proceeded from the outset along unique lines. Their forest-pasture type of mixed farming was perhaps the most distinctive of its kind in Oxfordshire, found over a compact area with its own name, matched and balanced only by the Cotswolds and Redlands. It sponsored a characteristic pattern of settlement, loosely arranged and scattered through the wooded country-side. The only interruptions in this habitat are formed by the beechwoods and heaths, and one gets the feeling that the farms and cottages appeared steadily through the centuries after the first breaches were made, without suffering much in the way of retreat or reduction. Certainly in the matter of what are known as 'deserted medieval villages' the Chilterns have very little to show (Fig. 9), and seem not to have experienced this phase of landscape-history, in sharp contrast to the rest of Oxfordshire where lost villages are pretty common. Indeed in some districts the village pattern is a mere skeleton of what it was between 1300 and 1500.

The desertion of medieval villages

A working principle in the study of landscape, already hinted at in the replacement of old Combe by a new village in the fourteenth century (p. 89), is that the pattern of settlement and the form of individual places are volatile and apt to change. This is a good argument against trying to classify villages into various types of plan and layout, for instance, on the basis of how they appear on the earliest maps. Such portrayals are generally no older than two or three centuries, and there is no guarantee that a village clustered around its green in 1700 was like that when recorded in Domesday Book; we shall take the argument farther in Chapter 6. Nowhere has this lesson been learnt more fruitfully than in the realisation that thousands of English villages, registered as prosperous places in Domesday or during the 'high culture' of the medieval expansion to 1300, have since lost their standing in the landscape.

Disappearance, shrinkage, and transference: these are the terms in current use by students of the deserted medieval villages.[3] Some have vanished virtually without trace and are still being searched out, others have dwindled to a single farm or a handful of cottages, still others have shifted from an original or previous site to a different location. We know roughly how many cases have been identified in Oxfordshire (Fig. 9), but the map shows they are not evenly distributed. As we have seen, the Chilterns have none, nor are they common in the Redlands; while they are not unknown in most other districts, they are particularly concentrated in the clay lowlands below the Chilterns and in the upper Thames valley, notably in the angle of country between the

[3] The most recent general survey is *Deserted Medieval Villages: Studies* edited by *Maurice Beresford and John G. Hurst* (London, 1971).

DISTRIBUTION MAP OF DESERTED VILLAGES

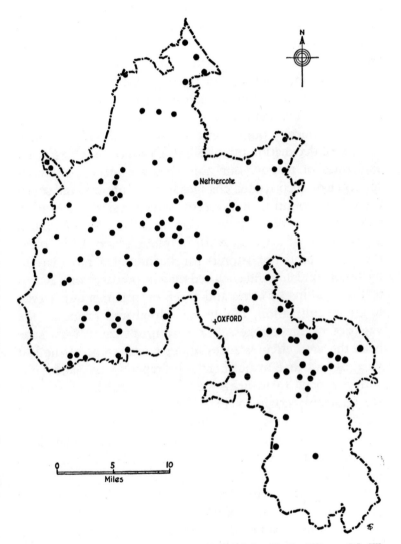

Fig. 9. The map shows the 101 sites listed by K. J. Allison, M. W. Beresford and J. G. Hurst, *The Deserted Villages of Oxfordshire* (1965), but in addition their pattern is supplemented by twenty-four fresh sites, including Nethercote, discovered since that survey. The map does not show the many rural settlements in Oxfordshire that have become shrunken since medieval or early modern times.

Thames and Windrush rivers. On the one-inch map these tracts of high-frequency DMVs are noticeable because of their blankness due to the thinning out of settlement detail: it is as if the map had worn threadbare. On the ground they are places of solitude where the walker has to look hard to catch a distant tinge of red from a tiled roof, and while doing so he may stumble across the hollowed site of a medieval village (Plate 11).

It was once thought that the deserted villages were victims of decimation by the Black Death of 1349 and other epidemics of plague. But now they are seen as the consequence of deep-rooted changes in the economic and social life of the country, one facet of which was the transition from an old order that was dominated by the communal organisation of a village with its plough-land. In its place there came more opportunity for the individual farm, larger, more consolidated and enclosed than its predecessors, geared to the handling of cattle and sheep on pastures rather than to grain cultivation, highly capitalised and prone to the vagaries of the market. A contributory cause may have been the very circumstances under which some of the lost villages had first made their appearance in the landscape, and the way their fields had been worked. As yet we are far from certain as to when and how these changes expressed themselves in different localities, but some of the Oxfordshire sites will help us to picture the complexities of this phase, really a transitory phase for the places involved.

We may begin with the sequence at Brookend, perched on the Gloucestershire borders. Not mentioned in Domesday, the village appeared between 1152 and 1200 as two hides of land which were colonised by Eynsham Abbey on the heath of Chastleton. With sixteen households it had grown to be as big as Chastleton by 1279, when the whole parish was fully productive of grain and pulse crops. Under the two-course rotation followed in the Cotswolds about

700 acres were sown each year, and smallish flocks of sheep were kept primarily for manuring the arable, none too adequately. Brookend survived the Black Death with scarcely any disruption, and while old village families were leaving and newcomers were entering the place later in the fourteenth century, the manorial rents did not suffer. Depopulation and the decay of farmhouses then struck hard between 1422 and 1441, when only three families remained, the rest having gone away "by night with their goods and chattels to a neighbouring village".

In the background was the consolidation of farms. What had been separate *virgates* (of thirty-two acres apiece) were gathered together in the hands of a few tenants. The abbey tried hard to check the disrepair into which their village was falling, but failed to stem the shift from a community of peasant holdings to a collection of yeomen farmers. At the same time the soil was becoming impoverished, so that larger farms were better able to offset their lower yields of crops. They were also prompted to replace crops and plough-land by livestock, perhaps accompanied by the enclosure of their pastures. Thus "the end of the village was brought about by a reversal of the processes which had given birth to it".[4] Brookend was the last corner of Chastleton to be colonised under population pressure in the twelfth century; after 300 years it was played out, maybe due to over-cropping. The place became so insignificant it did not figure in any of the early censuses, and all we can see there now is Brookend House.

Few sequences have been as thoroughly pieced together as that, but occasionally in the quite distant past (long before air-photography, field-archaeology and modern methods of research) a deserted village was detected and understood by an astute author. The best instance is Asterleigh, now a solitary stonebrash farm close to the A34 highway north of

[4] T. H. Lloyd, 'Some Documentary Sidelights on the Deserted Oxfordshire Village of Brookend', *Oxoniensia*, Vols. XXIX–XXX (1964–5), p. 128.

Woodstock. Like Brookend it did not flourish until the post-Domesday expansion of settlement, and even bears a clearance-name, rising to a village of twenty farms by 1279. Asterleigh was abandoned about the same time as Brookend, but the process was crystallised by the decision of the land-owning family to leave their house in the village to build a new one at Nether Kiddington. Its fate is beautifully discussed by Warton, including the *coup de grâce* when it was deprived of parish rank in October 1466 because (in the Bishop of Lincoln's words):

> the tenths, oblations, rents and emoluments of the rectory of Asterleigh were so diminished as to be insufficient to support a rector, or even a competent parochial chaplain, on account of paucity of parishioners, barrenness of land, defects of husbandry, and an unusual prevalence of pestilences and epidemic sicknesses.[5]

That sounds suspiciously like an all-purpose formula for what had become a familiar occurrence. Warton gave sound argument from the field ('inequalities of the ground') and from documents to support his idea of where Asterleigh had stood. We can confirm one of his points because, having thought the manor house had its own domestic chapel, Warton would have been glad to know that Asterleigh farm was not subject to the charge of tithe-rent in the nineteenth century, even though it ran to fifteen per cent of the area of the parish of Kiddington with Asterleigh.[6]

Sometimes we find a church standing among the fields with only a farmhouse or two for company. Outside the Chilterns, where they were late-built and sited in the midst

[5] Thomas Warton, *The History and Antiquities of Kiddington*, 3rd edn. (1815), p. 24; Warton's preface was dated 1782.

[6] One of the Bodleian's copies of Warton's book (G.A. Oxon. C.248) has manuscript notes of about 1900, including this reference to Asterleigh's tithe exemption.

of scattered settlement, such churches are generally survivors of a deserted village. They overshadow the dim vestiges of crofts, tofts and village greens, lanes, ponds, ridge-and-furrow. The best of its kind close to Oxford is Hampton Gay, but there is still more atmosphere at Shifford, adrift by the river meadows of the upper Thames, and it has long been appreciated:

> There is no doubt that Shifford was once a more important place than it is now, and perhaps contained several houses and streets. At present there is nothing but its solitary little church, four or five cottages, and Shifford farmhouse.[7]

But we can be surprised even at a relict site like this, because the church we now see was wholly rebuilt by the Victorians in 1861 to serve a wider area, and the old building Giles illustrated was quite different. This old church was reported as being 'almost down' in 1776 and repairs had to be carried out in 1785; the dereliction may have been caused by the deterioration in the churchyard, said to have become 'a common through broken rails' (1733).[8] As the fence of the cemetery at Asterleigh had to be kept in good repair even after the church went out of use, it may be that a village church would last only so long as that condition was properly maintained. Fortunately Shifford church is perched like a lighthouse on the island of its walled graveyard. The village had belonged to Eynsham Abbey since the foundation of that house, it had twenty-three households in 1279, but the value of its splendid pastures and meadows must have induced the canons to enclose and depopulate in the fifteenth century.

[7] J. A. Giles, *History of the Parish and Town of Bampton* (Bampton, 1848), p. 86.
[8] Bodleian Library, MSS. Oxon. c.99 (Oxford Archdeaconry Papers), ff. 3, 26, 27; MS. Top. Oxon. c.103, f. 42.

The discovery of Nethercote

After the scrutiny of Oxfordshire carried out by the Deserted Medieval Village Research Group it seemed improbable there was a single stone left unturned, but the finding of a fresh site has illustrated once more the scope for new discoveries in landscape-history, and it may be worth sketching its progress. Suspicion was first aroused when one of the best Victorian writers remarked in passing that there had been a village called Nethercote 'since reduced to a single farmhouse', in Steeple Aston.[9] No mention of it could be found in the usual check-lists such as *The Place-Names of Oxfordshire*, nor indeed in *The Deserted Villages of Oxfordshire*. Eventually it became clear that it has been overlooked because of a confusion in the editing of the text of the Oxfordshire Domesday. When this was compiled by Stenton he identified *Nidrecote* as Nethercott in Tackley, which happens to occupy a similar site four miles farther down the Cherwell valley.[10] But it is more likely that *Nidrecote*'s one hide recorded in 1086 was in the Astons, because by then the conventional scheme of five hides in Steeple Aston (presumably the oldest settlement), ten in North Aston (the second place to be founded), and five in Middle Aston (third in appearance) had changed to five, nine and six respectively. The one hide lost by North Aston to Middle Aston was in fact *Nidrecote*. Presumably after this debatable land was improved during the twelfth-century expansion, we find the ownership of half the tithes of *Nuthcote* in dispute between the rectors of North Aston and Steeple Aston by 1220. It went to a papal appeal before Steeple Aston secured them in 1239.

By then Nethercote was held of the king as quarter of a

[9] William Wing, *Annals of Heyford Warren, otherwise Upper Heyford* (Oxford, 1865), p. 18. Nethercote is also mentioned briefly in Wing's *Annals of North Aston* (Oxford, 1867) and in C. C. Brookes, *A History of Steeple Aston and Middle Aston* (Banbury, 1929).

[10] V.C.H. *Oxfordshire*, Vol. I (London, 1939), p. 406.

Plate 10 The countryside around Woodstock. Although now dominated by the geometrical shapes of the eighteenth-century landscaping within Blenheim Park and of modern farming, this landscape comprised the royal manor, forest and deer park of Woodstock in medieval times. Scale *c.* 1:126,720.

Plate 11 The deserted village of Caswell, near Witney. Its site is marked by the small closes in the centre of the air-photograph, with two moated sites, one unoccupied. Colonised from woodland on clay ground, Caswell was not recorded as a settlement until 1182. Its depopulation was completed by enclosure of the open fields in the early sixteenth century, when Richard Weynman of Witney, a wool-grower and merchant, rented pastures here from Eynsham Abbey. Scale *c.* 1:10,000.

Plate 12 Harpsden in the Chilterns, 1586: part of a manuscript plan by John Blagrove of Reading (Bodleian Library, MS. C. 17:49, 129). The *assart* settlement of Hunts Green lies centrally with four farms. By 1900 there was only one farm on this site. While some of the small Elizabethan fields have been thrown together, the pattern of the fields generally has not changed, many of the thick hedges persist even in the larger fields, Hunt's Wood and Lucy's Copse are still in the landscape, as are the tracks and lanes running along Harpsden Bottom. The chief modern intrusion is Henley golf course. Scale *c.* 1:10,000.

Plate 13 Alkerton: the Rectory House. The village is in the Redlands, on Lias clay close to the Warwickshire boundary. The rectory was built by Thomas Lydiat in 1625, using the local marlstone; its roof was stone slated in 1692, and a two-storeyed kitchen wing was added at right-angles to the original house in 1748 (to the left in the photograph).

knight's fee, but in 1257 Thomas Boffin granted his "whole
land in the parish of Steeple Aston called Nethercotes" to
Chetwode Priory, a new Augustinian house not far away
in Buckinghamshire. We should note in parenthesis here
that Boffin also gave to Chetwode his lands at Saxenton,
a few miles across the Cherwell, and *Sexintone* is among the
dozen places whose sites are listed as unknown in *The
Deserted Villages of Oxfordshire*: the similarity with Nethercote is obvious. By 1279 the prior held a tenement and
two and a half virgates of land at *Nithercot* hamlet, and
besides his two tenants there were eleven free tenants listed
by name: it was a small farming village dependent on Steeple
Aston for its parochial needs.[11] After 1461 it passed to the
rich house of Nutley Abbey, and by 1522 it was known as
the Grange of Nethercote, rented by a farmer who had a
large flock of 400 sheep. It seems likely that the desertion
and depopulation of Nethercote came late in the fifteenth
century when the canons of Nutley leased it as grazing
land.

'Nethercott Grange' kept the ancient name in currency
until the 1680s, when a map showed it as the only farmhouse
standing on its own beyond the village of Middle Aston.
It also had the only enclosed fields; two closes by the house,
Dovehouse Close (with dovecote), and another completed
a ladder of fields climbing from the Cherwell past the house
to the upper road. All this was essential background to
visiting the site to see if there were physical traces of the old
village. Immediately we find that the field next to Grange
Farm is so full of banks and hollows that it has not been
ploughed in the fourteen years the present owner has had
the farm; now known as Sheep Field, it consists of the four
enclosures shown in 1690 all thrown together.[12] Walking

[11] *Rotuli Hundredorum*, Vol. II (London, 1818), p. 862. Of the eleven
freeholders two had messuages, and eight of the others were also named under
Middle Aston or North Aston.
[12] Information kindly supplied by Mrs T. J. Davis.

into this field we see quite easily through the grass the house-platforms of Nethercote bordering two hollow-ways, one running down towards the farmhouse, the other towards its cowman's cottage. The old hedge between Dovehouse Close to the south and the other field to the west is visible as a lynchet cutting across Sheep Field: below it is the site of Nethercote (National Grid reference SP 481278), above it the ridge-and-furrow of the old common fields. Only the name of Nethercote Meadow still hints at this episode of transition in the landscape, reached by 'the monks' causeway' over the wet Cherwell flats to Somerton Mill, reminding us of the monastic owners whose agrarian policy disposed of Nethercote as a village.

The texture of early enclosure

The tracking down of Nethercote, its showing as The Grange on a map of 1690, and the sequence of causes behind the desertion of villages, leads on naturally to the general question of early enclosure. We have seen how the dislocation of a village and its common fields in the fifteenth century, bridging the context of late medieval to early modern times, could follow the consolidation of land and its rearrangement into compact single farmsteads with enclosed fields. Some of the free-standing farms we find in the Oxfordshire countryside may be of this *relic* type, survivors of an old village, but in other cases the depopulation and enclosure of village lands could disperse what may be termed *secondary* farms in the landscape, built afresh on their new spread of land.

Clare is a case in point, crowning the low ridge that appears beyond the Chiltern foot at Pyrton: thirty-seven households strong in 1279, its site now has just one farm and some cottages. By the early sixteenth century its arable land was being converted to pasture and then enclosed. We catch a glimpse of the rough-and-tumble of these innovations in a Star Chamber case brought against Sir William Barentyne, who had enclosed the northern part of Clare in 1515 "to the utter decay and desolation of the said town". When someone stood up to him Barentyne threatened, "whoreson boy and false crafty knave, I will sit upon your skirts", and "by many detestable oaths" promised to cut off his ears. By 1630 at least some of Clare's common fields had been enclosed by agreement, as well as the pasture and meadow; a century later the first plan of Clare showed four farmhouses, but two of them stood in isolation among their enclosed fields, i.e. of *secondary* origin.

Open farmland of various kinds—common fields for cropping, meadows for hay-cutting, waste for grazing—was steadily enclosed and replaced by a hedged landscape throughout the sixteenth and seventeenth centuries. Enclosure went on as a continuing process, not so much as a destroyer of villages but rather as a selective change towards more efficient farming with its heavier yields of grain and greater numbers of sheep, cattle and other livestock. If we take together the destructive or diminishing form of enclosure that thinned out the villages, and this less dramatic but determined enclosing in Tudor and Stuart times, we find they were responsible for putting about half of all the farmed land of Oxfordshire within hedgerows, fences or ditches before 1730. The scale of such early enclosing is impressive in itself, and saves us from exaggerating the impact of enclosure by Act of Parliament in the years after 1730 (see Chapter 5). But we would have found no more than three out of every ten rural townships in a completely enclosed state. The map of Harpsden in the southern Chilterns was drawn in 1586 and portrayed the manor entirely set out as eight compact farms with their hedged fields, but that was exceptional (Plate 12).

It is not easy to pin-point these field patterns in today's landscape, partly because they were created in smallish parcels in most parts of Oxfordshire, partly because they were refashioned when parliamentary enclosure took place around them. They are most likely to give themselves away by the physical conjunction of dispersed *secondary* farms, of ridge-and-furrow that corrugates the ground in the outlines of the old common fields as they were before enclosure (p. 137), and of their distinctive kind of live hedges. Clearly these hedgerows are more mature, diverse and luxuriant than the thin quicksets that were planted around the parliamentary enclosures in the eighteenth and nineteenth centuries. In comparisons of this kind, perhaps, lie the best opportunities for testing the ingenious hedge-dating method by which any given thirty-five yard stretch of hedgerow can be aged 100 years for each separate species of tree or bush it has growing in it, and so the date of its planting can be worked out. Thicker and denser, the early enclosures should be twice as abundant in species as their Georgian and Victorian successors.

Within Oxfordshire the intensity of Tudor and Stuart enclosing varied from one district to another because of the inherited differences of agrarian practice, of land tenure and the structure of estates, and local communities. These circumstances, after all, predetermined the usefulness of and demand for this costly business. The Redlands had very few early enclosures, in spite of their resources for a prosperous mixed farming on 'uncommonly good soil', as Leland put it. Corn yields were high on the marlstone plateaux, while the valleys of the Cherwell and its Sor Brook feeders were floored by clays of the Lower Lias that gave fine pastures. Not surprisingly a system of convertible farming had emerged at Bloxham as early as 1513, with leys lying intermixed with the arable strips in common fields. In addition the fields themselves had been restructured and reshaped into *quarters* by the sixteenth century—four of them in Bloxham South Field, but seven in the North Field. They were probably a complex device for providing a framework within which two separate rotations of crops

and grass could run their course over a large area of farmland (see p. 135). Enclosure was not part of these innovations
in the Redlands. In Bloxham hundred, to take one illustration, only fourteen per cent of the farmland was early
enclosed, only the villages of Adderbury, Broughton and
Drayton having much enclosure before the eighteenth
century. But the impact of this process on the local landscape was so variable: in Adderbury no more than eighteen
per cent of the parish was changed; in Broughton, however,
the castle demesne had been enclosed for pasture by Sir
Richard Fiennes in the 1590s, amounting to sixty-six per
cent of the parish; in Drayton the old enclosures ran to
seventy-one per cent.

In the Cotswolds and on the stonebrash about fifteen
per cent of the townships were entirely enclosed before the
Civil War. Most of the land still lay open in the seventeenth
century, following the two-field system with half of each
farm in fallow every year. For this reason and because of the
plentiful common grazings left on the bleaker ridges and
heaths, together with Wychwood Forest, there was no
shortage of pasture for cattle and sheep. To the majority of
small farmers the wholesale enclosing of their townships
was something they did not want. When Souldern was so
enclosed in 1613 the many freeholders (who were safe from
eviction) opposed it and their common pastures and meadow
were left open. Later in the seventeenth century, when new
crops like sainfoin and rye grass became well known, these
old fears were allayed by the extra feeding from sown grasses
raised in temporary enclosures within the common fields.
Also helpful in this way was the method of *hitching*, by
which peas and beans were sown in the fallow land. Such
devices came easiest to the larger farmers who had successfully engrossed and consolidated their land: at Lower
Heyford, for instance, between 1606 and 1689 two men had
consolidated for themselves blocks of twenty-five, twelve
and eight acres apiece, with many others of three and four

acres, and were probably sowing temporary grasses as ley grazing. This explains why *Sainfoin Piece* was such a common name for fields.

On the stonebrash, then, a moderate amount of early enclosure had buttressed the common fields by easing the demand for feeding livestock, but by 1730 only thirty-six per cent of the townships were enclosed, chiefly where the engrossing of larger farms into fewer hands had gone on apace. Gagingwell, enclosed in 1712, is a case in point. We find a different picture in the Chilterns, where population and settlement were a good deal sparser, scattered through a landscape dominated by woodland, scrub and heath. Most townships probably had some arable lying in common fields, but they were accompanied and overshadowed by many enclosed fields that were directly taken in from the waste or had long been 'in several'. Farms were of moderate or even large size by Oxfordshire standards, running to eighty acres and more of arable closes, with generous rights of grazing over the common waste. Given that enclosure had less headway to make, we would have found a good half of the Chiltern townships parcelled out in hedged fields by 1730.

Over the low-lying clay vales and riverine terraces of Oxfordshire the three-field system of working the common fields had traditionally held sway, since it replaced the two-field rotation about 1200 as more people required more grain, and a reduction in the fallow had allowed more crops to be sown. Studies of Watlington and Cuxham have shown that demesne farming was aimed at the commercial production of wheat in the medieval period, and although consolidation of the demesne within the three great fields was achieved by 1254 in the case of Cuxham it did not trigger off early enclosure. But we have also met clusters of deserted villages in this sort of countryside (p. 98), undermined as common fields were put down to grass and enclosed. Taken with piecemeal hedging and fencing we would have found about twenty per cent of these vale townships enclosed by 1640. At Eynsham, for example, it had affected a quarter of the manor, sixty-three per cent of which was pasture or meadow for dairying and fattening. There were cases of wholesale enclosure by agreement, particularly in small townships with few freeholders, as at Godington as early as 1603.

The pace of enclosure did not greatly advance here after the Restoration and by 1730 no more than thirty per cent of the vale townships were changed by it. Common fields went on being farmed without much interruption, and even showed themselves capable of adapting to new demands, new crops and methods of cultivation. More wheat and pulse crops were grown, the proportion of ley pasture and sown grasses was increasing. There was some piecemeal enclosing on the Oxford Heights, whose drier soils were better suited to long-term grazing, as at Elsfield (1692) and Forest Hill (1721). To sum up for the whole of Oxfordshire, when the distinctive process of enclosure by Act of Parliament made its appearance in the eighteenth century about one third of the open landscapes in the county had already been transformed by the early enclosers.

The Chronology of Enclosure (by townships)

Region	Before 1640	1640–1730	After 1730	No. of townships
Redlands	13%	nil	87%	39
Cotswolds and Stonebrash	15%	21%	64%	100
Chilterns	35%	17%	48%	23
Clay Vales	21%	10%	69%	121
Oxfordshire	19%	13%	68%	283

Finally, we shall look at Bletchingdon and find out how the early encloser went to work. We have already seen in another context that the Poure family had taken in about half of the three common fields between 1539 and 1596 (p. 93). Not surprisingly in the latter year Francis Poure was on the black list of enclosing landowners when a crowd of conspirators rioted against them, angered by such changes in the old agrarian order. Despite this protest the 1000 acres or so remaining open at Bletchingdon were finally, inexorably and completely enclosed, subdivided and hedged by the wishes of Sir John Lenthall in 1623. To the Queen's College, Oxford, as patrons of the rectory, he sent "a proposal of dividing the Heath and fields of Bletchingdon between me and my tenants". Following this somewhat blunt approach, in due course the lands were surveyed and allotted in a style that foreshadows the eighteenth-century enclosure awards, but in this case instead of a parliamentary bill there was the drawing-up of a tripartite indenture, carefully worded. It was later confirmed by a decree in the Court of Chancery. Agreement had to be secured from the fifteen freeholders of the manor who had land in the common fields. The outcome was that the last vestiges of an open landscape at Bletchingdon were carved up as compact blocks ready for the hedger and ditcher: Lenthall received 478 acres, the rector 192, and the tenants had farms varying in area from six to sixty acres.

After 1623 the only unenclosed land was a few acres of grazing along the verges of the roads and lanes, the Cow Common of the tenants and a few demesne acres. But the green in the midst of Bletchingdon village survived and remained open, as it still does, "a fine large breathing space and playground in its very centre".[13] As to the hedgerows at Bletchingdon there is no doubt they are taller and bushier than most, their thorn and elder thickets making good buttresses for the elm and ash growing in them. This is particularly true of the 'outer' lines of hedges where they fringe the roads or provide the ring fence to properties

[13] So described by W. Wing, *Annals of Bletchingdon* (Oxford, 1872), p. 28.

on the edge of the township. Not all the boundaries of the 1623 fields have survived, because we know that when William West came to Greenhill Farm in the 1820s and began the scientific breeding of long-woolled sheep he reclaimed quite a few acres by tidying up and reducing the hedges, which had been spreading themselves for 200 years since Lenthall's initiative in enclosing the surviving common fields.

Another and related characteristic of the Bletchingdon landscape is the presence of a striking number of single settlements away from the village, 'lonely farm homesteads' as Wing saw them a century ago. They are much thicker on the ground here than in any of the other places on this side of the Cherwell, as far north as Souldern. We can be sure that the oldest of them are of *secondary* origin, and were built as a natural outcome of the early enclosure of 1623.

Underdowns was certainly there by 1680, standing at the centre of its block of fields. Other seventeenth-century farmhouses, simple structures of two storeys with attics, built of coursed rubble and retaining many of their original features, were Diamond Farm, Grove (with early casement windows), and Stonehouse, dominating the north-eastern angle of the township, and still with its stone spiral staircase. Having once begun, the tendency to build dispersed farmsteads was taken farther in the eighteenth century by Greenhill, Staplehurst, Frogsnest and College farms. Even these symbols of modernisation were likely to run into problems because they broke the ancient ties of rural location. Whereas Bletchingdon village was sited on a patch of high-level drift with a definite capacity for storing water, and enjoyed a pure supply from springs and wells, farms like Stonehouse were out on the clay and their wells could not reach good water. One wonders just how difficult the problem of water supply had to be to deter the building of secondary farms. A little to the north on stonebrash lay "a district proverbially dry and badly off for water", where even the estate village of Middleton Stoney (p. 169) had to sink seven new wells (chosen by a water diviner) after the severe drought of 1884.[14] In such circumstances, as we saw at Caulcott in quite a different context, it is foolish to ignore the role of water supply as a conditioner in the spread of settlement.

New buildings in the countryside

The reality of early enclosure, newly accomplished, may be encountered in various settings, as in the complaint of tenant farmers at Standlake when their village was overrun by "a multitude of poor" in 1625. Not only were they losing poultry from their yards and corn from their fields after it was cut, they could scarcely keep

> any dead hedges standing, but that they shall be taken away by night. And oftentimes their quick Mounds [that is, quickset hedges] and other trees as ashes, willows, etc., be pulled or cut up by the ground, to the great hurt of the owners who planted the same to their own use and public good.

The true cause of such nuisances at Shiplake, according to the petitioners, was the way in which the village had recently become "much overcharged with poor people placed in cottages and new erected tenements". The covetous owners of "ancient cottages" (Standlake was said to have forty of these) and new houses alike had even placed "two couples or more of poor people" into a single building.[15] We might infer from this situation the problems of congestion arising as an eventual result of rapid

[14] J. C. Blomfield, *History of Middleton and Somerton* (London, 1888), p. 5.
[15] Bodleian, MS. Top. Oxon. c.118, f. 2.

growth of population, or as the more immediate effect of changes in the structure of farming. But the petitioners also tell us incidentally about another trend that gathered strength from the mid-sixteenth century: their "new erected tenements" point our attention to the building of many new farmhouses and cottages in the countryside, or the rebuilding of many others on a more ambitious scale.

This happened around Bletchingdon, as we have seen, after enclosure had made it feasible to build new farms beyond the village, but it was a widespread activity that could touch the whole landscape whether or not it had experienced early enclosure. Thus, not far from Bletchingdon the isolated farm of Begbroke Hill is known to have been built between about 1600 and 1630, but it retains part of the undercroft of a medieval house that preceded the new structure. Setting aside the parish churches and some great houses, however, as a general rule we must accept the fact that outwardly in the Oxfordshire countryside there are remarkably few surviving traces of ordinary domestic building of the medieval period. So thorough was the operation of the 'Great Rebuilding' from about 1570 to 1640 that the most recent count of medieval cruck dwellings could muster fewer than ten such houses from Oxfordshire in a total of more than sixty for the region around Oxford.[16] These were timber-framed buildings having a truss with cruck blades (i.e. curved timbers). Most of them are dwellings of three bays built in villages by peasant farmers who grew prosperous during the fifteenth century, as was probably the case with Crucks in Great Haseley, or Smith Cottage, Stanton Harcourt. Some have internal modifications of predictable date: The Old Cottage in Bright-hampton, for example, has a fireplace and first floor inserted about 1600. Other crucks surviving in the Chilterns, such as Carter's Cottage in Exlade Street, may be new or greatly

[16] John Fletcher, 'Crucks in West Berkshire and the Oxford Region', *Oxoniensia*, Vol. XXXIII (1968), pp. 71–88.

improved houses built in isolation from the main clusters of settlement in the century before 1550.

Perhaps better known than these medieval farmhouses is Rectory Barn at Church Enstone, one of four cruck barns in the Oxford region, and built in 1382 for the abbot of Winchcombe who had estates there. Its stone walls and stone-slated roof, however, place it close to the medieval stone-built barns of northern Oxfordshire and the tradition of vernacular building in this rich part of the county. Few parts of England can show a closer tie between geology and architecture than the Redlands. The red marlstone strata of the Middle Lias were quarried for a building stone that weathers to a rich honey colour; although not a very durable material, it stamps a local identity on the Redland district that surely distinguishes it from the inferior *rubble* used in stone buildings farther south in Oxfordshire. In turn the marlstone fabric is also distinguishable from the Cotswolds near at hand, where the finer oolitic building-stone was capable of inviting a superior kind of masoncraft.[17]

Given their identification by the colour and texture of farmhouse, cottage and barn, it is also true that the Redlands can scarcely be challenged by any other English region in the thoroughness with which they experienced the Great Rebuilding. It is hard to believe that the familiar marlstone was not widely employed before the sixteenth century, but the medieval villages must have been full of timber-framed houses (and poor specimens of their kind at that) because not one cottage or yeoman's farmhouse can be dated before 1500. Elsewhere the old framed structures, better built, were often retained as the nuclei of new buildings, but in the Redlands there was nothing less than the wholesale replacement of timber by marlstone. It took the form of a simple, unpretentious style with many modest refinements but little elaboration. The Redlands houses differed from their

---

[17] R. B. Wood-Jones, *Traditional Domestic Architecture in the Banbury Region* (Manchester, 1963).

Cotswold neighbours by not having gabled dormers; transomed windows were rare, porches positively luxurious (Plate 13).

Uniformity of this order in building-material and style does not carry from the stone belts into mid-Oxfordshire, as may be proved by going to the green at Marsh Baldon and seeing around it the colourful medley of houses in coursed rubble, brick or timber-framing, with roofs of thatch or tile. Even so, there are villages like Chalgrove and Chislehampton in which there is a predominance of timbered houses, while a few miles distant the changing geology is reflected by other villages such as the Haseleys or Great Milton, where all the houses and farm buildings are constructed of the sandy Portland freestone. Little Milton belongs in this latter group and it has been shown again here that before the sixteenth century the picture was quite different, giving a village of modest timber-framed houses of simple plan and construction. Only two houses now retain any evidence of this timber tradition, which was poor and curtailed by the costliness of timber in an open and long-settled landscape. One is the oldest surviving house in Little Milton, dating from about 1500, and although clearly built by someone of wealth it too shows such limitations as the use of very heavy timbers, widely spaced studs and frequent curved supports.

Like the rest of the village it was transformed by the energetic phase of new building that started about 1600 and continued through three or four decades to the outbreak of the Civil War. Old houses were improved, but many freestone farmhouses were built by the prospering yeomen and husbandmen: "within little more than a generation the face of Little Milton was almost completely changed".[18] Now of course they are outnumbered by later additions to the village, but at least one in ten of its buildings are still

[18] D. Portman, 'Little Milton, the Rebuilding of an Oxfordshire Village', *Oxoniensia*, Vol. XXV (1960), p. 55.

of this period. From time to time the process of rebuilding would have been speeded by the devastation of serious fires, a hazard that not infrequently tore gaps in the village fabric before the nineteenth century brought better means of limiting its ravages. At Eynsham, for instance, on the morning of Whit Monday, 1629, no fewer than twelve houses were burnt to the ground.[19] This destruction was also counted as 101 'bays of buildings', some of which must have been in the barns, stables and out-houses, but in this presumably random sample we also see something of the range of size of properties in a good-sized village at the time of the Rebuilding. At one end of the scale was the largest place with twenty bays, followed by others of seventeen, fifteen and twelve bays. The other eight houses were much smaller, ranging from tiny cottages of one and two bays to the more usual six or seven bays of building. The Eynsham picture fits well enough with that drawn from the farmers' inventories and other sources of the period, when the average Oxfordshire farmhouse rarely ran to as many as six rooms for living and working, interspersed with an unusually high number of one-roomed cottages.[20]

Taken together, however, these all formed the backcloth for the great houses, the new mansions of Tudor and early Jacobean times that were built for purely residential and servicing uses; all their farming was carried on from the manor farms as a separate concern from the home of the landowning family. But the ideas of comfort and convenience we have seen appear in the countryside at large had filtered down from these great households, doing so very rapidly from about 1500 under the stimulation of better

[19] Bodleian, MS. Top. Oxon. c.118, f. 6.
[20] M. A. Havinden, *Household and Farm Inventories in Oxfordshire, 1550–1590* (Historical Manuscripts Commission, H.M.S.O., London, 1965), pp. 15–27; M. W. Barley, *The English Farmhouse and Cottage* (London, 1961), p. 59, says that most of the one-roomed cottages were newly built in the period 1580–1630.

standards of design, building and furnishing. To discover how much the great houses added to the Oxfordshire landscape we may now look at them in the broader context of ornamentation and landscaping as deliberate actions.

SELECT BIBLIOGRAPHY

Allison, K. J., Beresford, M. W., Hurst, J. G., *The Deserted Villages of Oxfordshire* (1965).

Beresford, M. W. and Hurst, J. G., *Deserted Medieval Villages: Studies* (1971).

Havinden, M. A., 'Agricultural Progress in Open-field Oxfordshire', *Agricultural History Review,* Vol. IX (1961), pp. 73–83.

Havinden, M. A., *Household and Farm Inventories in Oxfordshire, 1550–1590,* Historical Monuments Commission (1965).

Lloyd, T. H., 'Some Documentary sidelights on the Deserted Oxfordshire Village of Brookend', *Oxoniensia,* Vols. XXIX–XXX (1964–5), pp. 58–70.

Portman, D., 'Little Milton, the Rebuilding of an Oxfordshire Village', *Oxoniensia,* Vols. XXV (1960), pp. 49–63.

Reeves, S. J., 'A Medieval Village' (probably Broadstone in Enstone parish), *Oxoniensia,* Vol. XXXVI (1971), pp. 49–51.

Sturdy, David, 'Houses of the Oxford Region', *Oxoniensia,* Vols. XXVI–XXVII (1961–2), pp. 319–35.

Victoria County History, *Oxfordshire,* ed. Mary D. Lobel and Alan Crossley, Vol. IX, 'Bloxham Hundred' (1969).

Wood-Jones, R. B., *Traditional Domestic Architecture in the Banbury Region* (1963).

5. Landscapes by design

Country houses.   Parkland.   The landscape of parliamentary enclosure.   Turnpikes and canals: new routeways

GENERALLY IT IS unwise to try to place country houses into hard and fast categories. They are reflective of individualism to a greater degree than houses in towns, and more likely to show change in their status because of expansion or contraction of their territorial support. Yet a line can be drawn between farmhouses that appeared in the landscape after early enclosure of common fields, as at Bletchingdon (p. 113), and the more substantial houses of those men who were responsible for the enclosures, and into whose hands more and more land came to be concentrated in the sixteenth and seventeenth centuries. As we saw in the case of Grange Farm at Middle Aston, marking the site of the deserted settlement of Nethercote (p. 104) it is quite usual for the larger farmhouses to stand as sole survivors of what had been a clustered hamlet or village under the old agrarian regime. So too with the next rank of houses in the hierarchy, where a modest country house was built on the profits of engrossing, enclosure and convertible agriculture in the Tudor period. They sprang from the transformation of what were typically small, late-founded settlements, and just as they did not reach the status of places with a clear distinction between the functions of residence and agriculture, so they have tended to settle back into life as the somewhat elaborate centrepieces of working farms.

A good instance is Hordley Farm, sited not far from

Plate 14 Wilcote Park, in the Wychwood country between Charlbury and Witney. The snow cover on 1st March 1929 throws into relief the outline of a formally laid out garden (centre of picture), otherwise hidden from view; compare Plate 4. Snow also etches out the pattern of ridge-and-furrow within the Park, showing how it was imposed on the old open fields. Scale *c.* 1 : 2000.

Plate 15 Blenheim Palace, looking east. The first gardens were laid out by Henry Wise, who transplanted 'elms out the country' for the main avenues (including that going off top left of the picture). The original designs were completed by Bridgman, and then by 'Capability' Brown, who created the lake (part of which is in the foreground) in 1764. The formal garden was laid out by Charles, ninth Duke of Marlborough, in about 1900.

Plate 16   Nuneham Courtenay, by Paul Sandby, 1760. In this landscape painting the outlook is upstream towards Oxford, and shows the newly-built villa perched on its commanding site above the Thames.

Plate 17   The new church at Nuneham Courtenay. Sandby's painting has the 'surprise vista' of the classical temple-church, as seen from the Terrace Walk.

Plate 18 Field patterns in the Cotswolds. The lower section shows the rectilinear fields created by parliamentary enclosure at Salford in 1770, with the old open layout persisting as ridge-and-furrow in some of them. The upper portion is different, with a spread of bigger pastures around Little Rollright, where the limestone slopes reach to 700 feet. A good-sized village in 1086 and still in 1279, Little Rollright was deserted later. The tenants of Eynsham Abbey converted arable to pasture, destroying houses, so by 1517 it was said that thirty-six villagers had been evicted. The fields reflect these two varieties of enclosure of common fields and waste. Scale *c.* 1:10,000.

Akeman Street's crossing of the river Glyme. There was no mention of Hordley, which has a 'clearing' name, in Domesday but by the thirteenth century it was a hamlet of the royal manor of Woodstock, probably the outcome of assarting, with its own chapel as a dependency of Wootton parish. In 1279 Hordley had nineteen households and 150 acres of land, whereas by the early sixteenth century only five residents' names were recorded; at this time the Gregory family leased most of the land. The Gregorys, like the Poures at Bletchingdon, were typical of the lesser gentry who were then benefiting from fairly stable costs and rising selling prices in farming. Having first applied their profits to securing more pastures or livestock (it is a telling point that the Gregorys also had interests in Dornford, another deserted village close to Hordley), such people were then able to turn to the rebuilding or enlargement of their homes. John Gregory probably built this house of stone about the year 1600, raising it around three and a half sides of a quadrangle, thus retaining the plan, perhaps, of a medieval house that had stood on the site. He built it of two storeys, with attics and cellar, and its period is reflected in many surviving details: the massive five-stack chimney on the south range where the hall was, with the great chamber above it; the wooden mullioned windows and elaborate four-centred doorway. The Hordley house stood thus unaltered for 250 years, and in essence it is still recognisably a product of the last years of Elizabeth.

Country houses

Francis Gregory of Hordley claimed the right to carry a coat-of-arms at the herald's visitation in 1634, but was refused, and here we touch on a source of information about the number of commoner families living in Oxfordshire who were entitled to bear arms. At the visitation that ended in 1574 the recorded total was 120 such families;

though incomplete, it showed there were twenty-six manor houses worth the heralds' visiting them. From Great Tew westwards into the Cotswolds, for instance, lay a group of houses at Swerford, Heythrop, Chadlington, Sarsden, Bruern and Chastleton. According to the later visitation of 1634 the number of gentle families seems to have fallen to ninety-seven, although many great names were in contempt (Spencer, Blunt and Dormer among them) for not having agreed to meet the heralds. A more pertinent point is that only twenty-nine of the families listed in 1574 were still included, suggesting the aggrandisement of the smaller gentry who had been inclined for whatever reason to sell their ancient estates.[1]

Few parts of the Oxfordshire landscape are without their manor houses of Tudor and Jacobean building. The common characteristic of the greatest households was a design with which to hold together their constituent parts— hall, kitchen, rooms for storage, accommodation for people of wealth and substance, with their attendant servants, for stables and barns that also demanded their place in the courtyard. New features appeared in the sixteenth century, such as the storeyed gatehouse that not only enhanced the mansion but also provided plenty of lodging space for servants. The plans of houses became more elaborate through the making of more rooms or parlours, and such rising standards of comfort were already to be seen in some of the last of the monastic buildings. At Thame Abbey the last Cistercian abbot was Robert King, who built a new range with oriel windows, stair turrets and a handsome parlour on the first floor; it remains as only one wing of Thame Park, but its early Tudor façade is unrivalled in the county.

The most lavish houses were designed for royal visits, with the emphasis on symmetry in their external appearance.

[1] J. Meade Falkner, *A History of Oxfordshire* (1899), pp. 195–6, 220, 293–300.

At first the elaborate stables with servant accommodation were built in separate courts, but by the early seventeenth century they were appearing on the flanks of the forecourt, adding to the first impression created by the house itself and echoing its symmetry on a simpler note. In Oxfordshire the expected setting for such splendours was the royal forest of Wychwood, where a royal lodge had been built of stone and timber by 1337. Its siting in relation to the mansion of Cornbury Park is not certain, but the Tudor wing of this great house dates from as early as about 1495 and was often visited by Elizabeth I and the Stuart kings. What is beyond doubt is that a royal master mason and pupil of Inigo Jones built the south-west front at Cornbury in 1631. It was done for Henry Danvers, Earl of Danby, who had been Ranger of Wychwood and Keeper of Cornbury Park since 1615. At the time of the building Danvers was also walling the Park, and in 1642 he saw it disafforested and put outside Wychwood. The masons used a local freestone of high quality, dry and hard, which did not bleach but weathered to a warm gold. The same material appears in the Clarendon wing that was added in high Renaissance style between 1666 and 1671. It was quarried at Bucksleap in the Park and was from the Great Oolite (Chipping Norton Limestone), and its special qualities were praised by Plot and Evelyn.[2]

Most of the more usual and modest run of country houses built in the sixteenth and seventeenth centuries may be viewed as points of stability in the landscape, even if in their externals they were prone to change in pace with affluence and taste. Continuity is perhaps more justifiable as an idea in their context than in those discussed earlier (p. 47), for they testify to the transition from late medieval events to the prosperity of the Tudor gentry who built them. Some like Broughton Castle were old structures that simply acquired a new structure and façade. Others

[2] Quoted by W. J. Arkell, *Oxford Stone* (London, 1957), p. 87.

appeared alongside the ruins of earlier castellated dwellings:
the Jacobean house at Rotherfield Greys in the Chilterns,
built by the Knollys family, accompanies the castle of the
de Greys in this fashion. There are more houses of this
kind in the Chilterns than one might expect, including
Mapledurham (completed in brick by the Blunts in 1588),
Hardwick, both of them by the side of the Thames, and
Stonor Park hidden away in the recesses of the wooded
Chilterns proper.

The stone country of the Cotswolds and Redlands is
predictably rich in mansions, a substantial response to the
Great Rebuilding. Chastleton House is one of the most
coherent and least changed, the handiwork of Walter Jones
between 1603 and 1618. Its symmetrical façade includes
five gables and terminates in a tower at each end, the eastern
one matching with the church tower close by. On a more
grandiose scale with seven gables is Wroxton Abbey, built
by Sir William Pope about 1620 (Plate 8). Although this is
manifestly the marlstone countryside, not far from Wroxton
there was an early use of brick at Hanwell, where Sir
Anthony Cope completed his castellated house in the 1540s,
possibly in emulation of Broughton; only one of its four
towers remains. Because of its royal associations, Wychwood Forest attracted an aureole of fine houses around its
margins. Cornbury we have already met; in Burford, one of
the forest towns, the Priory was built by Lord Chief Justice
Tanfield, a native of the place who served Henry VIII;
Shipton Court, Tangley Hall, and Asthall House are also
outstanding in this part of Oxfordshire. We find their
equivalents again at Kelmscott and Cote on the upper
Thames, at Fritwell and Water Eaton beyond the Cherwell,
or again at Yarnton where Sir Thomas Spencer (from
a powerful enclosing family) completed his house in
1612.

Ditchley was another Wychwood residence built in the
sixteenth century by Sir Henry Lee, Ranger of Wychwood,

but Ditchley Park as we now see it is later, superseding the old house in the 1740s. The tradition of country house building, based on a large number of Tudor and Jacobean forerunners, ran on without interruption through the seventeenth century, but with the emphasis falling more and more on fewer and more ambitious designs. Oxfordshire does not have much to show in the way of wholly new-built houses from the eighteenth century: there is the Queen Anne residence of the Harcourts at Cokethorpe Park; the house at Chislehampton with its unique and eye-catching church alongside; the Vanderstegen house at Cane End in the Chilterns; and, in a category of its own, Blenheim (Plate 15 and p. 128). It was more usual for the older houses to be extended and elaborated. Rousham was Jacobean by origin, built by Sir Robert Dormer, but its façade was redesigned and two new wings added in the 1730s. By this time the Georgian house improver was capable of a firmer manipulation of the designed landscape than before. Perhaps we can gauge this initially by keeping within the orbit of the building of a particular house, seeing the method and pace by which it was accomplished.

The influential family of Fermor had its seat at Somerton, but scarcely a trace is left of their Tudor house because they had moved a few miles to a new house at Tusmore in 1642. When that in turn was demolished, William Fermor laid the foundation stone of his Georgian mansion on 17th October 1766. The builder was Robert Mylne of Black-friars Bridge, who secured most of his materials from near at hand, the whole operation having the ring of self-sufficiency to it. Admittedly some of the freestone was brought from Totternhoe, near Dunstable, but the rest came from Glympton and Taynton, both of them Oxfordshire quarries of great age. Most of the 'common stone' was dug at Frit-well, two or three miles away, but the carriage of materials was costly at £500. Fermor's teams of horses were not always available for carrying to the house because simultaneously he was engaged in other improvements such as the enclosures at Somerton, building new farmhouses or altering others, installing barns and gates on the estate.[3] The bricks were made from local clay, all 323,000 of them, with furze from the commons providing the fuel for baking them and for burning the lime. Oak, ash and elm timber also came from the Tusmore woods. The fabric of the new house was completed by 1770, but the Fermors did not move into it until 1779. Its total cost was £11,305. Tusmore Park was then enlarged to its present area of seventy acres, surrounded by a stone wall, and set out with ornamental plantations, new drives and roads.

Parkland

This final phase of activity at Tusmore directs our attention to the full impact of country houses on the landscape in terms of the gardens and parks in which their builders set them. We can assume that most of the manor houses mentioned so far were accompanied by gardens designed at first with the "elaborate symmetry that delighted the Elizabethan eye".[4] The compact outline of a formal garden that must have had its geometrically designed terraces, parterres, box hedges and ponds may be traced in the snow-covered precinct of Wilcote House, near Witney, revealed to us on one of the first air-photographs of the Oxfordshire landscape (Plate 14). At Cornbury, again, a series of four enclosed gardens was laid out by the second Earl of Clarendon in 1689, while at the same time Plot enthused over the flight of five walks at Rousham, descending from the Dormer garden to the riverside, "having steps at each end parted with hedges of codlings". Only in early prints can we recapture the appearance of such ornamentation,

---

[3] J. C. Blomfield, *History of Cottisford, Hardwick and Tusmore* (1887), pp. 73–5.

[4] John Buxton, *Elizabethan Taste* (London, 1963), pp. 43–4.

as they have been obscured or replaced by more extensive schemes, but in them lay the seed of a succession of ideal formulations of the landscape as it could be seen and appreciated from the English country house.

The most dramatic manifestations of landscape design appeared in the eighteenth century. It was personal in the sense of individual designers being commissioned by men of property and ideas, so we may begin to follow its working in Oxfordshire by studying the career of one of the earliest of the 'gentlemen architects' who was born in the county. Sanderson Miller (1716–80) was the son of a successful Banbury mercer who came to enjoy a reputation as a builder in the Gothic style of houses, towers, sham ruins (even, in the disparaging words of a spiteful critic, "A Gothic Hog-sty for some customary freeholder in Oxfordshire"). His best work locally was at Wroxton Abbey and was done for Lord North.[5] As early as 1744 Miller began the ornamental lake and waterworks, the most original feature of the Wroxton landscaping. From a series of reservoirs by the house the lake was fed, dammed at its eastern end to form the Grand Cascade with a serpentine river below. The whole composition was "shut in with wood" as Walpole described it. Near the cascade Miller also made the Mount, crowned with a domed Gothic seat, an eye-catcher towards Drayton, as well as planning most of the plantations seen in Booth's engraving of about 1770.

By the time Miller began his creations, other and better-known landscapers were at work in Oxfordshire, producing the flexible, informal kind of parkland that ousted in fashionability the orderliness of earlier styles in gardening. William Kent's skill was applied at Ditchley Park by 1726 and at Shotover Park by about 1734. There is no questioning Kent's masterly achievement at Rousham between 1720 and 1738, still one of the best things in the Oxfordshire

---

[5] Anthony C. Wood and William Hawkes, 'Sanderson Miller', *Journal of Banbury History Society* (Winter 1969), pp. 79–110.

landscape. Approach it through the spacing of mature trees that unfold in changing perspective, and beneath which the undulations of ancient plough-land may be detected in low sunlight; cross the concealed fence or ha-ha by the house, to look over a perfectly-framed vista, ponds and basins underlying the natural foreground formed by the Cherwell; thickets of woodland shield a classical temple and statues, taken farther by the beeches and Kent's gothicised Cuttle Mill; on the far skyline poses the eye-catcher at Steeple Aston, tilted on huge buttresses to catch the light. Although the outlook is now broken by the intrusion of water towers at the Heyford air base, the delicacy and inventiveness of Kent's Rousham are undiminished.

Oxfordshire has more to show of Lancelot Brown's landscaping than most of the neighbouring counties. He realised the 'Capabilities' of Kirtlington Park (1751–62), of Blenheim for the fourth Duke of Marlborough (1765), and of Rycote for the Earl of Abingdon (1769). But his excellence is nowhere better displayed than in his last local assignment (1779–82), working for Lord Harcourt at Nuneham Courtenay. To appreciate fully the sequence of events there, so deliberate in their sense of design and the motivation to embellish a landscape, we begin in the 1750s when Lord Harcourt decided to move to Nuneham and build a new house. For centuries the locality had been thickly wooded on account of its poorish soils based on the Lower Greensand; there was a park by 1396 and traces of its pale survive as a low earth bank among the trees. Another precondition of the landscape changes soon to affect Nuneham was the London to Oxford road running close by; it was decided to turnpike and improve the highway in 1736, making the place more accessible. The original village stood above the Thames, but in Lord Harcourt's eye its "tumble down clay-built" houses gathered around the green were ripe for demolition. They were pulled down and the likelihood is that Goldsmith witnessed the demise of the old Nuneham, immortalised as 'sweet Auburn' in *The Deserted Village.*

But by the early 1760s a new village to replace the old had materialised on the London road, and in its paired brick cottages we can still savour something of the impression it made as "two rows of low, neat houses, built close to each other and as regular and as uniform as a London street". The chief attraction of the site of the old village was its riverside bluff, overlooking the Thames, and offering so much scope for landscaping on the grand scale. To Lord Harcourt and his Palladian ideal of 'a villa with a view' it was irresistible, and his house duly appeared on it by 1760 (Plate 16). It was accompanied by the formal clearings and aligned vistas of an Italianate scene; a classical temple-church, built on the site of the village church of All Saints took its place as what Walpole thought to be "the principal feature in one of the most beautiful landscapes in the world" (Plate 17). The former village green was planted with trees, and its pond transformed into a crescent lake with water pumped from the Thames. Ten years later the villa was too small and uncomfortable for the second Lord Harcourt, who also wished to have a Picturesque garden close to the house, with a corresponding parkland scene beyond. At this time William Gilpin popularised the Picturesque landscape in his *Tours* for travellers and *Essays* for artists, as scenery with "that kind of beauty which would look well in a picture". He introduced an alternative to the kind of landscape devised by Capability Brown, who usually worked on a lavish scale in clearing the countryside for a systematic imposition of new detail.

Instead, at Nuneham an informal flower garden was laid out by Mason in 1771, and afterwards Brown agreed to extend its picturesque quality to the park. To do so he broke the whole prospect enjoyed from the house and walks into a series of Thames vistas with hanging woods featuring the windings of the river, the spire of Abingdon church set against the Berkshire Downs, the village of Radley and the view towards Oxford.[6] Brown's landscape was completed in the autumn of 1782, shortly before his death, and so light was his touch that he and Nature shared a dialogue in William Whitehead's poem *The Late Improvements at Nuneham,* the last word going to the designer:

Dame Nature, the Goddess, one very bright day
In strolling thro' Nuneham, met Brown in her way;
And bless me, she said, with an insolent sneer,
I wonder that fellow will dare to come here.
What more than I did has your impudence plann'd
The lawn, wood and water are all of my hand.

Brown:
Who thinn'd, and who grouped, and who scattered those
   trees
Who bade the slopes fall with that delicate ease,
Who cast them in shade, and who placed them in light,
Who bade them divide, and who bade them unite?
The ridges are melted, the boundaries gone;
Observe all these changes, and candidly own
I have cloath'd you when naked, and when o'erdrest
I have stripped you again to your bodice and vest.

Farther north in Oxfordshire there are parklands designed subsequently by Humphry Repton, as at Sarsden House (1795) and Great Tew (1803), but they cannot rival the collective impression of planting and ornamentation that fills the Chiltern reaches of the Thames valley. Here the old woodlands were enhanced and emphasised in a succession of parks whose beauty is captured in the paintings of Joseph Farrington, and persists to the present. The sequence begins at Mongewell House and goes on to Coombe Lodge near Whitchurch, where by the early 1790s

[6] Mavis Batey, *Nuneham Courtenay, Oxfordshire* (Oxford, 1970), pp. 23–4.

A wide expanse of open fields on the Oxfordshire side of the river rise gradually to a considerable eminence, and afforded nothing but naked cultivation till Mr. Gardner began to build the mansion. When his plantations have risen into height, and thickened into shade, they will make to Basildon and its woods a return of equal beauty.[7]

The woods at Hardwick were "the pride of the country", not merely adorning the landscape but commanding it; Mapledurham had a mile-long avenue of elms; Caversham Park had an approach created by Brown; the picturesque lawns of Fawley Court were succeeded by Henley Park with "beautiful inclosures descending in natural waving slopes from the house". Such effects were repeated on the Berkshire bank of the Thames and we are left in no doubt that the special quality of a wooded riverside landscape was already exerting its appeal to the affluent.

The landscape of parliamentary enclosure

A graphic way of sensing the spirit of improvement that assailed the Oxfordshire landscape in the eighteenth century and introduced its various designs is to fan through the pages of a weekly newspaper, *Jackson's Oxford Journal*. There, in news item, comment and advertisement we see a reflection of many of the facets of innovation in the countryside and in its towns. From what we have just traced in the parklands, for example, it is natural that the *Journal* should give notice to the many nurserymen and gardeners who supplied the raw materials to ardent planters. There was Matthew Cook at Clay Hall near Oxford (1765), who was succeeded by John Rouse, gardener to Lord Wenman at Thame Park (1770); Laval Kent by the King's Head at Thame, and George Richards at Adderbury (1772); James

[7] W. Combe, *An History of the Principal Rivers of Great Britain* (1794), Vol. I, p. 230.

Wakelin in the Buttermarket at Thame (1775); John Whitton at Deddington and John Willis at Burford (1776).

Also noticeable is that some nurserymen advertised a special line of business: in November 1765 we read that William Poole of Charlbury supplied "crab setts to gentlemen concerned in enclosures", and in May 1773 Wakelin was selling whitethorns and elm trees for the same purpose. Enclosure itself was a persistent and continuing source of news. Rioters broke down the new fences and hedges at North Leigh in 1759, and two years later the Berkshire Militia was brought in to quell a similar riot on the Heath at North Leigh, but damage to William Perrott's gates, railings and walls at Lower Riding Farm still went on, as after Stonesfield Wake in August 1761. So many trees in new enclosures at Bicester were destroyed that the people of Market End clubbed together to detect and prosecute those responsible. The same problem arose at Bampton in 1777 and Stanton St John in 1780. Another pointer was that when Cottisford Manor was sold in 1773 it included '240 enclosed acres' as well as 800 acres in the common fields, and the *Journal* regularly advertised enclosed grounds or land as something of special value and interest. New farmhouses and new roads were other results of the reported activities of the enclosure commissioners, who were inaugurating a fresh farming landscape in Oxfordshire. In a more concentrated way than had been felt previously, the enclosure of common fields and wastes by Act of Parliament after about 1730 changed an open landscape into a closer-textured, parcellated pattern. Enclosure was revolutionary, it did away with the old, varied, haphazard scene inherited from centuries of piecemeal fashioning of the agricultural land, replacing it with a more systematic framework for improved farming. Nothing expressed more forcibly the change from instinctive actions to a deliberate, ordered layout of the working landscape.

The measure of this change impressed William Wing,

who was an eye-witness of what he called "the great
agricultural revolution of an inclosure of the open fields"
at Upper Heyford, in 1842. He remembered the intricacies
of the minute sub-divisions of the old unhedged arable, and
the terms by which they were known: *lands, acres* (two lands
lying side by side in parallel, irrespective of area), *foreshooters*
(lands adjoining at their ends), *hades* (headlands), *rick-pen
plots, men's maths in the meadows, closes* (narrow pasture fields
near the village). There were also the *baulks* or yard-wide
strips of untilled soil between the cultivated *lands*, smothered
in weeds and brambles before enclosure "reformed them
from the face of the earth".[8]

The open grazing of the cow-common also disappeared
among the new fields, but Wing could still recall the cattle
being herded to it each morning and brought back for
milking at the end of the day: "It was a curious sight to see
those animals enter the village at the western end, and stalk
onwards to the gate of their owner's farmstead." As a
consequence of enclosure these immemorial patterns of
Heyford life were swept away, new farms defined and farmhouses built on them away from the village, a new carriage-
way for public use was marked out, garden allotments were
set aside to compensate the poor who could no longer cut
gorse for their fuel on the old waste. Within twenty years
these expanses of furzy, rough grassland were "long since
nearly obliterated".

On the other side of the Cherwell valley the three Aston
villages show very well the different modes of enclosure
known in Oxfordshire. North Aston lost its common fields
and wastes early on, during Elizabethan times. The whole
of Middle Aston was in the hands of Francis Page by 1756,
when he secured the glebe and tithes (by a private Act of
Parliament) in exchange for lands at Steeple Aston. Accordingly he was able to go ahead with enclosing the open parts

[8] W. Wing, *Annals of Heyford Warren, otherwise Upper Heyford* (Oxford,
1865), p. 17.

133

of the township by 1763, without the expense of further
legislation, and divided it into three large holdings: Town
Farm (295 acres), Great House Farm (212 acres), and the
Grange (336 acres). On the other hand, the course of events
at Steeple Aston was entirely conventional, with an Act of
Parliament for its enclosure in 1766 and the award of
redistributed lands in the following year.

One special point about Steeple Aston is that the vestry
book shows how in the pre-enclosure years of 1762–5 the
nine holders of common land in the Lower and Upper
Fields were already introducing new methods of farming,
which could be accommodated within the old system. They
sowed sainfoin in one of the furlongs, and each farmer was
to *mound* or fence his crop, excluding horses and sheep
from the sown grassland. Part of the common land, Barley
Field, was sown with clover in 1762, another furlong with
turnips, and the fallow field with clover in 1764. They
planted quickset hedges around one of the *quarters* between
1761 and 1763, exchanged pieces of land in the Dean, and
stinted the grazing of animals on open land. These innovations were to be enforced by agreement for twenty years,
but were soon overridden by the Enclosure Act of 1766
which made them applicable on the grand scale.

We do not have so much as a hint from Arthur Young's
writings that such informal arrangements were even possible
under the old order of common fields, because he was a
propagandist for parliamentary enclosure as the means of
achieving an intensive kind of mixed farming with new
crops, rotations, implements and stock-breeding. Young
could look back with satisfaction on forty years' knowledge
of Oxfordshire and say that "more land has been enclosed
since I first travelled in it... than in any county in England."[9]
Between 1760 and 1800, according to his figures, thirty-four
Acts had been passed for enclosing 50,736 acres, while
another thirty-three Acts had not specified the area affected

[9] A. Young, *View of the Agriculture of Oxfordshire* (London, 1809), p. 87.

by them. The commissioners and surveyors were still very busy as he was compiling his figures, just after 1800. Even so, there were almost 100 townships as yet untouched by parliamentary enclosure, located chiefly on the good arable lands of the upper Thames-side gravel terraces, parts of the stonebrash, and most strikingly along the foot of the Chilterns. These held stubbornly to the old order: the last vestige of common field in Oxfordshire did not disappear until as late as 1886, at Crowell below the Chilterns. By contrast, the enclosers had made most headway in the Redlands, where townships with two common fields had split them into *quarters* before the eighteenth century; Young could not find any common fields surviving to the north of Deddington.

Phrasing it differently, eighty-seven per cent of the Redland townships were affected by parliamentary enclosure after 1730. In most other parts of Oxfordshire the proportion was lower and ran at about two thirds of the townships, save for the Chilterns where it was only about a half (p. 111). Townships are one basis for calculation, but to get some idea of what these figures mean as areas it has been worked out that about thirty-seven per cent of the county area was enclosed from common arable fields or meadow between 1755 and 1870. To this may be added the nine per cent of unimproved land, that is open commons and waste, which was also taken into the new fields.[10] In other words, again, if we add together all those townships where more than half the farmland was enclosed in this way, they cover just over half of Oxfordshire. So we should be prepared to find the pervasive results of the commissioners' redrawing of the agrarian landscape anywhere in Oxfordshire, not excluding the Chilterns and forest country (Plate 18).

The minute subdivision of lands in the old common fields was carried to an extraordinary degree, and so completely was it ironed from the landscape by the enclosers

[10] H. L. Gray, *English Field Systems* (Harvard, 1915), pp. 110–39.

that to see its like today we have to go to parts of southern Germany or France where the process of consolidation is still going on. Yet it was commonplace in the farming life of Oxfordshire only two centuries ago. On the road between Nuneham Courtenay and the Baldons, for instance, the farm Daglands consisted of eighty-six acres in all, but of this the six enclosed fields comprised only thirty-three acres, the rest being scattered in no fewer than forty-one parcels in the common fields of Baldon, still awaiting the enclosure that came half a century later.[11] Another farm of similar size in the Wychwood countryside at Hailey had only four small enclosures of meadow, from six to eight acres; the rest of its lands, two thirds of the farm, was dispersed in eighty open unfenced strips (mostly no bigger than half or three quarters of an acre), lying in various furlongs.[12] Totally different was the parliamentary enclosers' handiwork, already accomplished at Sturt Downs Farm on the Cotswolds beyond Burford. Now standing on the verge of the A40, its 245 acres had been contrived from the old common grazings, and it was composed of fourteen square or rectangular fields, varying in size from Sturt Home Ground at seven acres to Sturt Ground at thirty acres.[13]

As these three farms show, in various parts of Oxfordshire on differing terrain the scope for parliamentary enclosure was also variable, whole townships requiring it here, parts of townships there, whereas in other places the work of the early enclosers was so complete that only a tidying-up operation was needed. Aston Rowant, together with most other places along the foot of the Chilterns, was still wholly in common field in the early eighteenth century. Across the clay vale two-thirds of the tiny manor of Denton was in hedged pasture fields, but they still separated two

[11] Queen's College MSS. 4A, 5(A), *Survey and Terrier of the Manor of Toot Baldon, March 1770*, ff. 10–12.

[12] Bodleian, Gough Maps 27, f. 36: *Plan of a Farm belonging to University College in Hayley Common Field, July 1758*.

[13] Bodleian, MS. Maps Oxon. a.2(5), *c. 1780*.

blocks of common arable running in the Upper and Lower Fields: contemporary plans confirm the proportions of early and parliamentary enclosure at Denton as calculated by H. L. Gray from other sources.[14] At Gagingwell on the stonebrash, by contrast, there were a series of small homestead closes near the village (clearly enclosed, nevertheless, from what had been common field), while beyond and all round them the farmland lay entirely in very big fields of fifty or sixty acres, the work of pre-parliamentary enclosers.[15] Many of the old forest townships were wholly enclosed, too: Studley is so shown on a plan of 1641, and Elsfield— a neighbouring village on the Stowood hills north of Oxford—must have been finally enclosed by private agreement between 1689 and 1703, when it was mapped.[16]

The redrawing of the farming landscape by the enclosure commissioners as they made their awards is comparatively easy to identify, and so are the new features they brought into being as the direct or longer-term results of their planning. Consolidation of scattered strips and parcels into compact farms, each within its ring fence, meant that a totally new pattern of fields could make its appearance. We are still reminded of the common field complexities, all the same, by the ridge-and-furrow that can give a corrugated, corduroy look to the ground anywhere in Oxfordshire between the Cotswolds and Chilterns, especially in the *highbacks* of fields in the clay country. The ridges show where the medieval peasant ploughed up his open *lands* so that the intervening furrows could help the drainage of the soil.[17] The enclosure of the old common fields at Lower Heyford in 1802 was promoted by William Filmer who came

[14] Gray, *op cit.*, p. 541; *Plan of Denton by William Burgess, 1736*, Bodleian Maps, (E) C17:49, Oxon., 140; *Map of Queen's College Inclosed Lands in Denton, 1770*: Queen's College MS., 4A, 5(A), f. 54.
[15] Bodleian Maps, (E) C17:49, Oxon., 111; *Plan of Gagingwell, 1713*.
[16] Gray, *op. cit.*, pp. 119, 122: Bodleian Maps, (E) C17:49, Oxon., 88, 92.
[17] J. E. G. Sutton, 'Ridge and Furrow in Berkshire and Oxfordshire', *Oxoniensia,* Vols. XXIX–XXX (1964–5), pp. 99–115.

from Kent and introduced new methods in farming his rectorial glebe, including better drills and ploughs as well as new crops like swedes and lentils. As enclosure was usually the prelude to introducing an intensive kind of mixed farming, the number and size of the new fields bore a relationship to the intentions of the new farmers. Thus if the commissioners set out a new farm of 150 acres, if fifteen acres were set aside for the buildings and a few closes near to the farmhouse for handling young livestock, and if the farmer intended to follow a five-course rotation of crops and grass, then the remaining 135 acres were divided into six fields. Each field would therefore be twenty to twenty-five acres in area. Around Bicester the enclosed arable was usually divided into seven parts, one seventh under sainfoin, two sevenths under grass seeds, three sevenths under corn and one seventh under turnips.[18]

For such reasons we find a high degree of similarity in the field patterns created by the enclosure commissioners: on the same kind of land, whether it was in Oxfordshire or Durham or Dorset, the economic circumstances of improvement gave rise to a predictable, almost blueprinted layout of the new fields and much else that appeared with them. We can appreciate this in the work of John Claudius Loudon, famous as a designer of gardens, houses and modernised farms, who took in hand nearly 2000 acres of Redland at Great Tew in 1808. His intention, at least, was to create there a model estate, demonstrating in miniature the new principles for integrating the farmland, farmhouse, outbuildings and park.[19] Even though what he transformed was mainly old-enclosed pasture, Loudon's advice was also suited to the enclosure then being effected by parliamentary act. In uprooting the old hedges and making new fields he was guided by four requirements: to regulate the size of

---

[18] H. Wyndham, *A Backward Glance* (London, 1950), p. 17.
[19] J. C. Loudon, *Observations on laying out Farms in the Scotch style adapted to England* (1812).

the fields so that they ranged from fifteen to twenty-five acres apiece; to connect them to his new roads; to make their open ditches serve as drains; and to plant hedges for shelter without hiding the fields from Tew Lodge. On the high ridges his fields were smaller (fifteen to twenty acres), on the sheltered slopes or hollows they were larger (twenty to twenty-five acres). Hedges ran north–south wherever possible to protect the fields from prevailing winds, as a plantation running along the margin of the estate already sheltered it from northerlies. The two longest sides of a field were drawn parallel so as to avoid short ploughing-ridges at the angles. Laid up and down the natural slope, if it was not too steep or the soil impermeable, they would also allow good drainage along the furrows.

Loudon thought field boundaries should serve to separate land of different qualities and uses, also ensuring each field was supplied with water. By clearing the old sprawling boundaries at Tew he freed forty acres of land from copse, blackthorn and pollards. In their place he planted hawthorn hedges, simply laying the quicksets below the turf. They were protected by hurdle fences for two years in five, when (under the Scottish rotation he hoped to adopt) the fields were under clover. Timber trees were preserved in the new hedges, and Loudon was flexible in his programme of reform:

> The hedgerows in elevated situations, the acute angles formed by the intersection of the oblique lines of fences, the abrupt spots too steep for the plough, dells favourable for game or furzy knolls for the fox, we left either wild or planted as rows and thickets.

Great care was evident in designing the roads which linked these new fields with the farm. To avoid carrying heavy loads by cart up and down the steepish slopes at Tew, the ideal of 'a shortest mode of communication' was sacrificed to making the roads follow the contours, with easy access from the fields on either side. It was a circuitous but efficient pattern, surviving intact and in working use to the present day. Loudon made them twenty-two feet across, but within this only a nine-foot strip to one side had a stone-packed core for use by loaded carts or in winter. The whole road was sown with grass for grazing, because carts would not be using them for two years in every five-year rotation. Hedges were planted along the margins of the roads, with a single row of oak and elm trees on the northerly side, so as to leave the road open to the drying sun. Such minute care for detail of agrarian improvement is impressive, and the Tew landscape retains many relics of Loudon: the most obvious are the splendid exotic trees and rhododendron plantation (now overgrown) with which he ornamented the fifty acres of parkland around his model farm. Only the site of Tew Lodge remains, marked by old brickwork and a trace of driveways, but the surrounding fields offer more, here the channel and sluices that effected his drainage to the water meadows and ponds, there a fragment of slotted fencing.

In the stone country the new fields were demarcated by drystone walls, which cost no more than quickset hedges, railing and ditches. This was true of the Cotswolds and across the stonebrash to places like Wendlebury, enclosed in 1800. It was also the case that new farmhouses could be built away from the villages, when the enclosure commissioners had parcelled out the compact farms. If these lay at a distance of a mile or so from the old nucleations, it was sensible to have a freshly-built house, barns, stables and yard on the site, standing among its fields. This may have taken place gradually, first a barn and later the completed farmstead, but it amounted to a major wave of secondary dispersion in the countryside (p. 113). Most of the single farms in the Redlands originated at this time, five of them in Bloxham parish after 1794; Alkerton Heath Farm and

Alkerton Grounds Farm on the limits of the county, and Drayton Fields Farm after the enclosure of 1802. Typically they have 'Grounds' or 'Fields' in their names, revealing how they assumed the identity of the common lands from whose reorganisation they sprang. They are often imposing Georgian structures with strong visual appeal in their clean lines, stone- or brick-built according to their situation, shielded by plantations of Scots pine.

Sometimes enclosure was the means of encouraging new settlement of a more elaborate kind, as at Kidlington. Before 1818 there was a big common for grazing cows in summer and horses in autumn, with sheep commons at Campsfield. All this open ground was replaced with cultivation, substantial farmhouses, cottages and farm buildings when the Duke of Marlborough enclosed. Those commoners who could not afford their share of the enclosure sold out to William Turner of Shipton, who was awarded fourteen acres in lieu of these rights and added them to his park, "so enhancing the beauty of a Maisonette and its surroundings".[20] Further, the centre of gravity of the village was pulled westwards as new houses were built on the enclosed lands along the main road from Oxford to Banbury. When such changes happened on Oxford's doorstep, however, there could be criticisms of enclosure on the grounds of amenity and aesthetics. Thus the disappearance of the commons at Cowley and Bullingdon in 1850 stopped riding, the pursuit of natural history, and "cut off fresh air from Oxford students in general". The old trackways had led to open country and "were in themselves pretty, natural and winding", whereas enclosure reduced them to eight, "dull and dusty, as being merely footpaths by the new roadside, and formal as being all in straight lines".[21]

The commissioners introduced mile after mile of new access roads to the Oxfordshire countryside. At Somerton

---

[20] W. Wing, *Annals of Kidlington* (Oxford, 1881), p. 8.
[21] G. V. Cox, *Recollections of Oxford* (Oxford, 1868), p. 352.

it was thought they overdid it (1766) and marked out more than the parish needed. In 1769 appeals were made against the roads staked out at Chapel Heath, and at the Quarter Sessions they were altered for the benefit of the townspeople of Chipping Norton. More usually they took existing tracks and improved them, elsewhere they struck afresh along new lines. Akeman Street was cut down and narrowed by the Heyford enclosure in 1842, changed from a carriage-way to a bridleway and footpath, nothing more. The new public roads were fixed at forty or sixty feet across from hedge to hedge, a sufficient breadth being necessary because the road surface was poor and alternative courses were followed by road-users in wet weather. Now that macadamised surfaces have solved that problem, with a narrow central ribbon of roadway, the enclosure roads give themselves away by their surplus grass verges, with a summer growth of willowherb and cow parsley (where the herbicide sprayer is not at work).

Five Mile Drive in suburban North Oxford is of this origin. When the Wolvercote enclosure award was drawn up in 1834 it was in deep country, and the only track connecting the Woodstock and Banbury main roads was a green lane called Horslow Field Way, taking its name from one of the four common fields. As the newly allocated enclosures along its course had to be "guarded with good and substantial posts and rails" with ditches on either side and gates and stiles where needed, Horslow Field Way was established as a broad public highway, and still preserves this spacious quality as Five Mile Drive. The 1834 Act also made a new road at First Turn, directly linking Wolvercote with the Woodstock road. The award was typical in its framing, with its emphasis on allotments made in the "open and common fields, meadows, pastures and other commonable and waste lands", when they were divided, allotted and enclosed. Within six months they "should be inclosed, and the fences thereof composed of and planted with young quicksets";[22] in due course Red Barn Farm and Peartree Hill Farm came into the landscape for the first time, at a distance from the old villages.

The full and concentrated weight of the changes induced by the encloser, finally, may be illustrated from the actions of John Sibthorp at South Leigh. Three thousand trees, oaks and pollard elms among them, were cut down on his orders in the spring of 1793—"for my repairs and my enclosures", as he put it. Later that year he had fifty-four men working as carpenters, masons, hedgers, ditchers, roadmen and woodmen.[23] The energy of the improving landowner sparks from Sibthorp's letters as he played his part in this most influential phase of landscape-making: in ten months from the enclosure award

I have worked up between 2000 and 3000 trees to posts and rails for my enclosure, besides a great quantity of timber used in the general repair of the farmhouses and cottage. I have quicked [i.e. hedged] near upon 100 furlongs and fenced with posts and rails one-half of it. Gates and gateposts on the enclosures. I had three teams of horses constantly employed during the summer, yet unequal to my work.

Turnpikes and canals: new routeways

From its earliest issues in the 1750s *Jackson's Oxford Journal* reported new initiatives in the transport network—the making of carriage roads, the widening of causeways, the building of bridges. A meeting at the Crown in Witney, for instance, decided in 1766 to apply for an Act of Parliament to make a turnpike road from Witney Town End,

[22] Bodleian, MS. D. D. Par. Wolvercote a.1.
[23] M. R. Bruce, 'An Oxfordshire Enclosure, 1791–94', *Top. Oxon.*, Vol. 18 (1972), pp. 2–5.

via Ducklington and Standlake to the Thames crossing at Newbridge. Again, it was reported in 1772 that all turnpikes between Deddington and Chipping Norton were thoroughly repaired and "will be safe for carriages all summer". Conversely we read in 1775 how the road from Watlington to Oxford across the clay lowlands was often impassable. Just as the archaisms of the common fields were being changed by the enclosers, so with the traditional pattern of the highways along which people and goods made their way as speedily as conditions permitted. From this quarter, too, we can expect a measure of fresh design in the landscape.

It is a complicated story because of the extremely large number of roads, tracks and paths of varying degrees of importance that run through the Oxfordshire countryside. A quick glance at the one-inch map will confirm this, as we see in the district between the Cherwell and the Evenlode north of Oxford, which is as seamed with them as the veins on a leaf. Their status is also very sensitive and apt to change, so what may be an overgrown path today could have been a main road 200 years ago, whereas a modern trunk road may invigorate a disused Roman alignment. Sited on the ancient highway from London to Worcester, Enstone is a better place than most to illustrate these things, following Jordan's reconstruction of roads "in use when the saddle, the pillion, and the pack were the chief means of conveyance".[24] The medieval highway swung from the bottom of the Glyme valley at Cleveley and Radford to enter Neat Enstone village. It then crossed the hillside south of the river and on the opposite side from the modern A34. The section as far as Lidstone has vanished, "the old green lane forming it having been blotted out by the 1854 enclosure"; it reappeared by Chalford Green and looped on as Cow Ditch Lane, "enclosed between two high hedges and banks, in parts not so wide as bridle paths are now set

[24] J. Jordan, *A Parochial History of Enstone* (Oxford, 1857), pp. 375–81.

out", and significantly for its great age serving as the Enstone boundary. Chalford Green now is the meeting place of half a dozen roads and tracks, their verges a dumping ground for road metal by the local authority and impartially by users of the B4026; only the northerly 'boundary' side of the medieval road has a high hedge, the other being a crumbled drystone wall.

Having become inadequate for the growing volume of traffic by about 1800 the medieval highway was replaced by a new road (now the A34) from Woodstock to Chipping Norton, made as follows:

> the way in which it was commenced was by ploughing up the whole length of it, and the furrow thus ploughed was six miles in length, the team ploughing the whole length from end to end.

Along this road moved a great volume of traffic from Oxford to Birmingham and the Midlands; twenty-two four-horse coaches passed through Enstone each day and night, many of them changing teams there, and at least half a dozen heavy waggons did likewise. Other roads of merely local importance were also in need of improvement, such as that from Enstone to Bicester: before this was turnpiked in 1794 it had high sloping banks

> along which stood very lofty trees, growing in such a manner that their roots spread from one side of the road to the other, intertwining in the middle, so any vehicle passing up or down was severely tried and bumped.

So bad was it that the villagers of Westcott Barton and Middle Barton refrained from using it to take their corn to Oxford market. Instead of following it to the Banbury road at Hopcroft's Holt they preferred to strike across the open fields to the ten-mile stone on the Banbury road, leaving their waggons there overnight, continuing to market on the second day, and not returning to the Bartons (fourteen miles at the most from Oxford) until the third day.[25] Similarly, the way from the Astons to Oxford was not along the Banbury road but via Rousham Gap and then down what they called 'the Green Riding' to Woodstock: this was the *mereway* or boundary track discussed by Hoskins and of more practical use than he assumed.[26]

Before parliamentary enclosure we know there was an abundance of open commons, heaths and warrens over which people moved freely, around which they could build cottages, or on which race meetings took place without disturbance, in an altogether more spacious and informal landscape than ours. So too with the old roads before the age of design and improvement, when Bampton-in-the-Bush deserved its name prior to the enclosure

> no stoned road of any kind led from Bampton to the neighbouring towns and villages. Travellers were in the habit of striking across the common by which the town was surrounded, and finding their way to Witney, Burford, Oxford or any other place in the best way they could, as is done to this very day in the deserts of Arabia and Africa.[27]

The modern road approaching Bampton from Oxford is unusually straight and wide, with broad grass verges, as one would expect from its lateness and deliberate design through the open commons.

Clayland surfaces were the most difficult for the old highways, but thanks to the spread of gravel terracing or the outcrops of limestones and sandstones in the Oxford

[25] Jenner Marshall, *Memorials of Westcott Barton* (London, 1870), p. 51.
[26] C. C. Brookes, *A History of Steeple Aston and Middle Aston* (Oxford, 1929), p. 16; W. G. Hoskins, *The Making of the English Landscape* (London, 1955), p. 234.
[27] J. A. Giles, *History of Bampton* (2nd edn. 1848), p. 17.

Heights, which intervened very conveniently between the claylands, the old roads were able to avoid them and the damp alluvial tracts to a great extent. They chose to run on the marlstone ridges above the Lias Clay valley floors, or veered from gravel patch to patch in the Thames valley with a minimum of clay crossing, as on the roads from Oxford to High Wycombe and Henley. Even so the quality of the road surfaces was moderately good only on the higher Cotswolds and better-drained sandstones.

Road maintenance had relied on the Tudor statutes requiring the householders in each parish to give six days' unpaid labour each year under the parochial surveyor. It was unpopular work, ridden with abuses, and thoroughly inadequate by the eighteenth century when longer distance traffic put a far greater volume of stress on the highways. In response to these new demands there had to be a better system under the Turnpike Acts, by which justices of the peace and turnpike trustees were authorised to improve stretches of road, and collect tolls from goods and passenger traffic in order to do so. By the terms of the Acts the trustees enjoyed powers to make bridges and causeways and do whatever was necessary to produce a serviceable turnpike road. Eventually even Arthur Young, as a confirmed coach-traveller, had to admit in 1809 "a noble change" in the Oxfordshire roads as he had experienced them over forty years; the turnpikes he thought to be "very good and where gravel is to be had, excellent".[28]

At first only the principal through-roads from London to the Midlands were turnpiked, but by 1760 the network had grown to include others like the Oxford–Cheltenham–Gloucester and the Oxford–Banbury–Stratford roads. Under the old system the road from Gloucester to Oxford split into two on the eastern outskirts of Witney, at Staple Hall Inn. What was called the 'Wheel Road' for heavy waggons and coaches followed a dry route of fourteen miles (the

[28] Young, *op. cit.*, p. 234.

modern A4095) through Long Hanborough, Bladon and Begbroke. Passengers on horseback preferred the 'Bridle Road' of ten miles via Barnard Gate, Eynsham and the Swinford Ferry across the Thames. Although shorter this ancient road was "so deep and very much out of repair" (1751) it was positively dangerous for travellers in winter. Eventually, however, it was widened and improved; then the Earl of Abingdon built his private toll bridge at Swinford (opened to traffic in 1769); and with the reconstruction of the Botley causeway leading into Oxford this 'ancient horse road' became the main thoroughfare to the west for all kinds of vehicles from Oxford, remaining so until the new A40 was made in the 1930s.[29]

Adequate bridges and the raised causeways leading to them were of prime necessity in Oxfordshire with its many rivers which were more prone to flooding then than today (p. 152). It was boasted in *Jackson's Oxford Journal* in 1767 that there were six new bridges either planned or being built in or near Oxford. The oldest stone bridge on the Oxfordshire Thames is at Radcot, the first to span the river after it enters the county. It was there by 1209 but now crosses a backwater, because in 1787 the main channel was dug as an aid to river navigation, and a new bridge thrown over it. Until Tadpole Bridge was built in 1802 the next bridge downstream was the other surviving medieval structure, Newbridge, dating from the fifteenth century. When Tollit, the county surveyor, inspected it in 1878 he found Newbridge in good order and likely "to last another 300 or 400 years".[30] As at Radcot, so at Godstow there was a new two-arched bridge to supplement an older one, required by the digging of a new cut for navigation leading towards Godstow Lock.

It was the unreliable nature of the Thames for barge

---

[29] E. de Villiers, *Swinford Bridge, 1769–1969* (Eynsham, 1969), p. 17.

[30] H. J. Tollit, *Report upon all the County Bridges in Oxfordshire* (Oxford, 1878), p. 73.

traffic that prompted people to think of having in its place an artificial, regulated means of navigation, designed for use throughout the year. Thus the Oxford Canal came to take its place in the eighteenth-century landscape as a corollary of new bridges and turnpike roads. There was a coincidence between the succession of very bad floods on the Thames in the late 1760s, disrupting its navigation, and the first moves towards having the canal. As an experiment to judge if it was feasible to open a canal northwards from Oxford, in January 1764 a boatload of coal was taken by the Cherwell to Sir Edward Turner's house at Ambrosden, returning with a freight of barley. A few weeks later Captain Toovey and two passengers sailed up the Cherwell towards Bicester. Early in 1768 the plan for a canal was accepted, £50,000 subscribed at once, and the town clerks of Coventry, Banbury and Oxford prepared a bill that received the royal assent in April 1769.

By then James Brindley was already surveying the ground along which the navigation was to be cut. Only forty miles were finished by 1774 when contracts were made for bringing coal to the Oxfordshire towns. It was within two miles of Banbury by the end of 1776, but the first barge-load of coal did not arrive in the town until March 1778, when it was welcomed by peals of bells and brass bands. There was cause for rejoicing, because in a part of England where domestic and industrial fuel was scarce and costly the canal brought Warwickshire coal at eleven pence per hundred-weight. The cut was not brought on to Oxford for another twelve years.

The Oxford Canal certainly added to the distinctive landscape of the Cherwell valley through which it makes its way like a second river (Plate 19). On a minor scale Brindley proceeded in such cavalier fashion in its construction that at Upper Heyford he diverted the Cherwell from its course, gave it a new channel in the next parish, and used the old river-bed as part of the canal on the inside of a valley meander. Farther downstream at Shipton the canal and Cherwell are fully merged as a single waterway for a mile. It was also thought that the canal so interfered with the natural drainage that it increased the risk of summer flooding by the river (p. 155). There were eighteen locks between Banbury and Oxford, the largest at Somerton Deep with a twelve-foot fall; they are even more plentiful beyond Banbury, the Claydon Flight taking the canal to its summit. More noticeable are the many new bridges, built of brick, that frequently span the canal along its length.

On a more general scale, by providing an artery of cheap transport, especially for coal and bulky materials, the canal introduced to the Cherwell valley a potential for new industries (at Banbury in particular, p. 199) and a new kind of settlement. The 'semi-detached hamlet' of Enslow, for instance, consisted of the Rock of Gibraltar inn where the old London road crossed the Cherwell; a wharf on the canal with the wharfinger's house and stables; a water-powered corn mill; brickyards, tileries and quarries; and, later on as a reinforcement of the same locational ties, the railway station serving Kirtlington. Wharves also appeared at Lower Heyford, again because a good road crossed the river and so made it possible to distribute or collect goods carried by barge and the market boats plying between Oxford and Banbury; at Souldern, Twyford, and of course at Banbury itself. As a natural extension of its activities to the river trade, the canal company also built a wharf on the Thames at Eynsham, together with the Talbot Inn. With the decline in water-borne goods traffic the canal has assumed a different role: under the 1968 Transport Act the whole of the Oxford Canal was scheduled as 'a recreational and amenity waterway'. Where it leaves the Cherwell at Thrupp, another canal hamlet, the basin and wharf are now used as a service centre by the holiday cruisers that have superseded the old narrow boats bringing roadstone from the Midlands. Future plans for using the canal in its scenic setting include a riverside hotel and picnic site near Flights Mill in Kirtlington, sponsored by the British Waterways Board, and a country park provided by the Oxfordshire County Council. From being one element in the designed landscape of the eighteenth-century improvers, then, the canal and its vicinity have entered the competitive area of the planners' landscape, and we shall find other cases of such linkages in re-creating the Victorian scene.

SELECT BIBLIOGRAPHY

Batey, Mavis, 'Nuneham Courtenay: an Oxfordshire 18th Century Deserted Village', *Oxoniensia,* XXXIII (1968), pp. 108–24.

Batey, Mavis, *Nuneham Courtenay, Oxfordshire* (1970).

Green, David, *Blenheim Palace* (1957); *Blenheim Park and Gardens* (1972).

A Handlist of Inclosure Acts and Awards Relating to the County of Oxford, Oxford County Council, Record Publication No. 2 (1963).

Jaine, T. W. M., 'The Building of Magdalen Bridge, 1772–1790', *Oxoniensia,* Vol. XXXVI (1971), pp. 59–72.

Jourdain, Margaret, *The Work of William Kent* (1948).

Pantin, W. A., 'Houses in the Oxford Region: 2, Hordley Farm', *Oxoniensia,* Vol. XXV (1960), pp. 126–30.

Prince, Hugh, *Parks in England* (1967).

Stroud, Dorothy, *Capability Brown* (1957).

Sutton, J. E. G., 'Ridge and Furrow in Berkshire and Oxfordshire', *Oxoniensia,* Vols. XXIX–XXX (1964–5), pp. 99–105.

Young, Arthur, *View of the Agriculture of Oxfordshire* (1809).

6. The Victorian countryside

The gradual conquest of the Thames. The disappearance of Wychwood Forest. The changing village. Closed and open villages. Industrial villages. Railways in the landscape. Victorian building in the countryside

THE CHIEF JUSTIFICATION of a chapter such as this is to examine the way in which forces making for designed change in the landscape went ahead with fresh intensity from about 1840 to the close of the nineteenth century. This period of time has been a little neglected by writers on the making of landscapes, perhaps on the assumption that innovation discussed in the context of, say, parliamentary enclosure could be presumed to have gone on running its course as before. But the Victorian decades were so distinctive in their economic and demographic life that they deserve to be looked at in their own right, to see if new intensities appeared in established modes, as well as those wholly new actions in the landscape, such as the building of railways.

The gradual conquest of the Thames

We can illustrate the point by investigating how the river Thames ultimately passed under human control in this Victorian period, being changed from an unpredictable stream running wild with costly floods to the disciplined river that fits into the contemporary scene. To one modern observer, the Thames "now tamed and channelled, feels as though it long ago went into enjoyable retirement",[1]

[1] James Morris, *Oxford* (1965), p. 31.

Plate 19 The Oxford Canal. This stretch of the navigation, close to the canal village of Thrupp, runs along the natural course of the river Cherwell, which was diverted by Brindley into the new channel he made for it.

Plate 20 The Thames in full flood, 1875. In this photograph by Henry Taunt the main line of the Great Western Railway, just to the south of Oxford, has been breached by the flood waters that can be seen spreading across the river meadows.

Plate 21 The Thames flood plain above Oxford. This view, looking upstream, shows Pinkhill lock and weir (bottom left), part of the Thames Conservancy's design to control the serpentine river's regime in the late nineteenth century. The dense hedges in the right foreground are associated with early enclosure at Pinkhill, and the wide riverside meadows occur all the way upstream to the Bampton Polderland.

Plate 22 Landscape made at the final clearing of Wychwood Forest in 1857–8. Potter Hill Farm, whose huge stone-walled fields fill the centre of the picture, was marked out as 475 acres of corn and fattening farmland. The new settlement of Fordwells (bottom right) has the smaller enclosures of Broadquarter Allotments close to it. At the top of the air-photograph is the Leafield radio transmitting station. Scale *c.* 1 : 10,000.

but its status as a most regulated river is recent. It was not always so: a century ago its floods were a great nuisance to those living above its natural constriction at Sandford. In that flattish riverside country around and above Oxford, some 600 square miles of the 'Upper Division', a series of dangerous floods in the nineteenth century finally but gradually forced people to understand their causes, effects and control.

After the floods of 1821 the surveyor for the Thames Commissioners found that the river "would be running in its natural course" were it not for its contraction at a large number of man-made weirs. Thus at the outset it seems that flooding was being induced by those who built flash-weirs for the better navigation of the river by barges and other craft, as well as fishing-weirs and mill-streams. All the weirs needed rebuilding, it was advised that they should be wider and their sills and high-water marks should be deepened. The river flow could also be helped by dredging the shoals and clearing the banks. Another bad flood in 1825 was worsened by a further complication, "the general enclosure and draining of lands". Because of the improvement of farmland on the clays and alluvium by means of ditching and field-piping or tiling, more water from the surface of the fields and their subsoil was finding its way more rapidly into the river. Under-draining the heavy farmland went ahead on a big scale after 1840, when cheap machine-made cylindrical tiles became widely available and were encouraged by government grants. Thus more and more run-off water entered the Thames without anything being done to expedite the extra work the river was asked to do.

Predictably there came the disastrous floods lasting from September 1852 to February 1853, destroying the grazing that followed hay harvest and causing a public outcry. The investigators found all the old causes and some fresh ones: six dilapidated weirs in a stretch of seven miles of river near Bampton, islands "entirely of alluvial creation" encouraged in their growth by the fishermen, sluices across the backwaters, hedges (some recently planted at enclosure) going at right-angles to the Thames and so ponding back the floodwater. The spoiling of so much meadow ground was too high a price to pay for "the naviga- tion of a few boats and a few baskets of fish". On the posi- tive side, however, the flooding problem was better understood, and it was more complex than we might imagine. Rapid flooding in winter was beneficial to the land, but it had to be short-term or it became injurious. Summer floods were a menace, spoiling the hay and bad for the health of stock. Therefore the ideal was to guarantee a good high-water level throughout the year; to tolerate some moderate, speedy winter flooding; to remove the danger of excessive floods in winter and floods of any kind in summer. "A partial and not a total remedy is required for the floods of the Thames."

The 1852-3 floods led to the formulation, on paper at least, of a feasible scheme to remove the bottlenecks above Sandford, as a prelude to removing the weirs and other snags farther up-river. It was not implemented, unfortu- nately, because the various users of the Thames were still locked in a feud of opposing interests. First came the riparian owners (and drainers) of land, with their tenants of weirs and mills, who wished things to remain in *statu quo*; while the financing of improvement had to come from this quarter little would be done. Secondly, the barge- masters saw the Thames simply as a thoroughfare for traffic, with clear navigation and deep water. There was also "the dim Riverside population", as Thacker called them, whose houses and other property were at risk from worsened flooding as weirs were continually heightened.[2] Here, too, the city of Oxford came more into the picture as its better

[2] Fred. S. Thacker, *The Thames Highway. A History of the Inland Navigation* (1914).

drainage and the spread of building to more riverine sites involved it more intimately with the river.

External events helped to break this traditional impasse, with the eclipse of one of the river users, the Thames Commissioners who had managed the business of navigation since 1751. Their use of the river and its extensions in the Thames–Severn or Kennett–Avon Canals had been undermined by the railways, whose competition impoverished and put them out of business as carriers of goods. In 1866 they gave place to the Thames Conservancy, which began its career (due to end in 1976) with some slight improvements to the Upper River. Not enough to meet the problem, they were swept away in the series of destructive floods in 1875, and 1876 and (worse of all) 1877, when Queen Victoria was marooned in Windsor Castle for a week and London's water supply was in jeopardy. Plate 20 shows the floods at Oxford. Afterwards an 'Enquiry into Flood Prevention' was set up, but again nothing was done before Oxford was damaged by heavy flooding in the winter of 1882–3. It was then admitted that because of human interference in many directions, "the state of the river is less favourable for the removal of flood-waters than when the river existed in its natural condition".

A more effective bid was then made to widen and dredge the Thames, restoring as far as possible the natural fall to the river-bed, as well as digging the New Cut on the lower Cherwell, because that tributary had always generated its own rhythms of flooding in cycle with the main stream. The Drainage Commissioners were hampered in these works by shortage of money, as the rating area did not coincide with the drainage basin, even to the exclusion of Oxford. Luckily the Thames Preservation Act was passed in 1885, also mentioning for the first time another use, 'the purposes of public recreation' and 'regulating the pleasure traffic'. Yet another serious flood had to come before the Conservancy's responsibilities were confirmed and extended by a really powerful Act in 1894. At last in the 1890s they had enough money to start building pound locks and weirs on the Upper River (Plate 21). Forty years after the dismal inundations of 1852–3, and a saga of truly Victorian dimensions when bitter experience alternated with bluster and inaction, there was the hope of controlling the Thames floods.

It was realised as emphatically as the solid lock-keepers' houses with their country gardens, marking like so many fingers the human hand that confined the stream. Only the aberrations of climate can now lead to serious flooding, as in 1918 or 1947, and the question has swung instead to maintaining enough water for all the new demands, even by resorting to permanent flooding of the land (p. 223). Directly or indirectly, the Thames and its tributaries impinge very much on the lives of Oxfordshire people, despite their modified regimes. Nowhere is this clearer than in what we may term 'the Bampton Polderland', a splendid riverine landscape lying between Newbridge and Radcot. It was transformed by successful draining in the mid-nineteenth century, and in its scale as well as its moods it outshines for some the better-known 'mysterious bowl of Otmoor'. Floods were very bad here, thousands of acres being inundated each winter, cutting off places like Shifford and Chimney.[3] As the first edition of the Ordnance Survey one-inch map shows, major settlements like Bampton, Aston and Cote were set back from the unpredictable river, and surrounded by extensive tracts of common pasture on land too damp for other uses. All this was transformed by the skill of William Bryan Wood, who was responsible for the enclosure of the common lands in the 1850s. In a bold piece of engineering he straightened the course of the Isle of Wight Brook flowing on the north side of the Thames, deepening it to serve as an artery for draining floodwater. In continuation with the Sharney Brook it

[3] J. A. Giles, *History of Bampton* (1848), pp. 17, 86–7.

provided a direct cut-off channel on the very side of the Thames that had been most afflicted by floods. On the map, where it is named 'Great Brook' it looks artificial and designed, an impression sustained by its canal-like appearance and that of the embanked, tree-lined road that goes with it. Drainage ditches run deeply into it, it was carefully bridged "to accommodate the passage of a large quantity of water at flood times", and it released much riverside land for more intensive use.[4] People were unwilling to build on the flood plain, apart from Meadow Farm near Tadpole Bridge, whose builders prudently gave it three storeys.

Closer to Oxford, another 'wetland' was brought under control. "Otmoor for ever!" With this cry of defiance the enclosure of Otmoor and its consequent riots have entered not only the social history of Oxfordshire, but its folk mythology as well. Behind the familiar story lies another facet of the taming of wild places, by the draining of an ancient freshwater fen whose resources were used for a thousand years by the 'seven towns' grouped around it. They were the villages of Oddington, Charlton, Fencott, Murcott, Horton, Beckley and Noke, and the changes they so resented were bound to add to the volume of water the Cherwell and Thames were expected to cope with, as we have just explained. The carving up of Otmoor was mooted by Sir Alexander Croke as early as 1787, and loudly championed by Arthur Young who thought it "a scandal to the national policy" that it was not enclosed and converted to farms for tillage and pasture. In spite of his moral indignation, the legal process dragged out for so many years—a bill in Parliament in 1815, the final award not until 1829—that the reaction of the people when it came in 1830 seems all the more explosive (Plate 1).

The improvers had to dig a new and more efficient channel for the river Ray, but in June 1830 a group of farmers blamed it for flooding their hay meadows and

[4] Tollit, *op. cit.*, p. 69.

accordingly destroyed its embankments. They were acquitted of a felony, the judge declaring that the Enclosure Commissioner "had very much exceeded the power granted to him by the Act, in thus altering the course of the river". The Otmoor people were quick to take this to mean the nullification of the 1815 Act, and for years they fought against the consolidation of their old common, vowing "to have the Moor" again. As many as 150 men cut down miles of new hedges at night, smashing fences, gates and bridges; shots and intimidation plagued the Otmoor Committee of magistrates that was specially formed, parties of troops and police were brought in. Men let loose their cattle in the new allotments, and (because the magistrates were anxious to persuade farmers to cultivate their enclosures) the freshly-ploughed fields were turned in again by gangs at night. Only when the fencing was complete and ploughing going ahead by the spring of 1835 did the rioters give up. The magistrates (somewhat cautiously) relaxed, "Otmoor being now, it may be hoped, in a state of permanent tranquillity".[5]

The disappearance of Wychwood Forest

By contrast the extinction of Wychwood, just as revolutionary in its way as the enclosure of Otmoor, went ahead as a peaceable exercise in agrarian change. The forest, as we have seen (p. 85), was one of the most ancient forms of institutional landscape in Oxfordshire, hunted by Saxon royalty, its bounds expanding and contracting at the wish of later kings, even being walled round by Cromwell. But by the beginning of the nineteenth century it had lost status. The *cover* of the true forest was much interrupted and the woodland interspersed with clearings. This was

[5] A. V. Brown, 'The Last Phase of the Enclosure of Otmoor', *Oxoniensia* Vol. XXXII (1967), pp. 34–52; V.C.H. *Oxfordshire*, Vol. V (1957), pp. 70–1.

to be expected near places like Ranger's Lodge, with its stone-built dwellings, stables and coach-houses of a forest official; it had an enclosed *lawn* of pasture running to sixty acres, and thirty acres of plough-land, some of which was recently "taken out of one of the coppices and cleared of wood" in 1792.[6] More seriously in terms of land use the regulation of the resources of royal timber was slipshod and irregular. Forest courts were no longer held, the trees were damaged by deer and trespassers, the coppices leased to outsiders.

Traditionally the king had eighteen coppices or stands of woodland, one of which was cut each year, when its underwood was of eighteen years' growth; before cutting the coppice was enclosed with a strong hedge and ditch, staying closed for eight years before it was again thrown open to deer and cattle. Throughout Wychwood, however, the royal woods of oak, ash and beech were thinning out and unprofitable due to the unlawful cutting of saplings and timber trees in the coppices, as well as to grazing by deer and farm stock. By right, common pasture was confined to cattle and horses, but the more destructive feeders, pigs and sheep, had become very numerous. Such was "the fine, wild tract of country" seen by Arthur Young, who added predictably that Wychwood should be enclosed without delay.

It was a long time coming, as a parliamentary Act for the disafforestation of Wychwood was not sponsored until 1853, and even then its terms were modified before the award was finally signed in 1857. It swept away all that remained of the ancient forest recorded in Domesday; 3378 acres were subject to the rights of the Crown, the hereditary Ranger and the commoners, half of them in the coppices, the other half in open forest with a fair amount of timber and brushwood. Another 3000 acres comprised the 'Purlieus' of Wychwood, being in various ownership,

6 V. J. Watney, *Cornbury and the Forest of Wychwood* (London, 1910), p. 203.

especially the Ranger's, as coppice or common disposed from the forest by royal grant. In all, then, when the Commissioners of Woods and Forests and their lawyers were penning its demise, Wychwood still cast a certain amount of shade over ten square miles of Oxfordshire.

The full force of most intensive change fell on some 2000 acres of unreclaimed forest in the Crown allotment. Over this area an entirely new landscape of farms replaced the woodland, designed in every detail by the surveyor, the Hon. Charles Gore.[7] First the timber trees were felled and sold for £34,000, leaving a few stands for ornament and shelter. The underwood was stacked, the tree stumps and roots burned: clearing the ground cost £6000. Next, seven new farmsteads were created "on sites judiciously selected in reference both to the occupation of the land and the beauty of the prospects". The farmhouses and outbuildings were constructed of local stone, well-proportioned and laid out on a generous scale; they cost £11,000. Then the field boundaries and division fences were set out, water supplies provided, and the land prepared for cultivation. The whole plan cost about £10 per acre to complete, and in addition the surveyor made ten miles of new roads for access and fenced them.[8]

All this was achieved in a dramatically short space of time. The first trees were sawn down in October 1856; sixteen months later, in January 1858, the first tenants were living in their farmhouses and sowing their first crops. Royal forest had given way to harvested fields in under two years. The new farms were let on thirty-one year leases, and although the rents were high they were offset by benefits such as having no tithe-rent charges, and minimal poor rates, because some of the farms were in a new parish of Wychwood created under the disafforestation.

[7] Bodleian, MS. G. A. Oxon. b. 115.

[8] For the sequence of events that disintegrated Needwood Forest in Staffordshire, see P. H. Nicholls, 'On the Evolution of a Forest Landscape', *Trans. Inst. Brit. Geogs.*, Vol. 56 (1972), pp. 57–76.

Now the view from Leafield Barrow northwards is over open farmland, and it is difficult to believe it is some of the newest of its kind in Oxfordshire, cleared from woodland only in 1857. It was all marked as 'Wichwood Forest' on Richardson's map of Leafield in 1764, and all we have to suggest its origin is the preservation of a few ancient forest names like Kingstanding Farm, or a dark wooded skyline where the Wychwood remnant stubbornly beautifies the landscape.

The disafforestation also gave birth to Fordwells, one of the most secluded of Oxfordshire's settlements (Plate 22). One looks in vain for a reference to Fordwells in *The Place-Names of Oxfordshire*, omitted simply because it is such a new place and so falls through the net of enquiry. It has a sprinkling of cottages along the roadside, a Primitive Methodist chapel, and a water supply still provided by the powerful springs thrown out in this narrow valley. 'Fordwell Lane' is all we find on the Leafield map of 1764; Davis did not mark a single habitation on his *New Map of the County of Oxford* (1797), while on the first edition of the Ordnance Survey one-inch map (1830) there was merely the name 'Fords Well' at an intersection of forest tracks in the valley. It was one of the boundary marks of Wychwood, marked as such on Pride's plan of the Forest (1787), and appearing again as 'Ford Well Spring and Duck Pool' in 1854.⁹ Thus the place originated as a farm labourers' hamlet after Wychwood disappeared in the 1850s. Land was set aside there as allotment gardens for the unpropertied men who populated it and whose labour was needed on the new farms. Typically it stands on the very margins between Asthall parish and the Wychwood parishes, tucked away in the debatable no-man's-land so favoured by the squatter and the poor countryman.

⁹ *Plan of Whichwood Forest, made by Thomas Pride, 1787, corrected by F. I. Insall, 1849; Map of the Forest and Purlieus of Whichwood, 1854, by William Bryan Wood.*

L

There were other places of this nature around the periphery of Wychwood, for instance the hamlet of Mount Skippitt between Ramsden and Finstock. In this spatial context of late medieval clearance and settlement, a cluster of farms and cottages had grown around an arm of Ramsden Heath, with small encroachments on the heathland between a pool and Skippitt Copse. They lay just within the limits of Wychwood, and by their origins as intermediate, ill-defined settlements were likely to become 'open' hamlets by the early nineteenth century (p. 170).[10] We see the same thing in New Yatt on the road from North Leigh to Witney, also omitted from *The Place-Names of Oxfordshire*. It was marked characteristically as 'Newgate' on Davis's map of 1797, a group of dwellings sited between Wychwood and Eynsham Heath; southwards from it Davis showed a broad-hedged ribbon of *greenway* that would fit as the eastern boundary of Witney as demarcated in the pre-Conquest charters (p. 62). New Yatt's tiny, box-like cottages are also reminiscent of the Victorian open settlements; so too are the neighbouring parts of North Leigh on the hill above the church ('Providence Cottage, 1863').

The changing village

Against this background of new settlements like Fordwells, we should now look at how certain villages could grow from nothing while others experienced considerable change in the nineteenth century, a process of rural settlement that has not always been suspected of being so significant. We can begin with a study of Freeland, one of the fraternity of villages now inundated with so much new housing that they threaten to form a continuous belt of residential growth from Long Hanborough through Freeland and

---

[10] *Plan of the Hamlet of Ramsden in the Parish of Shipton-under-Whichwood, 1838, for the Tithe Commissioners*; Wood's plan of Wychwood, 1854, showed 'Mount Skippert' as lying within the Purlieus.

North Leigh to Witney. But Freeland is not an old place, despite its superficial likeness to other, really ancient street-villages. Again, it is omitted from *The Place-Names of Oxfordshire*, notwithstanding the interest of its name. It also grew on the margins of older places, in this case between Eynsham and Hanborough, and it materialised as the result of redevelopment of the agrarian landscape.

We trace it first of all as a field-name on the Hanborough map of 1605, close to the Frith, a boundary woodland in dispute between Eynsham and Hanborough. In fact *Free-landes* was almost certainly the land called *terra de Frithe* in 1150, when the abbot of Eynsham granted it to Nicholas of Leigh: although literally 'free land' on this account the name probably comes from *frith*, meaning simply a wood.[11] A few houses had appeared there by 1650, sited on that part of the open heath closest to Eynsham itself. They had grown somewhat by 1738: of 160 houses in the parish of Eynsham "near 20 are situate upon a large Heath a mile from the church". They lacked status because the vicar thought there were no hamlets in Eynsham parish "unless the houses upon the Heath may be taken for one".[12] The legislated enclosure of Eynsham (over which there was rioting on the heath in 1780) was achieved by 1784, and there is no doubt that the parcellation of the commons was to consolidate the growth of the squatter settlement at Freeland. In 1800 there was a cluster of houses around the green, close to Freeland Gate, and they still look like the oldest dwellings in the village. There was another group of houses to the north where Merry Lane joined Freeland Road, and it is from this point northwards that later settlement was to grow.

Expansion was also affected by the building of two mansions nearby. The larger, Eynsham Hall, was a residence

11 E. K. Chambers, *Eynsham Under the Monks* (Oxfordshire Record Society, 1936), p. 51.
12 *The Primary Visitation of Dr. Thomas Secker, 1738* (Oxfordshire Record Society, 1957).

of the Earl of Macclesfield and by 1800 its extensive parkland had spread over most of the old heath (Plate 25). Freeland Lodge then appeared in the landscape to absorb in its own ornamental park the portion of old heath known as Merry Hill. Between them these country houses would have given Freeland an element of being an estate village, as it grew from 1819 (when its Wesleyan chapel was finely rebuilt) to 1868, when a new church was built there. For by 1847 the *Post Office Directory of Oxfordshire* was referring to 'Freelands' as 'a village in the parish of Eynsham', its community including seven farmers, a mason, a carpenter, the publican of the New Inn, and two shopkeepers. Victorian Freeland grew along the ancient axis of the *via regia*, the road from Eynsham to Charlbury, now marked along its length by ribbon development of houses of mixed age and origin: at present a single field makes the only green break in a mile of housing from the church to the Witney road. But, as we have seen, this is not the fabric of an old street-village, and is far younger than the sunken course of Merry Lane that dips between Devon-like banks to the Caverswell stream and then on to Church Hanborough.

Nor is Freeland unique in the way it came into the landscape. We can learn a good deal from the hamlet of Juniper Hill as portrayed in the 1880s,

> about thirty cottages and an inn, not built in rows but dotted down anywhere within a more or less circular group. A deeply rutted cart track surrounded the whole, and separate houses or groups of houses were connected by a network of pathways. The church and school were in the mother village, a mile and a half away.[13]

The beginnings of Juniper Hill (Lark Rise in the book) may be first traced to the building of two cottages on Cottisford Heath in 1754, followed a little later by two others; they

[13] Flora Thompson, *Lark Rise to Candleford* (Everyman edn., 1945), p. 16.

were meant to house the paupers of Cottisford, and the parish paid for their construction.[14] For a century the poor remained in solitary occupation, until the heath was enclosed for cultivation by Act in 1854. Flora Thompson found in the 1880s that

> Some of the ancients still occupied cottages on land which had been ceded to their fathers as squatters' rights, and probably all the small plots upon which the houses stood had originally been so ceded ... A road had been cut when the heath was enclosed, for convenience in field work and to connect the main Oxford road with the mother village and a series of other villages beyond ... A few of the houses had thatched roofs, whitewashed outer walls and diamond-paned windows, but the majority were just stone or brick boxes with blue-slated roofs.[15]

The distinction in many respects of village from hamlet is an interesting reflection of the way the landscape was settled over varying scales of time. It was certainly ingrained in the contrast between Cottisford, the village, and Juniper Hill, the hamlet, by Victorian times:

> The village was a little, lost, lonely place, much smaller than the hamlet, without a shop, an inn, or a post office. Its squat church, without spire or tower, crouched back in a tiny churchyard surrounded by tall, windy elms. Next came the Rectory, so buried in orchards and shrubberies that only the chimney-stacks were visible from the road; then the old Tudor farmhouse with its stone mullioned windows and reputed dungeon. These with the school and about a dozen cottages occupied by the

[14] J. C. Blomfield, *History of Cottisford, Hardwick and Tusmore* (London, 1887), p. 37.
[15] *Lark Rise to Candleford*, pp. 15–16.

shepherd, carter, blacksmith and a few other superior farm-workers, made up the village. Even these few buildings were strung out along the roadside, so far between and so sunken in greenery that there seemed no village at all . . . The hamlet laughed at the village as 'stuck up'; while the village looked down on 'that gipsy lot' at the hamlet.[16]

We may add here, however, that the character of the village was due to the recent handiwork of one man, William Turner, who lived in Cottisford House. One of his family had pulled down Ambrosden House "in a sudden and capricious whim", and about 1840 he made substantial changes in the village structure at Cottisford. He diverted the main road from its old course in front of his house to a new east–west direction, he demolished all the houses standing by the church and replaced them with plantations of trees. "The landmarks and peculiar features of the old village have thus disappeared," wrote Blomfield, leaving the Cottisford described forty years later by Flora Thompson. In the neighbouring village of Hardwick, too, the layout of the village was reshaped by the landowner. When the Earl of Effingham came to live at Tusmore House in 1857 he not only rebuilt the church at Hardwick, but also pulled down the old stone-built cottages clustered around it. In their place he put up "the comfortable brick houses which are now seen".[17]

So many forces have worked to loosen, modify and distort the structure of our villages in quite recent times that we must be prepared to explain peculiarities simply as residual features left as the result of change. Why, for instance, does the fourteenth-century church at Kidlington with its magnificent spire stand so far to the margin of the village? The truth is that originally it stood more centrally in the settlement, but in response to two events the houses

---

[16] *Lark Rise to Candleford*, pp. 43–4.   [17] Blomfield, *op. cit.*, p. 58.

of Kidlington have spread farther afield from the Port Way on which the church is sited. One was a fire in 1638, which may have thinned out the older houses.[18] Fires were likely to do this in villages as much as in towns before the nineteenth century, when inflammable building materials were more usual and houses closely packed together. There was the Eynsham fire of 1625 (p. 118); other cases were at Great Milton in 1762, when sixteen houses were destroyed, and Great Barford in 1775, the fire spreading from a bakehouse to burn down nine buildings before fire engines from Deddington and Bloxham stopped it from harming the church.[19] More villages provided themselves with fire engines because of the rick-burning riots of 'Captain Swing' and his followers in 1831; Steeple Aston, for instance, joined with seven neighbouring parishes to buy one.

Fire on its own would scarcely have been a major modifier of the village fabric, but it could serve as a trigger for the changes due to other circumstances. Thus the second factor at Kidlington was the breaking-up of the manor into several estates and parcels, leading to building on many sites and so accounting for its scattered layout. The single coherent manor was subdivided after 1546, and its effects were felt again in the Victorian period (p. 141). A similar institutional change is argued for the neighbouring village of Yarnton, "the present aspect of which only dates from the breaking up of the manor upon the sale of the Spencer property".[20] That was in 1712 and before then most of the houses stood along the east side of Church Lane, opposite the park carved out by Sir William Spencer in the 1590s. After the estate was fragmented it was possible to build new houses elsewhere on many small properties, especially along the Oxford road.

[18] B. Stapleton, *Three Oxfordshire Parishes* (Oxford Historical Society, 1893), p. 258.
[19] *Jackson's Oxford Journal*, 481, iii; 1154, iii.
[20] Stapleton, *op. cit.*, p. 314.

From these and other cases it is plain that we should budget for radical changes in the form of villages. Sometimes because of the effects of continuing parliamentary enclosure, sometimes because of the ideas of an influential landowner (whether or not he had a park around his house), places in the countryside were more prone to late reshaping than is usually supposed. Nothing could be more misleading than to accept the form of a village as shown on the Tithe Maps of the 1840s or the first six-inch Ordnance Survey plans as being in any sense that of the original settlement, and then again to classify the various forms in the time context of their foundation. In the last two centuries alone so much has happened to morphology that it is at least as necessary to work out the degree of likelihood of such changes. We saw these at work gradually in Freeland and abruptly in the arch-typical estate village of Nuneham Courtenay, where a new linear settlement superseded in 1770 the old village grouped round its central green.

There are echoes of Nuneham in the changing form of Pyrton, below the Chilterns (p. 64), although the transition was more gradual and did not involve the making of an entirely new village. As it now stands Pyrton is a linear settlement strung along the ancient highway of Knightsbridge Lane. But this is a comparatively new development, because on a plan of 1730 the village appeared tightly clustered around the church and an open space beside it; the manor house, rectory, big farmhouses and other buildings were grouped round about. From this central nucleation a line of settlement branched away, standing on Knightsbridge Lane, but consisting of smaller houses. When we look at Pyrton as it was a century later, however, we see at once that the grouping of houses around the church was much less distinct. Instead the main focus of settlement by 1835 had shifted to the axis of Knightsbridge Lane. Due to encroachment by the manor house and its park in the intervening period (it was landscaped by

1792) the village had been thinned out at the park approaches, and deflected away in the direction of the Lane. By the end of the nineteenth century, and as we find it today, the village had shrunk overall but unequally so. Pyrton church ceases to be a centralising feature, the park dominates what was once half the village, and most of the houses range along the Lane.[21] Some figures will summarise this surreptitious transformation:

	1730	*1835*	*1900*
Buildings close to the church	29	18	11
Buildings on Knightsbridge Lane	20	19	17

Somewhere between the experience of Nuneham and Pyrton lies the sequence of events at Middleton Stoney, where the village nucleus was originally close to its church and the site of a medieval motte-and-bailey castle. By the 1820s the Earl of Jersey had extended his park to occupy nearly half the parish, and in so doing absorbed the old village. Accordingly the houses were demolished and new ones built outside the park gates, under the personal direction of Lady Jersey; the village road was extinguished in favour of the Oxford–Brackley turnpike. To a contemporary the new cottages, with their rustic porches and flower gardens, gave "an idea of comfort and respectability seldom enjoyed by the lower classes".[22] For this very reason of their being designed all of a piece such model villages divert our attention from the many other places where villages were modified in a modest but tangible way by the great landowner, as at Cottisford, Hardwick and Pyrton. Much more fundamental and widespread, however, was the acceptance in the Victorian countryside of two distinct

[21] The sequence is based on Bodleian Maps (E), C17:49(66), (181), (182), (184), and on O.S. six-inch plan Oxon. XLVII (S.W.), 2nd edn. (1900).

[22] J. Dunkin, *History and Antiquities of the Hundreds of Bullingdon and Ploughley* (1823), Vol. II, p. 57.

kinds of village environments. Thomas Hardy took them for granted in his novels and tales of Wessex country life and we should now consider them.

Closed and open villages

It was said of Steeple Aston in 1846 that it had many labourers' cottages and poor people, the complaint being that neighbouring villages like Middle Aston "belong each to one single proprietor, and it has been the policy for some years past of such single proprietors to destroy existing cottages and to prevent the erection of new ones".[23] Thus the Steeple Aston ratepayers found themselves supporting poor persons who had moved away from the closed villages where new housing was not encouraged. The structure of Steeple Aston as an open village still reflects this trend. It consists of two streets of buildings, the older one containing the church, rectory, school, The Grange and big farms, whereas South Street has most of the nineteenth-century cottages, and a Methodist chapel, the significance of which we shall see later (p. 175). Accordingly the village population was growing in marked contrast to Middle Aston, which was as closed a village as it was possible to find:

	Population in		
	1831	*1841*	*1851*
Steeple Aston	441	469	601
Middle Aston	123	111	101

To set the scene, the early nineteenth century was a time of rapid increases in population: Oxfordshire had a population of 153,000 in 1831; 163,000 in 1841; and 170,000

[23] C. C. Brookes, *A History of Steeple Aston and Middle Aston* (Banbury, 1929), p. 146; the note is in the Vestry Book of Steeple Aston, 26th November 1846.

in 1851. There are plenty of indications of the pressure to find new housing. Sometimes the large farmhouses in a village centre, replaced by new farms built at a distance among their newly enclosed fields, were split into several tenements, as happened at Pyrton. Another way of meeting the pressure was to build on waste land near the village in squatter settlements. Such cottages often encroached on roadside verges and were placed end-on to the highways. Precisely this kind of development brought into being in about 1820 a street of new cottages leading up the hill from the old centre of Lower Heyford; some years later the landlords (an Oxford college) asked for a nominal quit rent for these houses and provided them with gardens. It was not always so easy; the Stratton Lyne cottagers whose dwellings had encroached on Stratton Lane were brought to an 'ejectment trial' at the assizes in 1860, and as they were unable to prove title the verdict went against them.

Regrettably the most obvious outlet, that of building new houses as an integral part of existing villages, ran into serious difficulties due to the administration of the Poor Law, and in turn this gave rise to the separation of closed from open villages. The visible effects of this distinction are still there in the fabric of many places in Oxfordshire. In practice a parish was financially responsible for the paupers who belonged to it, so it had the incentive to control the number of houses in which its paupers might live, or to discourage the immigration of those who tried to become settled in it. Where the vestry was small, that is where the number of major landowners was few, they could make this restriction by ensuring there were just enough houses for their own agricultural labourers, indeed sometimes not enough for them. They could thus slam the door on persons who might otherwise move into the parish, gain a legal settlement and, should they become destitute, then claim poor relief levied on the parish rate. The only check on this reaction was the distance between such closed villages and other places from which labour could be drawn to the estates and farms of big landowners. These others were the open parishes, "in which dwelling places are numerous and always to be had", as Grenvil Pigott, a Poor Law inspector, phrased it in 1849. On the whole he found the Oxfordshire landowners unwilling to build new cottages, a liability that might "absorb their whole rental" due to "the ever-varying and uncertain laws of settlement".

Over the previous ten years Pigott found that in eighty-six open parishes in Oxfordshire there had been a net increase of 1352 new cottages; in thirty-four closed parishes only seven had appeared. There was also a problem of quality, because many of the houses in open villages were small, without gardens, primitive, expensive to rent by those who were denied a residence in their place of work, overcrowded. Most of them were jerry-built as a property speculation by small tradesmen, builders and farmers. Such were the 100 cottages owned by twenty-five different proprietors at Steeple Aston, according to a report of 1869. By contrast the twenty-two cottages in Glympton, a closed village, although too few to house all the farm labour, were soundly built and let at thirty shillings a year, "often paid by selling the product of the apricot tree planted against the side of the houses". Similar closed villages "lying under the eye of a resident landowner" were Stanton Harcourt, Kirtlington, Tackley, Swyncombe.[24] Such differences persisted well after the Union Chargeability Act of 1865, which came too late in taking the pressure of poor relief from the open villages.

This dualism took many forms: whereas the closed villages had their 'squire and parson' orderliness and adhered to the church, open villages were more indepen-

---

[24] George Culley, reporting on Oxfordshire to the Royal Commission on the employment of children, young persons and women in agriculture, *Parliamentary Reports*, 1868–9, Vol. XIII, pp. 74–98.

dent and turbulent (Tetsworth was known as 'Botany Bay' for this reason), welcoming the various nonconformist chapels. From them, too, went the bands of travelling harvesters who found work in the meadows and cornfields of the London region. One was compact and well-shaped, the other sprawling and haphazard. It is still possible to see these contrasts preserved in the outward appearance of villages in the Oxfordshire countryside, sometimes in neighbouring places. Turn off the Oxford–Banbury road at Hopcroft's Holt, for instance, and the B4030 will take you through Middle Barton, a Victorian open village by any standard. It was always a formless place as we see from a plan of 1795 and the account of its origin given by Hoskins,[25] but this characteristic is now lost because of its 'infilling' with a vast spread of modern housing: like so many other places in the countryside it looks like a portion of suburbia come adrift. A mile up the road is Sandford St Martin, a closed village, its trim marlstone houses all lining the single village street, set off by the courtyard and parkland of Sandford Park and the Manor House. It all looks as if it had changed very little in 100 years, and there is no more than a small, discreet close of new housing. Middle Barton is at the other extreme, and it is worth explaining the gulf between them as elements in the landscape (Fig. 10).

When Sandford was enclosed in 1768, it had seventeen proprietors of land, only four of whom had more than 100 acres. During the early nineteenth century the small holdings were absorbed by two principal estates which controlled most of the farmland. The Park estate owned all the farmhouses and cottages along the eastern side of the village street, and in 1849 it was bought by Dr Edwin Guest, Master of Gonville and Caius College, Cambridge. He soon began to rebuild his houses, "of which the altered appearance of the village to which he so much contributed

[25] W. G. Hoskins, *The Making of the English Landscape* (1955) p. 52.

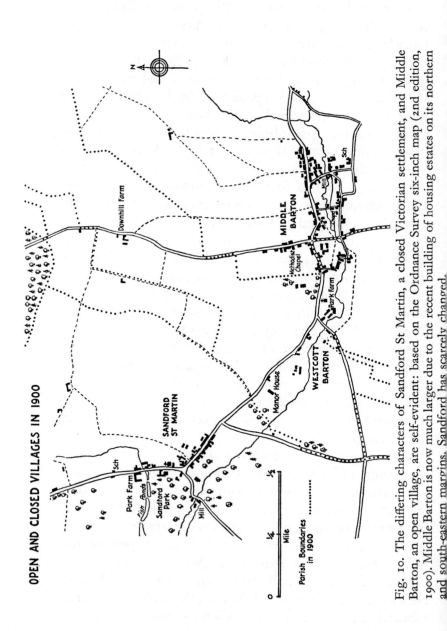

OPEN AND CLOSED VILLAGES IN 1900

Fig. 10. The differing characters of Sandford St Martin, a closed Victorian settlement, and Middle Barton, an open village, are self-evident: based on the Ordnance Survey six-inch map (2nd edition, 1900). Middle Barton is now much larger due to the recent building of housing estates on its northern and south-eastern margins. Sandford has scarcely changed.

is a lasting proof".[26] Guest lived at the Park until 1880. Then along the western side of the street stood the property of the Manor estate. The manor house had originated as a hunting-box built by a London merchant in 1715. It was enlarged before the Rev. Edward Marshall moved there in 1862; he was resident until 1899. He worked in concert with Guest to improve the quality of housing, "approaching more to what the habitations of a village population ought to be", as he phrased it.[27] Sandford was a closed village of the kind where its own labour force was decently housed, but stabilised to a level that checked increase from within or from other places; it was losing population by 1851 and there were eight fewer houses by 1861.

Some Sandford people moved to the next village, contributing to "the recent growth of the hamlet of Middle Barton", which must have seemed a different world to them. It was another no-man's-land settlement that had grown at the meeting place of older (and fissiparous) village territories. Indeed, the boundaries were so confused that the liberty of Middle Barton was debatable land between the parishes of Westcott Barton and Steeple Barton; under the enclosure award of 1796 a line had to be drawn specially to separate the responsibility for road repairs between the intermixed parishes.[28] At the same time the village highway became part of a turnpike from Bicester to Enstone, and people began to encroach on the roadside to build cottages. Middle Barton was a community of many small holders of land: "there was not a single proprietor of six acres resident in either Barton, and absenteeism was the rule".[29] In the absence of resident clergy, too, and with Steeple Barton church some distance away, nonconformity flourished. In 1738 the only dissenters were some Quakers,

[26] E. Marshall, *An Account of the Parish of Sandford* (1866), p. 51.

[27] *Ibid.*, p. 47.

[28] J. Marshall, *Memorials of Westcott Barton* (1870), p. 42.

[29] W. Wing, *Annals of Steeple Barton and Westcott Barton* (Oxford, 1866), p. 12.

but a Wesleyan chapel appeared in 1835, the Primitive Methodists built a large chapel in 1860, and by this time the church was noting "an almost universality of Dissent".

By this time, too, the village had acquired a great majority of the 270 houses in the Barton parishes, where the 1801 population of 417 had been trebled. In these circumstances it is not surprising to find Middle Barton in the various reports dealing with Poor Law administration. It was criticised by Culley in 1869 as being badly congested; the Westcott portion of it alone carried fifty cottages, belonging to twelve assorted small tradesmen, some with a dozen, some with one piece of property. These houses were let at as much as £4 a year (contrast with Glympton's thirty shilling rents), and a 'one room up and one down' cottage could be occupied by as many as nine people. In all, the 150 or so cottages in Middle Barton were owned by some forty different owners, very few of whom were farmers. Culley found up to thirty young men without work and not looking for it, instead putting themselves 'on the Union'. Besides farming there was some employment in the flour and malt mill powered by the waters of the Dorn, in the claypits, brickworks and tileries and limekilns. Here, having explained the open antecedence of Middle Barton as we know it now, we should go on to establish the place of industrial activity in the rural landscape of Victorian times.

Industrial villages

Open and closed villages were found in all parts of Oxfordshire without exception; it is not possible to say, for instance, that only closed villages were typical of the Cotswolds and stonebrash country. But it is true that the countryside that had been cleared and settled at a relatively late stage, in the medieval and early modern periods, were more likely to have open villages rather than closed. The forest landscapes of Wychwood illustrate this association, the reason being that such settlements as they had were from the outset less ordered and stratified socially and in terms of land tenure, with more freeholders and a general lack of manorial forms. Forest villages also offered common rights that helped poor people to follow their meagre living. Such places were thus more likely to be open settlements whose inhabitants resorted to by-employments, such as the glove-making industry that came to be centred on Woodstock.

By contrast, wherever large estates and their country houses had emerged by the nineteenth century, with a restricted base of land ownership, then the likelihood was that closed villages would result. We can also accept from this a distribution of such estates as more typical of the best agricultural land, but this association is more valid for the clay country than for the prosperous Redlands. Here on the marlstone plateaux the social and institutional characteristics could be of a different order. Places like Adderbury, Milton and Bodicote were notable freeholding communities, engaged in dairying and cloth-working, with nonconformist traditions. The freeholder class was strong in this area in the seventeenth century, and related to it may be the late enclosure and a cultivation of special crops, e.g. woad, as being labour-intensive and profitable on the small farms. Here and there, as at Wroxton, the landowner was powerful and a strong body of freeholders had not emerged. The character of manorial ownership thus had real social consequences for the village community, seen in the contrast between places where the lord was resident and visibly influential, and other places where he was absent or sometimes negligent, and where freeholders were plentiful.

It is in this light we should view the localisation in the Redlands of the plush industry. Against the background of a traditional manufacture of woollen cloth, the weaving of fine plush was taken up from about 1750 in Banbury and

M

many villages around it in north Oxfordshire.[30] Plush was usually made of an intermixture of worsted warp and silk or hair weft. From Coventry and the North came silk and worsted; there was no need to scour or full this fabric, so as a region of small streams and hard water the Redlands was at no disadvantage. Yarn was sent out to villages from Banbury, which was the distributing, dyeing and marketing centre: Wardington, Bourton, Bloxham and Adderbury shared this industry by 1831. Two thirds of England's plush-weavers worked in and around Banbury, but by 1850 the competition of power-loom weaving in Coventry had seriously weakened the local industry. For its tenacious survival we look to the industrial village of Shutford, which came to specialise in fine plush for liveries, upholstery and furnishings, requiring skilled handling. Power looms were introduced in 1885, and scarlet plush from Shutford was supplied for the coronation of the last Czar of Russia. Due to failure to find craftsmen who would live and work in a country village the factory finally closed in 1948, terminating an industry that had helped to keep people and sustain housing in these large Redland villages.

Besides textiles, we have already found an association between an open village, Middle Barton, and simple extractive and processing industries (p. 176). Other cases can be cited from the pottery, brick and tile-making at Leafield in Wychwood, and from the stone-working village of Stonesfield (Plate 23). In the 1860s there were 120 cottages in Stonefield, and with only about 1000 acres in the parish it was obviously a settlement from which most of its farm labourers travelled to work elsewhere. But there was also work to be found in the local stonepits and slate mines: here was the source of Stonesfield Slate, the best, lightest and least porous of the 'flat-stones' used for roofing in Oxfordshire. Stonesfield's industry dates at least from the

---

[30] R. P. Beckinsale, 'The Plush Industry of Oxfordshire', *Oxoniensia*, Vol. XXVIII (1963), pp. 63–7.

sixteenth century, when the process of splitting the 'green' rock by frost seems to have been discovered. In the 1820s horizontal galleries were still being driven into the side of the hill, but by the end of the nineteenth century only shallow mines were in use for getting at the *pendle*. This was dug from Michaelmas to Christmas, when it was hoped that a week's frost in January would yield well-split slate and so plenty of work for the slaters through the year. It was a favourite form of by-employment, and the debris of spoil-heaps is still to be seen even though the last shaft was closed in 1909.[31]

Of course, quarrying and stone-working were traditional openings for the labouring men of Oxfordshire's stone country. If Stonesfield gave its village name to a distinctive kind of roofing material, so did Milton, Wheatley, Headington and the rest become known to the medieval masons as sources of superior stone. Taynton may be the most venerable of them all, its quarries in the Great Oolite already worth listing in Domesday Book. North of the village we can see, along the flank of a tributary valley running to the Windrush, the bays, notches and pock-marks created by generations of quarrymen, their spoil-heaps now softened with vegetation. From these pits came a splendid stone for such buildings as the Norman tower of Burford church, Blenheim Palace (1704–22), and the many railway bridges with which the Evenlode was spanned in 1846–52. Besides these and a host of other uses in Oxford and the surrounding countryside Taynton stone also went farther afield to Windsor Castle and Eton.[32]

Quarrying was also present in Wheatley and Headington before they became suburbanised, prompting us to ask if such open industrial villages so much closer to Oxford itself had a different character from the usual run (Plate 24). We find a positive answer from studying Wolvercote at this time,

[31] W. J. Arkell, *Oxford Stone* (London, 1957), pp. 128–42.
[32] *Ibid.*, pp. 54–64.

when it stood in open country a few miles north of the city. Ownership of its cottages was very mixed, including stable-keepers and college servants, as were the tenants: besides farm labourers there were artisans working in the city, masons, shoemakers, railway platelayers, and workers in the paper mill. They enjoyed the common right of keeping geese and other stock on the prairie-like expanse of Port Meadow. There were two Wolvercotes, the Upper village being typical of many early settlements around Oxford, with its parish church perched on the edge of terraced gravels. In 1834 the enclosure plan shows it as having four farmhouses and fifteen other dwellings; all but two of the properties were freehold, and Upper Wolvercote was settled in its open character. There was virtually no change in its form before the close of the nineteenth century.

Its companion settlement, Lower Wolvercote, was larger and showed more of the usual characteristics of an open village, and it was partly an industrial village as well. Only two farmhouses stood there but they were reinforced by as many as thirty-five other houses and cottages; again, there was a complete predominance of freeholdings, with three public houses and a chapel. In 1834 half the houses of Lower Wolvercote lay in a ring besides Port Meadow, with their orchards, gardens, bakehouses and out-buildings; two large ponds and open ground have now disappeared into the front gardens of these houses. All this represents the maturing as an open settlement of an offshoot from Upper Wolvercote, making the most of common grazings.

The other half of Lower Wolvercote in Victorian times was dominated by its paper mill. The Thames had supplied clean water and power for the manufacture of white paper here from 1683, but there was no inkling of an industrial village until Thomas Combe built a new steam-driven mill in 1856. Combe was superintendent of the Clarendon Press, and his mill made the paper for millions of Bibles published by the Press. Known as 'Patriarch' before his death in 1873, Combe had built new cottages and a school at Lower Wolvercote, making the 'Street' of houses running from the mill to the open green at the other end of its alignment.[33] Some of Combe's work has disappeared but there is still enough to remind us of this Victorian enterprise. Were it not for their separation by the canal and then the railway the two Wolvercotes might have fused together into a single settlement by now.

Railways in the landscape

Railways came relatively late to Oxfordshire. Not until 1844 was Oxford linked by rail with the Great Western line at Didcot, so strongly and effectively had its opponents fought to keep the railway from Oxford. Subsequently the main lines continued north to Banbury (and so Birmingham) by 1850, and via Bicester towards Bletchley (originally the Buckinghamshire Railway, opened in 1851). The main line of the Oxford, Worcester and Wolverhampton Railway, 'the Old Worse and Worse', was opened in 1853, passing through the Wychwood and Cotswold country to Kingham and beyond, but important also because of its branch lines. In particular, by 1887 a link ran from Kingham to Banbury, which helped to precipitate a special impact on the Redlands through the quarrying of its ironstone (p. 183). By then it was part of the Great Western Railway, which had also run a line from Oxford eastwards through Thame by 1864.

Predictably the making of the railways wrought changes along their courses as the engineers had to come to terms with the terrain. On the open lowlands and flooding valleys they had to build embankments; in the deeply-incised twisting valleys of the Evenlode and Cherwell (which

[33] Harry Carter, *Wolvercote Mill. A Study in Paper-making at Oxford* (Oxford, 1957), p. 39.

naturally attracted the railways as relatively easy going) they had to dig cuttings through the spurs and build frequent bridges over the streams. Their most impressive single piece of construction is the viaduct at Somerton, on the old London and Birmingham line. The effects of such engineering in the Cherwell valley were thought by those who knew it of old to be harmful to agriculture. In 'this alluvial territory' as Wing called it there had always been the risk of disastrous summer floods that destroyed the hay harvest, as in 1829, 1854, 1876 and 1879. One of the reasons why floods were 'now so common' (1880), he argued, was the disturbance to natural drainage caused by the Great Western Railway's works, chiefly the various embankments between Somerton and Kidlington. These interrupted a free flow of water into the Cherwell; in fact the railway line occupied the former bed of the river, a channel having been cut for it by the engineers—reminiscent of Brindley's cavalier treatment of the Cherwell when he made the canal (p. 149, Plate 26).

The University had made the same argument when it successfully opposed the railway's advance from Didcot to Oxford in 1838, that the Thames would be impeded by embankments and flood more tiresomely than it already did. It must have seemed like divine retribution when the floods of 1852 damaged the new banks and cuttings; in November of that year the line was so badly flooded that engines could not pass and carriages were drawn through the water by horses. Not until after the floods of 1894 was this hazard checked by modifications to the line.[34] Ironically, too, when the line first reached Oxford the city supplied itself with water from the 'Rail-road Lake' at Hinksey, formed when springs filled the gravel-pits dug by the railwaymen for ballast. On the other side of Oxford to the north, the impact of railway-making was at its heaviest:

[34] E. T. MacDermot, *History of the Great Western Railway,* revised by C. R. Clinker (London, 1964), Vol. 1, pp. 343-4.

just beyond Wolvercote three main lines funnelled out to the north-west, north and north-east, and were linked or crossed by the Yarnton loop, taken farther by the Witney Railway (1861). Given a close mesh of intersecting trunk roads, and the Oxford Canal as well, this landscape is hopelessly dissected by thoroughfares of one kind or another, and the consequences are many (p. 222).

The railways made it easier to embark on a more ambitious working of mineral resources. Traditionally the bulky loads of building stone were transported laboriously by waggon, the hauls being kept short by the supplementary use of river carriage wherever possible, as in the movement of Taynton and the other Windrush stones down the Thames. After about 1850 industry could make itself felt by the freer use of the new railways. One of the first exploitations of ironstone took place at Fawler in the Evenlode valley close to the Oxford, Worcester and Wolverhampton line; the site is now overgrown with trees, but it tempts the industrial archaeologist as a complex of quarries, mines, limekilns, claypits and brick kilns. These ironstones (belonging to the marlstone of the Middle Lias) and other outcrops were on the property of the Duke of Marlborough. The geologist Phillips noted their working, and the more grandiose quarrying of rich ironstone near the railway at Adderbury, where his estimated yield of 30,000 tons to the acre pointed the way to drastic stripping of the Redlands by modern open-cast quarries (p. 223).[35]

The railways also undermined the existing modes of long-distance road traffic, and access to the lines of rail became a prime conditioner of vigour or stagnation in the countryside. Stagecoaches and spring-vans for passengers and goods began to disappear from the Oxfordshire roads in the 1850s. The eight-horse waggons to London had gone earlier. Wing could remember when as many as seventeen

[35] John Phillips, *Geology of Oxford and the Valley of the Thames* (Oxford, 1871), pp. 115, 496.

coaches each way changed their teams of horses every day at Woodstock, where the innkeepers also kept relays of post-horses and post-chaises for hire. Small towns of this type on the main highways lost one of their major functions to the railway, and did not recoup their loss until the appearance of the petrol engine and motor traffic on modern roads. In residential terms, on the other hand, the railway could have a positive value for country places through which it ran. Kidlington in the 1880s was thought to be "a village second to few in Oxfordshire" (in Wing's cautious words) simply by virtue of several "respectable residences, some of which are occupied by traders in Oxford".[36] From 1855 they could use its railway station on the Banbury line, first known as Woodstock Road and then, after 1890, as Kidlington. At a more elevated plane the accretion of new houses in the Bicester hunting country was helped by the fast rail services to London. When the Earl of Effingham bought Tusmore House in 1857 it was advertised as being "in a district studded with Gentlemen's Seats and Hunting Boxes, affording society of the most agreeable kind",[37] close to five railway stations that placed it within a two-hour journey from London.

Victorian building in the countryside

Only three Oxfordshire villages can be dated precisely as to their first appearance in the landscape: they are the Victorian new village of Charterville, which materialised in 1847; Summertown (1820), now an Oxford suburb and discussed in its own right later on (p. 212); and Carterton, founded in 1901. Together they throw into relief the mainly relative arguments we have been forced to adopt in earlier chapters when trying to explain how the countryside was settled. Charterville was unique both for the exactness with which we know its date of birth and the circumstances of its

36 W. Wing, *Annals of Kidlington* (Oxford, 1881), p. 6.
37 Blomfield, *op. cit.*, p. 75.

Plate 23 Stonesfield village, looking east. Above the trees in the foreground the edge of Stockey Bottom is lined with chipping banks, waste stone tips, quarry faces; other slate mine-shafts are marked by bushy patches (upper right). The sprawling shape of an open village is plain to see.

Plate 24 Wheatley village, looking east. This large village is centred on Church Road and the curved High Street, once part of the London to Oxford highway over Shotover Plain that was used until 1775. Its villagers had a range of employments besides agriculture, in the coaching trade, in stone-quarrying, in the working of clay, ochre and ironstone, and other industries. The plurality of landholders also helped make it the prototype of an open village, known for its turbulence in Victorian times—"a refuge for all the worst characters in the neighbourhood", whose inhabitants "lived much as they pleased".

Plate 25 Eynsham Hall and its nineteenth-century parkland. The first hall was designed for the Earl of Macclesfield in 1843, but the present house, —'a large hard Elizabethan mansion in bright red brick'—dates from the remodelling of about 1880. It was the work of Sir Ernest George who also built Shiplake Court, on the Thames near Henley, in 1899.

Plate 26 The lower Cherwell valley at Tackley. At the top left is the tree-fringed outline of Tackley Park, its southern boundary marked by the straight line of the Roman road, Akeman Street (compare Wilcote Park, Plate 4). Parallel with the curves of the river Cherwell runs the Oxford Canal, with Pigeon Lock in this section. The main railway line from Oxford to Banbury cuts its way indiscriminately north–south through the countryside. At the bottom left is the white scar of a limestone quarry near Enslow (p. 150). Scale *c.* 1:10,000.

Plate 27 Photograph of the Bayswater Brook, about 1900. Sheep-dipping in the wooded, early enclosed landscape of Shotover Forest, just to the north of Oxford. The evidence of early photographs such as this is full of potential for studying the changing landscape, although most of them were taken in urban or domestic settings. This scene is now replaced by a housing estate.

foundation, because it sprang from the Chartists' idea of transplanting 'back to the land' those industrial workers who had grown tired of life in the towns. By creating new villages for them there would be the incidental gain of increasing the numbers of forty-shilling freeholders who were entitled to vote under the Reform Bill of 1832, and who would be bound to support the Chartist cause in Parliament.[38]

As in the other five Chartist villages, the design of Charterville owed much to Feargus O'Connor, whose Chartist Land Company bought 300 acres of land in 1847. The location was a bleak spot on the main road above Minster Lovell, quite out of keeping with the traditional siting of Cotswold villages (such as Minster itself), which sought the shelter and water of the valleys and avoided the exposed ridges. O'Connor nevertheless built the Charterville cottages quickly and solidly, twin lines of single-storey houses spaced along a by-road, the meeting house and school taking the place of a church. Each settler had between two and four acres of land, and in spite of legal difficulties there was always a keen demand for properties at Charterville because of the security and independence that went with them; it was an open village with a difference, tailor-made for the smallholder. The colony's most rewarding period was between 1858 and 1887, when its cultivators grew potatoes for the Oxford market.

O'Connor's buildings are easy to distinguish, still in remarkably trim condition, each single-storey house marked with an ornamental tile set over its front door. They have been castigated as an early prototype for ribbon development, 'hideous' in appearance, a charge refuted in 1931: "This is too severe, as the little houses of standardised design compare favourably with recent developments."[39]

[38] A. M. Hadfield, *The Chartist Land Company* (1970), p. 20.
[39] The Earl of Mayo, S. D. Adshead, P. Abercrombie, *Regional Planning Report on Oxfordshire* (Oxford, 1931), p. 19.

This can surely be endorsed in 1974, when the Chartist houses are far outnumbered by modern in-filling and the extensions that have swamped Victorian Charterville.

A few miles away, and also vastly expanded, is another linear settlement of somewhat similar origin: Carterton was founded in 1901 when William Carter bought land from the Duke of Marlborough with the intention of subdividing it for a colony of smallholders living off the land.[40] It did not prosper as originally planned, but served a useful residential purpose after 1920 by focusing on itself the considerable volume of new housing then being built. The same is true today, because it is in the context of Charterville, Carterton and the special housing needs generated by the astonishingly built-up area around the R.A.F. station at Brize Norton that we may understand the forty-four per cent increase in population during the last ten years in Witney Rural District.

As the industrial towns of England continued to grow on a massive scale in the nineteenth century, it is not surprising that we associate Victorian architecture primarily with cities and suburbs. More than that, we are even assured that after the 'Battle of the Styles' between the adherents of late Georgian classicism on the one hand and neo-Gothicism on the other, the outcome was that "the characteristic Victorian creations are all urban".[41] This view, however, should not tempt us to overlook the presence of many notable Victorian buildings in the countryside, not all of which invariably "keep a rather urban look".[42]

What we can best do here to illustrate this theme is to record some of the rural handiwork of William Wilkinson, who lived from 1819 to 1901, and who is most famous, admittedly, as the virtual creator of the Victorian suburbs

[40] A. W. Ashby, *Allotments and Small Holdings in Oxfordshire* (1917), p. 131.
[41] Joan Evans, *The Victorians* (Cambridge, 1966), p. 161.
[42] See, for instance, Mark Girouard, *The Victorian Country House* (1971). The Oxfordshire houses described in the catalogue are those at Eynsham, Heythrop, Kiddington and Shiplake (see Plate 25).

of North Oxford (p. 214). He was the most prolific of a group of local men emerging after about 1850 as representatives of a new class of professional architects. Coming from a Witney family of builders and auctioneers he probably did not receive a formal training in architecture, and this may explain why his creations are thought by some to show "a lack of full sophistication".[43] His first known building is the new church at Lew, not far from Witney, and dating from 1841; it is typical of the revival of 'Christian architecture'. He helped to make his name in the 1850s (he first worked in Oxford in 1856) by designing a dozen or so sets of agricultural buildings on some of the biggest farming estates in Oxfordshire. These included 'model farms' incorporating new features for a more ambitious style of agriculture, bailiffs' houses and keepers' lodges, as well as cottages, at Shirburn, Cote and Aston (probably after their enclosure), Northbrook Farm at Kirtlington, with others at Black Bourton, South Leigh and elsewhere. New farms were also appearing around Wychwood, partly as a result of the disafforestation (p. 158), partly because of development on the Marlborough estate. In this latter context Wilkinson built Chasewood Farm, near Hailey, for the duke in 1874; it was widely copied as a model, with farmhouse, offices, stables, out-buildings and a covered yard, all constructed of local stone for £3000.

His subdued Gothic style was not inflexible, as we can still see in Upton Down Farm, a prominent building just off the A40 beyond Burford, where he blended Gothicism with the familiar vernacular tradition of the Cotswolds. This farmhouse is every bit as ample in plan and elevation as Wilkinson's town houses in the Banbury Road, Oxford, and cost only slightly less to put up; it is now empty as some of the farm buildings across the road have been made

[43] Andrew Saint, 'Three Oxford Architects', *Oxoniensia*, Vol. XXXV (1970), p. 55.

into a less pretentious residence. At the smaller scale, his labourers' cottages were carefully designed. Their ground floor had a living-room, scullery and pantry, and another room for aged parents living with their married children; above there were two or three bedrooms, depending on whether the cottages were single or paired. Whatever the nature and purpose of his buildings in Oxfordshire, we have Wilkinson's assurance that he always tried to make them "suited to an English landscape".[44] Thus he used local stone and Stonesfield slates (or Welsh slate, occasionally) as building materials in the countryside, in place of the Oxford brick and Broseley tiles he favoured in the town.

A number of large country houses were designed by him, starting with Hollybank at Wootton (1863), with others at Chadlington, Bignell (now demolished), Brashfield (now in military hands), and Shelswell (1877). No fewer than eight vicarages and parsonages in Oxfordshire villages originated on Wilkinson's drawing boards, ranged in time from Hailey (1843) to Studley (1880). So, too, with his school buildings: besides St Edward's in Summertown he was responsible for village schools (for example, Clanfield, 1872), and others in small towns, e.g. the Lord Williams school at Thame (1879). Indeed, Wilkinson's stamp is to be traced in practically all the small towns of Oxfordshire, because he became architect to the county Police Committee at an early stage of his professional career. He built as many as eight police stations in the country towns, beginning with Watlington and Witney (1859–60), and finishing with Deddington (1871). He was also responsible for a number of other structures in his native Witney, including six almshouses for the Holloway Charity (1868), a chapel and a cemetery.

It is clear, then, that we can find in this single career of a practising architect whose origins lay in the Oxford region where he did almost all his work, a representation

[44] W. Wilkinson, *English Country Houses* (2nd edn., 1875), p. 10.

of the vigorous phase of Victorian building experienced alike in the farming countryside, in villages, in small towns and, on a concentrated scale, in the phenomenal expansion of suburban Oxford.

SELECT BIBLIOGRAPHY

Arkell, W. J., *Oxford Stone* (1957).

Beckinsale, R. P., 'The Plush Industry of Oxfordshire', *Oxoniensia*, Vol. XXVIII (1963), pp. 53–67.

Brown, A. V., 'The Last Phase of the Enclosure of Otmoor', *Oxoniensia*, Vol. XXXII (1967), pp. 34–52.

Graham, Malcolm, *Henry Taunt of Oxford: A Victorian Photographer* (1973).

Moreau, R. E., *The Departed Village* (1968).

Morris, R. J., 'The Friars and Paradise: an Essay in the Building History of Oxford, 1801–1861', *Oxoniensia*, Vol. XXXVI (1971), pp. 72–98.

Saint, Andrew, 'Three Oxford Architects', *Oxoniensia*, Vol. XXXV (1970), pp. 53–107.

Thacker, Fred. S., *The Thames Highway. A History of the Inland Navigation* (1914).

Watney, Vernon J., *Cornbury and the Forest of Wychwood* (1910).

Wilkinson, William, *English Country Houses* (1875).

7. Towns in the landscape

Simple boroughs and market towns. The bishops' new towns. Full boroughs: planned towns. Oxford. North Oxford: a Victorian suburb

OLD AND NEW WOODSTOCK, Old and New Thame were terms of reference in common use for these towns until recently. To some extent they linger on, although the dominance of Oxford now gives greater currency to Old and New Marston as modern parallels for describing parts of a suburban district within the city. It is also the case that several of the smaller towns of Oxfordshire have neighbourhoods within them known as Newland or Newlands, so there is clearly scope here for determining the meaning of precedence and subsequence as implied by 'Old' and 'New'. The problem prompts us in this chapter to unravel the age and chronology of towns, when and in which sequence they materialised in the landscape, and to what extent their origins and subsequent growth are reflected in their nature as places, in the patterns of their streets and principal parts, or in the impression made by what some call their townscapes.

It is notoriously difficult to define in absolute terms what constitutes a town, and we meet this in Oxfordshire as elsewhere. Places like Watlington and Charlbury, for instance, are understandably regarded by those who live in them as small towns rather than as large villages, and it is true that in the past they attracted urban functions such as regular weekly markets. We shall look at Bampton as representative of this sort of place, never a town in the formal sense of the term, and at Bicester where the doubling of its population in the last ten years hides a similar lack of formal urban status in earlier times. Otherwise we shall follow as a general framework the ranking of towns according to the status they enjoyed as boroughs, that is to say the legal character of their original 'township', so far as it is known. Oxford was the only borough to be mentioned in the Oxfordshire Domesday, and it is likely on other evidence that its companion boroughs were not founded in any full sense until the twelfth and thirteenth centuries. Thus the creation of new towns goes along with the other developments we met in the context of medieval expansion (Chapter 3). Leaving aside Oxford, each and every borough was the scene of deliberate acts of urban genesis during the twelfth and thirteenth centuries, so the landscape of medieval Oxfordshire had to accommodate a series of new towns, the nature and spacing of which is vital to the structure of the region today.

Simple boroughs and market towns

Because the borough status of Deddington and Eynsham was so rudimentary they must be placed in the lowest category of towns.[1] They were essentially small market centres with a minor ranking in the legal sense. *Eynsham* was invariably omitted from the Assize Rolls in medieval times, and could boast no more than the possession of burgage tenure. Of itself this did not raise a place far above any manor of ancient demesne, but it was popular because money invested in such property could become more liquid, since the burgages could be freely sold or bequeathed by will. The old borough at Eynsham was held by the abbey under the Bishop of Lincoln, with burgage tenure, and dated from the early twelfth century; it had a mayor and the right

[1] Bodleian, MS. Top. Oxon. c. 43b: ff. 102–11, notes on the Oxfordshire boroughs by H. E. Salter.

to hold weekly markets, close to the abbey. Then in 1215 the abbot founded a new borough alongside the old by dividing a twenty-acre portion of the common fields into eighty equal plots of land, granting them out as burgages for ground rents of one shilling apiece. This was Newland, *Nova Terra*.

Despite its charter it was a minor place, its court meeting only three times a year and differing from manorial courts only in that it did not deal with the admission of new tenants. By 1366 there were twenty-seven tenements, some of them divided by the building on them of subordinate cottages; the pattern was similar in 1650.[2] The main point is that the abbot's foundation shows how all creations of boroughs were for the economic gain of the lord. The offer of burgage tenure to small freeholders added to the value of the land, and by increasing the number of residents it also increased the perquisites from the courts and market tolls. Newland did not grow much physically, and is easily recognised in the straight but curtailed lines of building along a spacious Newland Street, a deliberate-looking appendage to the old core of Eynsham. Newland also points to the kind of planned layout we shall meet in other Oxfordshire towns.

Deddington, too, had little more than burgage tenure and the right to hold markets. Unlike the abbot of Eynsham and his foundation at Newland, the founder of the borough is not known; nevertheless upon the large village (one of the richest in the county in 1086) was grafted the structure of a trading centre, probably before 1190 and possibly by William de Chesney. Physically there are similarities with Eynsham: the association of an old core of settlement, church and market place, with tangentially to them the laying-out of New Street, in which many of the burgages were situated. New Street is now part of the main A423,

[2] E. K. Chambers, *Eynsham Under the Monks* (Oxon. Rec. Soc., 1936), pp. 84–8.

indeed the motivation behind the founding of the borough
was its favourable location at a crossing of highways,
Oxford–Banbury, Buckingham–Chipping Norton. But it
failed to attract enough trade to sustain its growth into a
larger urban place of the self-governing kind. To its mis-
fortune it also had a near neighbour at Banbury which
prospered at the expense of Deddington.[3]

In next considering *Bampton* we have to remember that
it was outside the simplest legal category of borough, not
even having had burgage tenure, but its known life as a
market town cannot be ignored. As with Eynsham (which
it also resembles through its site on a gravel terrace by the
upper Thames), Bampton is one of the oldest settlements
in this part of England (p. 54), a royal manor of high value
by 1086. It was also the only place besides Oxford described
as having a market in the Oxfordshire Domesday; and its
Saxon standing may be gauged from its annexation to the
diocese of Exeter by Leofric, the first bishop. But its
institutions were as simple as those of any village, the
constables and other officers being appointed at the court
leet of the joint proprietors of the manor. Its market
flourished nevertheless, and in the eighteenth century it had
the cachet of being in good sporting country and a genteel
neighbourhood, with its weekly card assembly, physician
and apothecaries. By the early 1800s "the town now wears
the tranquil appearance of a large village, has a nominal
weekly market, but very little business is conducted".[4]
Ironically the Town Hall was built too late, in 1838: it
stands in the open market place at the town centre where
three main roads converge, giving the least sophisticated
town plan in Oxfordshire. Stylish houses line the streets,
reminiscent of the range of retail and other services in
Victorian Bampton, with five schools and sixty-five tradesmen, among them a printer and bookseller.

[3] H. M. Colvin, *A History of Deddington* (1963), pp. 55–7.
[4] Bodleian, MS. Top. Oxon. d. 171, f. 16: notes of Charles Richardson.

Bicester was another early English village sited on the dry cornbrash (like Witney), near the Roman road from Alchester to Towcester, and possibly it was a fortified place or *bury* like Burford and Banbury. As in Bampton there is no evidence of deliberate design in the layout of the town. The medieval plan consisted of two streets separated by the Bure stream: King's End was the more southerly, and had the church (with Romanesque features of the twelfth century), an Augustinian priory founded about 1180, and the Causeway. Bury End lay north of the stream, better known as Market End, with Sheep Street running on to the Market Square. In this triangular market space the two Ends meet, giving Bicester (if we take the open Roman road as its base) a stirrup-shaped plan distinctly set among its common fields. The Earl of Salisbury secured the grant of a free market in 1239, followed by a fair. It is possible that he encouraged traders to settle on burgage tenure, and as Bicester was located advantageously on the main roads the speculation met with success; its monastery, both for its own needs and as a place of lodging, helped the market to function profitably.[5]

As frequently happened (compare Thame and Chipping Norton) the market place was partly built over in the sixteenth century, when the Town House and Shambles appeared there. Many town houses were rebuilt in Elizabethan times, using coursed rubble, brick and timber. A series of destructive fires early in the eighteenth-century likewise opened the way for new building. Bicester came to have trades and industries of the kind found at Burford (p. 201), and by 1800 much of its prosperity stemmed from its sporting activities in horse racing and fox hunting (p. 184). The streets of the old town present a striking variety of building styles and materials, Elizabethan and Victorian nestling side by side. Its outskirts have expanded greatly with new housing estates, private

[5] V.C.H. *Oxfordshire*, Vol. VI (1959), pp. 14–21.

and council-built, especially on the northern side. More than any other Oxfordshire town of its size, Bicester responded to the wartime and post-1945 presence of airfields and the largest Ordnance Depot in southern England (p. 223). This was the first wave of a residential tide that has enveloped every town (and many villages) in Oxfordshire during the last twenty years. Bicester's population doubled from 6000 in 1961 to 12,000 in 1971, and shows no sign of halting.

The bishops' new towns

At a more sophisticated level we can subdivide the other medieval boroughs on the basis of those having a merchant guild and those without a guild. Far more than burgage tenure, the guild meant an elected body of men, perhaps with a common seal, certainly with power to hold property, which met often and made rules for the guild. No one could have a shop in the town unless he was of the guild, but it did not include regulation of the market. A considerable degree of self-government is implied by the possession of a guild merchant. In the first place, however, we shall look at three boroughs that do not seem to have had a guild, but whose foundation was by powerful tenants-in-chief— bishops in each case—who alone could secure the privileges of market or fair, and moreover whose early days were marked by town planning to a degree not met in the towns already brought into the discussion.

Witney again is among the oldest recorded settlements in Oxfordshire (p. 55), sited on an island of cornbrash breaking through the wet alluvial flats and clayland of the Windrush valley (Plate 28). It is also in the most complete sense an early industrial town, with a commitment to wool-spinning and the weaving of heavy broad-cloth, a foundation upon which other industries have built themselves in the last thirty years. As a possession of the Bishop of Winchester, it is likely that the woollen industry was fostered at Witney in the twelfth and thirteenth centuries. Fine wool was produced in the Cotswolds, water power for fulling mills was provided by the Windrush, the London road was at hand, while (beneficially in a manufacturing context) there were no guild regulations in the town to concern the broad-weavers, cloth-workers, clothiers, tuckers and fullers who, by the seventeenth century, had made Witney famous as a centre for making white blankets. There were sixty blanketers at work then, with 3000 people of all ages employed in carding and spinning the wool into yarn, many of them living in the forest hamlets of Hailey and Crawley.

In its structure and layout Witney, like other small towns in Oxfordshire, shows evidence of medieval planning. It consists essentially of a single axis of buildings running from Bridge Street over the Windrush to the High Street, Market Square, Buttercross and Church Green, which faces the town church. At this upper end of the axis, close by the church, the bishop probably had his palace, and his residence viewed in conjunction with royal visits to the hunting in Wychwood, would have benefited the town. The main civic services, such as the Town Hall and Blanket Hall, have always remained close to this planned focus of the market, which instead of disappearing under later buildings now survives in part as a town green fronting the church. Witney also experienced, like medieval Banbury (p. 199) the appearance of a Newland. Very close to the town across the Windrush ("a sort of outlying district or hamlet belonging to Witney"),[6] Newland seems to have been a new village founded in the thirteenth century by the lord of neighbouring Cogges (possibly the Archbishop of York), at a time when land clearance was active and also generated an outlying settlement at High Cogges. Newland can still be appreciated as a street-like *faubourg* where the Oxford road enters Witney.

[6] J. Giles, *History of Witney* (1852), p. 11.

The essence of its original townscape was sketched in 1815 by Charles Richardson:

> The principal street is about a mile in length, adorned with many domestic buildings both handsome and spacious, while the remainder are of a respectable character; the custom of colouring the fronts with a light yellow gives the town an air of cleanliness and cheerfulness. As the High Street draws towards the south, it progressively expands, and in the broad area is preserved an extent of greensward, through which is formed a wide gravel walk leading to the church, which gives a fine architectural finish to that part of the general view.[7]

The industrial sector of Witney lay in the weaving shops of West End and Newland, close to the river, with the mills spaced along the Windrush on old sites at Woodford Mill (now part of Witney Mills), New Mills, and as far upstream as Crawley. The substantial stone buildings of the nineteenth-century mills, factories and warehouses, with their recent extensions, confirm that the Witney manufacturers were able to modernise and stay in business at a time when most old woollen towns in the south of England were being undercut by the Yorkshire mills. A main reason for their success was the concentration of blanket-making in the hands of the Early, Collier and Marriott families, with informal co-operation between them in the critical first stages of modernisation. About 1800 the fly-shuttle or spring-loom was adopted, and in 1818 John Early went to Rochdale to order spinning machines which were installed in New Mill and powered by the Windrush. These spun yarn not only for the Early blanketers but for all who needed it in their manufacture.[8]

[7] Bodleian, MS. Top. Oxon. d. 171, f. 16.
[8] A. Plummer and R. E. Early, *The Blanket Makers, 1669–1969* (1969), Ch. 4.

Witney had six factories at work by the middle of the nineteenth century, when the railway brought cheaper coal. Charles Early who successfully directed the family business from the 1850s to the 1890s introduced power-driven looms at Witney Mill, with a steam engine aided by water power. Subsequently industry spread through the town, such as the Mount Mills built by the station, or the various engineering works that have come since the Second World War. More people now work at making car heaters or machine tools than in the blanket factories, and a totally 'New Witney' provides acres of housing for them and for others who work in Oxford and elsewhere in West Oxfordshire. The town's population has advanced from 9000 to 12,500 in the last ten years, and the sharpest of lines between town and country may be seen where the new houses of the Abbeyfield Estate seem poised to spill over the western boundary to make Burwell Farm and its environs a thing of the past.

Modern *Banbury* conveys the same impression, all the stronger for its status as an expanding town that absorbs new industries from the Midlands and people from London. It has had this kind of potential through much of its history. Compared with Burford, for instance, with which it shared a similar genesis as seigneurial boroughs, Banbury was larger and more prosperous by virtue of its better geographical location. It took full advantage of a more central position at the intersection of ancient route-ways from north to south and east to west. Originally an early English settlement, perhaps a *bury* stronghold like Burford and Bicester, it was one of the richest places in Oxfordshire by 1086: compare Deddington and the Redlands generally (p. 71). Banbury had sufficient status as a minster parish to enjoy a connexion with the earliest Bishops of Dorchester-on-Thames, whose estate it was.

It is not surprising, then, that Banbury owed its creation as a seigneurial borough to a churchman. A castle was first built by Alexander ('the Magnificent'), Bishop of Lincoln from 1123 to 1148. It is also likely that (as at Sleaford) he founded beside it a new town for traders and craftsmen, laying out nearly 200 house plots.[9] Attracted by low money rents and the other privileges of burgage tenure, the immigrant townsmen would generate income for the bishop through market tolls and other returns. The market was flourishing by 1138, using a new market place by the bishop's castle with good access to the Oxford–Coventry road and the Cherwell river crossing. The oldest tenements were probably upslope between the market and the Oxford road, near the church that Alexander may also have built. New quarters had spontaneously grown up by 1225, by extension along the southern side of the market place, in a growing town of about 1300 people. Between 1250 and 1285 another planned action took Banbury farther into the fields and meadows on this side, by creating the suburb of Newland. It was probably the first step to build beyond the original boundaries, taking Banbury to its medieval peak in area and population. There was little basic change in the next 500 years, before industrialisation began to prompt new forms of urban work and living, as Banbury responded to its location first on the Oxford Canal and then an important railway line. More than Oxford itself, it grew to be a Victorian manufacturing town of a familiar Midland kind (agricultural machinery was one of its specialities), as its townscape still testifies. At Banbury, too, we now find the largest twice-weekly cattle market in Europe, attended by many continental buyers. In this we see a modern expression of the town's place in the English network of drove roads for cattle, especially the great midland thoroughfare of Banbury Lane, much used between 1600 and 1800.

There was much in common between the origins of

9 P. D. A. Harvey, *Banbury*, pp. 1–8 in M. D. Lobel (ed.), *Historic Towns*, Vol. I (1969), p. 181.

Witney, Banbury and *Thame*, but the latter preserves more plainly the structure of the Bishop of Lincoln's creation of about 1150. Thame has expanded less than the others, and despite some in-filling by sixteenth-century buildings its ample High Street (which provided space for the market) still stamps it with the characteristic of a linear medieval town (Plate 29). Even so, Thame has prompted some questioning of what 'new towns' meant in the medieval landscape.[10] How should such places be defined? Were they new settlements planted on virgin soil, or the promotion of villages already there, or new boroughs added to old settlements? Many were created on the boundary of older places, and evidently the divorce of new from old was not always absolute. Thus at Thame in the late thirteenth century the bishop drew nearly £3 from the rents of seventy-six burgage tenements; his revenue from free and villein tenants holding virgates of the manor of Thame was over £18, so outweighing the new source of revenue. Some of the tenants held property in both the manor and the *burgus*, and one freeman held three virgates for eighteen shillings in *villa de Thame*. Thus the line between the old settlement and the new may not have been hard and fast, and it has even been suggested that New Thame simply grew along the road between the ancient village and the Cistercian abbey. Today it has a population of 6000 and due to its nearness to new motorways in the more metropolitan part of Oxfordshire it seems likely to grow at a much

[10] M. G. A. Vale, reviewing M. W. Beresford, *New Towns of the Middle Ages* (1967) in *Welsh History Review*, Vol. 5 (1970), pp. 72–7. Similar doubts are expressed by R. P. Beckinsale, 'Urbanization in England to A.D. 1420', *Urbanization and its Problems*, ed. R. P. Beckinsale and J. M. Houston (Oxford, 1968), p. 44. He prefers to call places like New Thame and Newland at Eynsham 'planned borough-extensions' rather than '*de novo*' plantations'. Thus all boroughs should be divided into unplanned and planned categories, the latter being then subdivided into planned extensions to existing settlements and newly-created planned boroughs. This puts too much stress on the physical form of towns and not enough on their institutional status and strength as boroughs.

Plate 28 Witney. In the centre of this photograph, taken in June 1969, the north–south axis of the planned town's market place is the principal feature. Scale *c.* 1:7500.

Plate 29 Thame. The view is south-east along the High Street. To the right of the picture some of the medieval burgages, running at right-angles to the High Street, are outlined as a separate block of land.

Plate 30 Burford. The view looks north from the junction of the High Street with the A40 (just off the photograph, in the foreground), towards the town bridge over the river Windrush. Again, the dominant feature of the town plan is provided by the axis of High Street, partly tree-lined.

Plate 31 Henley-on-Thames. The main street of the medieval town may be seen reaching from the bottom left towards the church, and so across the bridge; nineteenth-century building in the right foreground.

faster pace than in the past. A number of northern bypass roads are planned to take traffic away from the High Street axis of the old town, an ironic reversal of policy from that of the Bishop of Lincoln in 1219, when he diverted the Oxford–Aylesbury highway to a new course through his borough in order to increase tolls.

Full boroughs: planned towns

Farther up the pyramid of medieval boroughs were three that had merchant guilds, with all their implications for urban strength (p. 195). *Burford* was only a middling village in 1086, but before 1107 it was transformed into a seigneurial borough. The tenant-in-chief responsible for it was Robert fitz Hamon, Earl of Gloucester, who was also conquering territory in South Wales at that time. A broad street was marked out, running up the hill from the Windrush. On each side of it there opened out a series of long, narrow burgage plots ending in a back lane. Within this framework the town's life has run its course ever since. By their foundation charter the burgesses of Burford had a merchant guild, a weekly market held in the High Street and fairs.

When the ford was superseded by a bridge over the Windrush (it needed repairs by 1322) more trade came to the town: hides, fleeces and livestock, timber and charcoal from Wychwood, butter, wine. Burford dealt in wool and cloth, leather goods (especially saddlery), and became a stopping place for traffic on the Oxford–Gloucester road. Its medieval inns—the George, Crown, Bull—are grouped where this road met the High Street, and the rebuilding of its fine church in the early fifteenth century marks the prosperity of the medieval town. Never a large place, Burford retains its original form more closely even than Thame. A plan of 1800 showed about 100 houses on each side of High Street, much as it is today (Plate 30), and it had already reached its zenith because the new turnpike road to Gloucester had bypassed it so as to avoid the steep pitches imposed by its site.

Accordingly when Byng went there in 1781 he found Burford "a poor declining place, having lost the clothing trade and, almost, the saddle business".[11] But this retraction has meant the preserving of most of the town's original form. The fine stone houses are mainly Elizabethan or later rebuildings, as are the almshouses, inns, shops and Market House (*Tolsey*), but they stand on the footings of fitz Hamon's burgages. Narrow frontages on the High Street and long rearward yards and gardens are typical.[12] The main street must have been too narrow from the outset to allow building within the market place, as at Thame or Bicester; instead houses were already prolonging its course up the hill by the sixteenth century, and it has become hollowed out with use. Now the advent of a mobile road-using public in search of recreation has brought a modern tempo to this 'Cotswold Gateway'.

Much less is known about the growth and fortunes of *Chipping Norton*, although it almost certainly had a merchant guild. The town was probably founded by William fitz Alan who held the manor in the mid-twelfth century, and who founded Coldnorton Priory nearby. The physical form of the town centre is conventionally like that found at neighbouring Burford or at Thame (p. 200), with a widened High Street in which the market was held (the *Chipping* part of its name, meaning *market*, was first recorded in 1224). This space is now partly obscured with later building, while away on either side of this axis run the narrower, parallel plots of the medieval burgages. It is a Cotswold hill town, its High Street taking the 650-foot contour in its stride, surely one of the highest settlements of its size in southern England. Yet it has never been hampered by

[11] *The Torrington Diaries*, ed. C. Bruyn Andrews (1954), p. 33.
[12] M. W. Beresford and J. K. St. Joseph, *Medieval England. An Aerial Survey* (1958), pp. 165–6.

remoteness, because a main highway from London to the Midlands has always been at hand (p. 145). By contrast with Bampton, therefore, in the 1840s when its Town Hall was also being built and their populations were evenly matched, Chipping Norton ("one long and tolerably handsome street"), offered twice as wide a range of services. It had twenty inns and taverns, eleven bankers and insurance agents, and its 137 tradesmen included two wine merchants, three perfumers and hairdressers, and two booksellers and stationers.[13] In addition to its weekly market (which long antedated the borough charter of 1607), Chipping Norton had great cattle marts at the end of each month, and two statute fairs in October. Woollen cloth was manufactured, but only a single tweed mill survives in a grandiloquent but impressive Victorian pile.

Henley-on-Thames is at the opposite geographical extreme in most respects, ensconced in the wooded valley of the Thames barely 100 feet above sea level (Plate 31). It had a merchant guild by 1269, and it became usual for the Warden of the guild to be known as 'Warden of the Town', with admissions or elections to burgesshood being recorded in the guild's Assembly Books.[14] Guild and borough could scarcely have been closer. Henley did not appear in the records until 1199, and then simply as part of the grant of royal Bensington to Robert de Harcourt, who may have sponsored its urban growth on *terra regis*, land that was ancient demesne of the Crown. The tenurial links with Bensington were not severed until about 1330, just as St Mary's remained a chapelry of the mother-church; its advowson passed from royal hands to the Bishop of Rochester in 1272.[15]

[13] *Pigott's Directory of Oxfordshire* (1842).
[14] P. M. Briers (ed.), *Henley Borough Records* (Oxford Record Society, 1960), pp. 3–7.
[15] This reconstruction of the town's genesis and later growth is based on documents printed by J. S. Burn, *A History of Henley-on-Thames* (1861), pp. 7, 10, 12, 18, 27, 122, 290 and 293.

From the outset Henley was a river town and its bridge was its livelihood. The bridge was in being by about 1230, when indulgences were granted for its repair as well as that of the church which stands so close to it. Two of the town's most important officers were the Bridgemen, whose accounts go back to 1306. From 1385 they administered an estate whose rent was used for maintaining the bridge and a charity in St Mary's; some of these houses and granaries belonging to the corporation were on the bridge itself. When Leland saw it in the 1530s it was a wooden bridge on stone foundations; the present structure dates from 1786. The 'Town Water', a right of fishing in the Thames between known marks, was the property of the town at least as early as 1313. Records show that a substantial Decorated church was being built between 1400 and 1420, perhaps enlarging the older one, and by this time the essential form and layout of the town had come into being.

Opening from the bridge and running to the Hill was the main thoroughfare of High Street, now Hart Street, an axis divided in two parts by the cross in the Market Place. Close to the cross stood a Guild Hall, rebuilt in 1487, its site now marked by the Town Hall of 1796; it had shops under it in the fifteenth century. Henley may be unique among the small towns of Oxfordshire in having had its 'Walls', which are mentioned in the records from 1397. As in Thame or Bicester the market place came to be reduced by 'a stack of buildings' within it, Fisher Row on the north, Butcher Row on the south. This apart, the plan of medieval Henley was similar to that of Burford and suggests an element of design. Its medieval inns—the Red Lion, White Hart, Catherine Wheel—are close to the church and bridge or in High Street, which was intersected at right-angles through the market cross, for instance by "the south street of Henley called the Broad Street" in 1395 (now Duke Street).

The town had the usual complement of medieval trades-men for its region: millers, tanners, skinners, glovers, fullers, dyers, tailors, timbermen and carpenters. There can be no doubt that its prosperity grew in proportion with that of London in the sixteenth century, due to the streng-thening of its commercial links with the metropolis by river transport. Its charter of incorporation was granted in 1566. Blome captured its role in his *Britannia* (1673):

Henley has a considerable trade for malting, its inhabi-tants (which for the most part are bargemen or watermen) gain a good livelihood by transporting of malt, wood and other goods to London, and in return bring such com-modities as they and the inhabitants of the adjacent towns have need of, at easy rates; and its market is very considerable for corn, especially barley, which is brought there for their great malt trade, there being oft times in one day sold about 300 cartloads of barley.

Many of the town houses had malt kilns built behind them, and most of the wood sent to London was local beech from the Chilterns.

As its traditional trading strength began to weaken in the railway age, Henley found compensation in its attrac-tiveness for out-of-town residences built by rich metro-politans. The seductiveness of its riverside landscape, hanging beechwoods and plantations were drawing 'elegant villas' to the neighbourhood before 1800 (p. 131), but judging from the *Directories* their presence was slow to make itself felt in the number and nature of its shops: the town did not differ much from Chipping Norton in this respect, no doubt because the big houses were supplied direct from London. Before the railway arrived in 1857 a horse-bus left the Red Lion twice daily for Twyford station on the main line. Through-traffic by road still brought good business to thirty-two inns and taverns, although the day was passed when a dozen coaches stopped on their way to Oxford, Birmingham or Cheltenham. Victorian Henley was "one of the neatest and cleanest towns in the county", most of the new building having gone along Greys Lane and so in fact into the parish of Rotherfield Greys. The reason for this lopsided expansion to the south was that on the other side of the town growth was choked by three private parklands—Deanfield, Fawley Court and Henley Park, whose deer park was part of the manor since 1300.

Finally, at the summit of the borough hierarchy stood not only Oxford but also the other royal town of *Woodstock*. They differed from the rest through having more than burgage tenure, markets, or merchant guilds: they paid a *firma burgi*, having bargained to collect and keep the king's revenue themselves in return for an annual payment to him. Thus in 1199 Oxford agreed to pay £63 a year, more than the king's average profits from the city, and in return the burgesses could take the profits of the borough court, market, quit-rents of many houses, and so on. As Oxford also had a merchant guild at least as early as 1147, its primacy among the towns was unrivalled. But Woodstock enjoyed the same measure of independence and self-government. In all probability it had a merchant guild: admittedly it was not mentioned in 1279 in the Hundred Rolls but it was not necessary to do so, and when the town obtained its royal charter in 1453 the king did refer to a guild among the ancient customs and privileges of the borough. At the same time its burgesses rented the borough from the king at a very small *firma burgi*, the only town in the county besides Oxford to do so.

This achievement was in line with the rest of Woodstock's distinctive genesis in the landscape. Its 'Old' and 'New' sectors are more differentiated physically than in any other Oxfordshire town. Old Woodstock lies north of the Glyme valley and strung alongside the park (originally Woodstock, now Blenheim), the prototype of an ancient village shifted beyond the park wall at a command of its royal lord. New Woodstock came abruptly into the picture in 1163–4 when Henry II, who was fond of the park and often visited his manor house there, "gave and granted divers parcels of land of the said waste place to divers men for the purpose of building hostelries therein, for the use of the king's men".[16] The town had a market from the outset, later a fair, and by 1279 its restricted territory (cut off like an island within the royal manor) housed a community of something over 500, traders and craftsmen migrating to it from the surrounding countryside. Its burgages were grouped on all sides of a large triangular market place known as the Green, and lacking the focus provided in other Oxfordshire towns by a church, bridge, castle or palace. (St Mary Magdalene was only a chapelry of the mother-church at Bladon.) While the pattern of the burgage lots is still traceable in the back lanes marking their rearward limits, the market space is much obscured by a wedge of later buildings, the prow of which is formed by the Town Hall of 1776, replacing the old Guild Hall; a new Market House had been built ten years earlier.

If we wished to emphasise the differences in origin and standing between towns, finally, we could do so by re-defining the groupings within which we looked at each of them in turn. Eynsham, Deddington, Bampton, and Bicester (with the addition of Watlington, perhaps), would go together as unplanned places, or as old irregular settlements that grew into boroughs or market towns. Then the majority were planned places: Newland at Eynsham, Witney, Banbury and Thame belong here as the extensions to existing settlements, whereas Burford, Chipping Norton, Henley-on-Thames and Woodstock were newly created and planned boroughs. Oxford stands apart from the rest, not on the grounds of greater age but because it enjoyed a

[16] A. Ballard, *Chronicles of the Royal Borough of Woodstock, compiled from the Borough Records* (1896), p. 8.

unique status before it also went on to acquire burgage tenure, a guild merchant, and the payment of *firma burgi*. We must now try to explain its uniqueness.

Oxford

Until recently, and especially at times of river flooding, it was easy to appreciate the island-like site on which the city of Oxford originated:

> The gentle rise of the surrounding heights, the steepness of the (Cumnor) Hurst itself, and united waters of the Isis and Cherwell which, mingled together and swelled by the late rains seemed at a distance to insulate the town of Oxford . . .[17]

The role of Oxford's rivers in the origins of the place lay at two levels: on the broader scale a natural frontier along the Thames needed strongpoints to guard it, while on the local scale the Thames and Cherwell together served as natural lines of defence for a town. In this setting in the early tenth century a fortified town was established by Edward the Elder, King of Wessex, fitting into the southernmost tip of a gravel terrace running as a tongue of drier land between the flood plains of Thames and Cherwell. Here an ancient north–south trackway, probably prehistoric, crossed the braided river, and there was already in being a settlement that had grown to serve the monastic community at the eighth-century shrine and minster church of Saint Frideswide. Details of this earliest Oxford have been discovered since 1967 by the Oxford Archaeological Excavation Committee.[18]

[17] C. K. Francis-Brown, 'Sir Frederic Madden at Oxford', *Oxoniensia,* Vol. XXV (1970), pp. 34–5; the observation is from Madden's diary for 30th December 1823, when he first visited Oxford as a young man. The winter of 1823–4 saw serious flooding by the Thames (p. 153).

[18] T. G. Hassall, *Oxford: the City Beneath Your Feet* (1972), pp. 5, 10–11.

The site of the city thus had much in common with those of Eynsham, Dorchester-on-Thames and Abingdon, but what distinguishes the appearance of Oxford in the landscape was its status as a late Saxon planned town. Evidence for this kind of urban planning is only now coming to light. Archaeological, documentary and topographical sources all point to the making of the rectilinear street plan of Winchester as a planned system not later than the mid-tenth century, and probably before about A.D. 904.[19] The same kind of Saxon design is attributable to Exeter, Bath and Chichester, as well as to towns on non-Roman sites at Wareham, Wallingford and Cricklade. Like all these places Oxford was listed in the Burghal Hidage, embodying a strategic pattern for the defence of Wessex based on a series of fortified places or *burhs*. They were not so much fortresses as fortified towns, in which the rectilinear street plan was a conscious expression of the apportionment of land for permanent settlement.

While the extent of the early *burh* at Oxford is not fully ascertained, elements of its rectilinear street plan are easily identified and form the oldest ingredients of the townscape (Plate 32). Carfax marked the intersection of the main streets, lying centrally within the rectangular outline of the defensive earthworks that ran for some 2000 yards around the town. This was the framework in which Saxon Oxford grew to be a prosperous royal town, undisturbed until the physical shock that accompanied the building of a large Norman castle. As in other *burhs* such as Winchester, Exeter and Wallingford, the castle-builders were responsible for a second phase of activity that modified and distorted the old urban pattern. Probably in 1071 Robert d'Oilly sited his strong motte-and-bailey castle to the west of the town and close to the river Thames, dominating the *burh* and sitting astride the western road approaches.

[19] Martin Biddle and David Hill, 'Late Saxon Planned Towns', *Antiquaries Journal*, Vol. LI (1971), pp. 70–85.

The castle and its outworks brought a new physical presence at the expense of older houses that had to be demolished, old roads diverted and new ones laid out.[20]

Of this medieval castle we can still see the mound, standing eighty feet above New Road (which was cut across the northern part of the bailey in 1776), and St George's Tower, a blunt military landmark on the riverside. The shape of the bailey may be inferred from the grouping together of buildings always associated with it, such as the prison and the county hall, while the curving outline of the moat can also be detected in the course of Paradise Street, which succeeded it when it was filled in during the eighteenth century. Castle Street has just been realigned once more because of the development of the Westgate Centre, and further change will come to the castle precincts in the near future. Recent excavations hereabouts also revealed sections of the town wall, including a small postern known as the Little Gate. In its full extent the outer wall was carried farther to the east in the eleventh century, beyond St Mary's church, where the High Street makes its curving line towards the old Eastgate (Plate 33). Not until after 1226 was the city wall rebuilt in stone with its battlements and now vanished gates, and the bastions still surviving in New College.

From the outset the castle bailey protected the Chapel of St George, a collegiate church for secular canons, scholars whose presence may have helped the founding of the university when Oxford expanded in the twelfth century. As time went on the Franciscan order of Greyfriars acquired land between the castle and Little Gate, building a splendid church there in the 1240s, while not far away the Dominican Blackfriars also built their priory church.[21] Scholarly and influential, the friars were active in the growth of the university, which dominated Oxford

[20] T. G. Hassall, *Oxford Castle* (1971), p. 3.
[21] T. G. Hassall, *Oxford: the City Beneath Your Feet*, pp. 24–30.

by the end of the fourteenth century. Initially the students lived in private and licensed lodging houses, but in due course the fabric of the town had to accommodate college buildings as they came into being at the expense of the old tenements. This was especially noticeable in the eastern parts of the walled city, where Merton College and New College had their spacious freeholds. Gradually the heart of the medieval town was taken up by new foundations, culminating with Christ Church in the 1520s. The Reformation then swept away Oxford's abbeys and the friars' churches—Greyfriars was demolished in 1537 and the Blackfriars in 1544—before another phase of university and college building began early in the seventeenth century. Subsequently Oxford was to stay contained more or less within its medieval circuit, save for new suburbs at St Clement's, St Ebbes and Jericho,[22] until its metamorphosis to an industrial centre for the manufacture of motor vehicles in the twenties and thirties of this century.

North Oxford: a Victorian suburb

New housing spread beyond the walled city on its northern perimeter as early as the twelfth and thirteenth centuries, towards Broad Street and St Giles. Here, after all, the continuation of the gravel terrace offered the driest and most attractive site for further settlement, where life soon became rural (Plate 34). Number 22, St Giles, for instance, is an old town house close to the parting of the Banbury and Woodstock Roads, but it was a working farm when it first appears in the records. It was the home of Matthew Penn "of the parish of St Giles in the suburbs of the City of Oxford, yeoman", in 1640. He was a fairly wealthy man, living comfortably, and it is clear he was a farmer who sold

---

[22] Significant changes *within* the old city took place in 1771, when a local Act of Parliament set up the body known as the Oxford Paving Commission, with a special interest in improving streets, roads and market.

his produce, butter, cheese and bacon, in the town. His livestock "in the outward houses" included eighteen cows, heifers and calves as well as "little hogs", with a valuable hayrick for winter feeding and a woodstack of faggots for fuel. Penn's son had a bakery, and the house was partly destroyed by fire in 1669. Later occupants included a brewer, cook, rag and coal merchants, hatmaker, poulterer and butcher; only after 1842 did it become a purely residential town house.[23]

By then the wealthier tradesmen of the city were choosing to build new houses for themselves in what was open country, but within what we now call easy commuting distance of their business premises. Again they looked to the north of the old city, along the easier going of the main roads to Woodstock and Banbury. Here they could reinforce "the newly erected village" of Summertown, attractive for its fine views over the city, growing in spectacular fashion as an open settlement after its foundation in the fields in 1820. Few places can claim a horse-dealer as their first settler: James Lambourne was not only this but he gave Summertown its name as well, and his business flourished there beside the turnpike road. A row of twenty-five houses straggled along the eastern side of the Banbury Road, among them the hallmarks of an open village:

> eight tidy white-washed tenements, under one continued roof, for poor families, with green doors and window shutters. They have little slips of garden in front reaching to the road, and larger pieces at the back. These tenements were built about the years 1821–2 by a coal merchant in Oxford.[24]

The other embryonic half of Summertown was more of a

[23] Bodleian, MS. Wills Oxon., 83/2/39, 144/3/16; it is possible to identify the house leased by Penn through the muniments of Christ Church, Oxford, its owners since 1572.

[24] Quoted by Ruth Fasnacht, *How Summertown Started* (1969), pp. 6–7.

planned affair because of the careful subdivision into building lots and speculative sale of Whorestone Farm, sixty acres of it, in 1821. This led to houses appearing along both the Banbury and Woodstock Roads, along the South Parade ('Prospect Road') that connected them, and Middle Way that bisected the ground between them. Summertown had about 120 houses, mostly small and mostly leased, "in general miserably contrived and ill-built". In 1833 it became a parish with a church of its own when the most northerly portion of St Giles parish was lopped off, and remained an Oxfordshire village for most of the nineteenth century, refusing a "reckless and unnecessary expenditure" on drains and sewers. When it was finally absorbed by the city in 1889 it still stood clear of the northernmost margin of Oxford's suburban bricks and mortar.

Summertown preserves something of its village flavour, despite the growing uniformity caused by its physical union with the rest of North Oxford and the disappearance of some of its open land. Originally there were spacious grounds planted with trees and shrubs attached to the country houses built by Oxford citizens, such as Apsley Paddox or The Avenue. A twelve-acre nursery garden supplied ornamental conifers that we now see in mature growth, such as those planted at 333, Banbury Road, the best surviving example of the larger Summmmertown residences. This house was Summerhill Villa, built in 1823 by an Oxford butcher who may have carried on his business there. By 1846 it was the property of James Ryman, a city art dealer, whose family lived there until 1925. The estate Ryman pieced together around the house has been built over since, but much remains of his grounds with their "shaded walks, arbours, fountain, ornamental stone figures and terrace, with a large and varied assortment of choice forest trees and shrubs, conservatory, Palm House and summer houses".

Between the rustic variety of Summertown and the old

suburbs of St Giles lies the Victorian perfection of North
Oxford proper, now under siege by the developers. Few
English towns have anything to rival its architectural
wholeness or the very individual way in which it virtually
exploded on the landscape. As we have seen, Oxford in the
mid-nineteenth century had not much outgrown its
medieval circuit, and it was still a small town:

> . . . I used to get field-walks in what are now districts
> completely overrun by new Oxford suburbs. In 1878
> Canterbury Road was just being built—beyond it there
> were only farms and market gardens. There was no build-
> ing along the Iffley Road after the first 200 yards from
> Magdalen Bridge. In what are now Grandpont and New
> Hinksey there were not twenty scattered houses . . .[25]

North Oxford chiefly came into being on the property of
a single landowner, St John's College, and a comparatively
small number of architects saw it through from start to
finish. At the outset in 1853–5 the Park Town estate was
developed by S. L. Seckham, but William Wilkinson (p. 186)
inherited his design for the Walton Manor estate with large
houses along Woodstock Road, on either side of a corner
with a new Leckford Road. Wilkinson also assumed
responsibility in 1860 for work on the Norham Manor
estate, along the new lines of Norham Gardens, Fyfield
Road and Norham Road; domestic building had soon
spread from the Oxford Canal to the Cherwell. It was
Wilkinson who marked out these new residential quarters,
sited houses in the streets, approved the houses designed
by others (for instance, along the northern side of Keble
Road), and assessed the ground rents. After his nephew
Harry Wilkinson Moore joined the practice in 1881, building continued from St Margaret's Road (which followed
the line of Rackham Lane) northwards along the main

[25] Sir Charles Oman, *Memories of Victorian Oxford* (1941), pp. 78–9.

roads, including Frenchay Road, Staverton Road and Linton Road (pegged out on the line of an old farm track).[26] Moore was responsible for "an amazing number of picturesque and tasteful houses in North Oxford, the best of which are the latest, in Northmoor Road", pegged out in 1895. It is a unique family record in suburban design, now threatened by piecemeal development, as at 'Shrublands', Number 60, Banbury Road, completed in 1866 and regarded as the best surviving example of Wilkinson's work.[27] The whole of Oxford between St Giles church and Summertown is the conception of Wilkinson and Moore, who built large houses in brick with stone dressings, each with its spacious garden. In a single generation, to meet the demands of married fellows of colleges for family houses, and the aspirations of wealthy townsmen, they initiated a suburb that was more than double the area of the old city of Oxford.

SELECT BIBLIOGRAPHY

Beckinsale, R. P. and Houston J. M. (eds.), *Urbanization and its Problems* (1968), Ch. 1, 'Urbanization in England to A.D. 1420', by R. P. Beckinsale.

Beresford, M. W., *New Towns of the Middle Ages* (1967).

Betjeman, John and Vaisey, David, *Victorian and Edwardian Oxford from Old Photographs* (1971).

Colvin, H. M., *A History of Deddington* (1963).

Fasnacht, Ruth, *A History of the City of Oxford* (1954).

Hassall, T. G., *Oxford: The City Beneath Your Feet* (1972).

Hinton, David A., *Oxford Buildings. From Medieval to Modern: Exteriors*, Oxford Archaeological Excavation Committee (1972).

[26] Another of his nephews, C. C. Rolfe, worked in Oxford after 1883, having previously designed the row of model houses for artisans on the eastern side of Kingston Road: Andrew Saint, 'Three Oxford Architects', *Oxoniensia*, Vol. XXXV (1970), pp. 53–102.

[27] E. O. Dodgson, 'Notes on numbers 56, 58, 60, 62 and 64 Banbury Road', *Oxoniensia*, Vol. XXXII (1967), pp. 53–9.

Martin, A. F. and Steel, R. W. (eds.), *The Oxford Region* (1954), Ch. 17, 'The Growth of the City of Oxford', by E. W. Gilbert.

V.C.H. *Oxfordshire*, ed. Mary D. Lobel and Alan Crossley, Vol. VI, 'Bicester Hundred' (1959), pp. 14–21; Vol. VII, 'Thame Hundred' (1962), pp. 78–92; Vol. X, 'Banbury Hundred' (1972), pp. 5–39, for the town of Banbury.

Turner, Michael L. and Vaisey, David, *Oxford Shops and Shopping. A Pictorial Survey from Victorian & Edwardian Times* (1972).

Plate 32 The urban nucleus at Oxford. The view is east across the Thames (foreground), along the line of High Street (left middle distance) towards Magdalen Bridge and the Cherwell river meadows (background). Left of centre lies virtually the whole of the walled medieval borough; to the right is nineteenth-century suburban building, where new development has led to the demolition of hundreds of artisan cottages dating from 1830 to 1860.

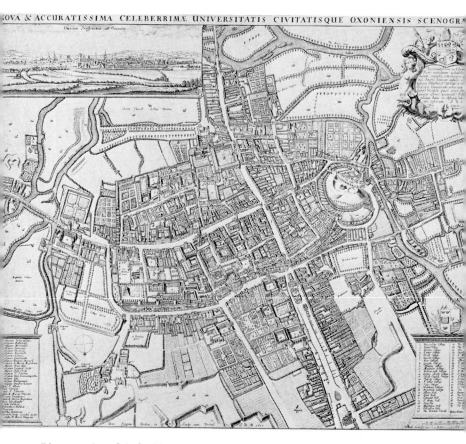

Plate 33 Plan of Oxford by David Loggan, 1675. Loggan published this earliest accurate plan of the city in his *Oxonia Depicta*. Compared with previous drawings like that of Agas (1578), Loggan recorded new buildings within the ancient city, as well as some extra-mural expansion, for instance along Broad Street. North is to the bottom of the plan. Scale *c.* 1:3250.

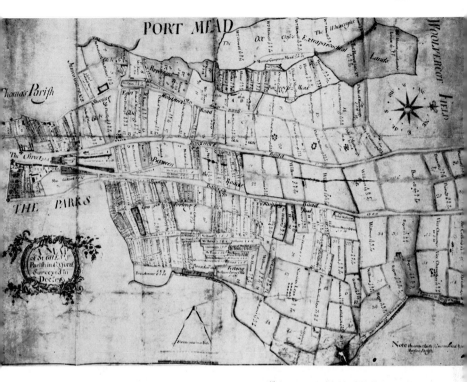

Plate 34 Plan of St Giles parish, Oxford, 1769. It shows the three roads running north in parallel from the city: Old Road (now followed by Kingston–Hayfield Roads), Woodstock Road, and the Parks–Banbury Road. The fragmented holdings of common fields were still well preserved near Oxford, but farther north they were consolidated and enclosed. This farming landscape was superseded and overlain by the suburban streets and houses of Victorian North Oxford. (Drawn by Edward and Thomas Smith, St John's College, Oxford, MS. Map No. 41. Scale *c.* 1:21,120.)

Plate 35 Clifton Hampden, looking north. The village is hidden among the trees on the Oxfordshire side of the bridge over the Thames. Beyond stretches the wooded terrain of the low Greensand hills.

Plate 36 The M40 extension under construction, 1972. Here the motorway makes a curving descent of the Chiltern escarpment to the Oxfordshire plain below.

8. The contemporary landscape

AT PRESENT THE Oxfordshire landscape is open to revolutionary changes of an order and tempo not previously experienced. Many of them are taking place on a national scale, and a single county is absorbed, pawn-like, into the planners' strategy for the whole country or one of its planning regions—in the case of Oxfordshire that of South-East England. So the total experience is increasingly subject to external decisions: as the national network of motorways is put together on the drawing-board, for instance, the need for a new M40 is translated into a line that may or may not bring yet another artery of communication to the Cherwell Valley. This eventuality then has to be faced by a Cherwell village such as Steeple Aston, which recently has also had to live with the discovery of a concealed coalfield that the National Coal Board may work in the long term, and drilling for natural gas— as well as the day-to-day issues of low-flying aircraft and building development.

Of three directions along which we may trace these current forces of change, the first is the result of new trends in agriculture. Industrialized farming is the outcome of larger farms and more intensive methods of production, and it is creating not only new biological problems but others of a visual kind as well. The farmers' response to market demands has introduced all manner of exotic touches to the landscape, some of them transient like the fields of maize for silage or sunflowers that puzzle or dazzle the beholder, but most of them permanent. First, the use of powerful machinery in the farming round—tractors, cultivators, hay-balers, combine harvesters—demands huge fields for efficient working. Hence the grubbing up and destruction of thousands of miles of living hedges with their trees, especially the slighter newer hedges brought into the landscape in the first place by the Georgian enclosers (pp. 131–43), which are most vulnerable. Bulldozers make short work of the job, for which grants were available from public funds. The cost of maintaining hedges is another reason for the big arable farmer, 'the barley baron', to clear the landscape of trees and shrubs that also cost him money in shade and roots.

We may calculate there are at least 10,000 miles of hedges in Oxfordshire, a figure to place alongside others such as the total of 5000 hedge-miles being uprooted each year in Britain. About fifteen per cent of Oxfordshire's hedge-miles are associated with medieval assarts, including those boundary hedges of pre-Conquest date that are mentioned from time to time in late Saxon charters. Early enclosure of common fields and waste, dating from about 1450 to 1750 and associated both with deserted villages and with the agreement enclosures of the sixteenth and seventeenth centuries, accounts for thirty-five per cent. The remaining fifty per cent of Oxfordshire hedges may safely be attributed to the Georgian and Victorian enclosures by Act of Parliament after 1750. The historical value of certain hedges, especially where they mark boundaries between parishes or estates, sometimes more than 1000 years old, should be a point argued in favour of keeping them in their landscape.

The clock is being put back in visual terms to the bare, open vistas of the ancient common fields: see the lifeless prairies at Ipsden in the Chilterns, or Great Milton in the vale, or on the low Cotswolds around Chadlington. The disappearing hedgerow also spells out problems in ecological and historical terms, and at present is as great a threat to trees in the landscape as Dutch elm disease. Nor should we forget that modern ploughing is levelling and obliterating many of the patterns of ridge-and-furrow that date from pre-enclosure days, taking them out of view at ground level. Here too lies the conflict over the destruction by farmers of ancient footpaths, bridle paths and other rights of way: it required a civil action in 1971 to restore the status of public road to Holcombe Lane between the villages of Chalgrove and Newington.

When the fields become larger, so do the farm buildings. As modern farming systems have advanced there has come a need for bigger buildings with a wider span. Gone are the simple groupings of barn, stable, byre and rickyard. Instead we see from afar the looming cattle sheds, grain and potato stores holding 1000 tons, all achieving their span thanks to the successful design of pre-cast concrete frames. Such concrete buildings are made near Thame, and by paying special care to the cladding and enclosing of the frames the manufacturer aims at structures that will merge as harmoniously as possible with the landscape. As to new materials, farmers now use coloured sheeting in asbestos, cement and plastic-coated sheet steel. It is as well that the Country Landowners' Association holds competitions for the best design of 'farm buildings in the landscape', although little can be done about the 400-ton tower silos that make farms look like something from Cape Kennedy. Push-button farming reaches its peak in big units like the 2000 acres of Glympton Home Farm, which looks what it is, a well-run factory astride the road.

As a second phenomenon we have an invasion of the countryside by those who live and sleep there but work and shop elsewhere, so reflecting the blurred relationship we now have between town and country. Villages fall into two broad classes on this very point of how much new housing they provide for an outgoing population. Some villages, and more often than not they were closed settlements in the nineteenth century (p. 170), remain unaffected by the waves of new building because of their relative isolation and lack of services. They are apt to be called 'copy book villages, almost too good to be true', or 'picture postcard villages'. It is noticeable that the stone-built places of the Cotswold and Redland regions, thanks to their share in the 'Great Rebuilding' and particularly if they retain a village green, score time and again as 'Best kept villages' in competitions arranged by the Oxfordshire Rural Community Council—places like Kingham, Spelsbury, Shenington, Adderbury, Bloxham and Wootton. Other villages, beautified by a riverside location and sylvan surroundings, have managed to keep their appeal despite the demand for housing by those working elsewhere (Plate 35). At Great Tew, where a start is being made with restoring some of the houses, it is the intention of the landowner to keep the village as a home for country workers, not outsiders; this may prove to be a source of stability in the current situation, when the number of full-time agricultural workers in Oxfordshire has dropped to only about 3000. Ascott-under-Wychwood is the home of 370 villagers, for instance, but only eighteen of them work on the land, whereas 100 men and women work outside the village in Witney, Oxford or elsewhere.

By contrast, many Oxfordshire villages (as well as the small towns within the county) are washed by the rising tide of new housing. Often they were open settlements in the nineteenth century (p. 172), where runaway development triggers off new tensions within communities faced with the transformation of the character of their villages. Stonesfield, for example, has grown threefold in population since 1951, and some of its 1200 inhabitants wish to see no more than an increase of 200 by 1980; but this could be accomplished now at one go by the proposed building of forty houses in the village centre. At the adjoining village of North Leigh the population is about 2000 and a proposal to develop new housing on a nineteen-acre site would lead, if implemented, to a strain on facilities such as water supply, sewage, roads, schools and recreational space. Such are some of the facts and figures of this particular kind of landscape change, the like of which has not been experienced since early in the nineteenth century. The county's population (omitting Oxford itself) grew by thirty-one per cent in the ten years before 1971, the third fastest growing county in England; and even this rate soared to forty-four per cent in Witney R.D.C. and forty per cent in Henley R.D.C.

The chief difference, admittedly, is that nowadays the county planners can try to guide the course of new developments on a rational basis. The results of natural growth are at their most obvious in the country around Bicester, where population grew by 24,000 in the last decade. Planning now requires the selection of *specified villages* where development has most room to run its course, but the pressures for scarce building land are so strong that the list of such villages is never closed. These growth villages are expected to house between 3000 and 5000 people, while only infilling and renewal is permitted in other villages. On visual grounds, again, one hopes that decisions are guided not simply by the capacity of social and public services (and there are peculiar problems of draining surface water in this low-lying countryside), but also by the design and appearance of villages like Bletchingdon, Chesterton and Kirtlington as vital parts of an inherited landscape. We should also remember that modern building regulations on such matters as room heights can make it more difficult to attune new structures to existing forms, unless the rules are made more flexible.

The dramatic expansion of the small towns underlines the curious situation of Oxfordshire being officially regarded as a non-growth area in the South-East planners' strategy, while it ranks as one of the fastest growing counties in England. Better communications by trunk roads and motorways (as in the sub-Chiltern villages near the M40) are partly responsible (Plate 36). So too is the policy of restricting new housing within the city of Oxford, and when the new Oxfordshire comes into being in 1974 the county and city will be divided in this respect. All its satellite towns have been encouraged to expand, Banbury with a population of 29,000 most of all, buying land for new industrial estates and housing as well as carrying through the redevelopment of its town centre; villages like Bodicote, a mile away on the Oxford road, face being absorbed as Banbury suburbs. In Woodstock a survey found that about 200 of its 886 houses had been built during four years before 1967, bringing with them thirty-five per cent of the town's householders; nearly half the town's newcomers arrived from other parts of Oxfordshire—shades of the medieval borough (p. 207). Aesthetically, too, the bonding of new building to old townscapes without spoiling the prevailing character is a contemporary issue. When old listed buildings are developed for new shops and offices in the High Street at Witney, for example, it is right to expect the use of Cotswold stone, and conformity of roof heights and style of façade with neighbouring sites. Within Oxford itself, the Victorian suburb of North Oxford has its watchdogs, rightly claiming that its individuality is at risk if development goes on piecemeal rather than as a whole for what should certainly be a conservation area.

Finally we have the result of piling detail into the modern landscape without thinking about its co-ordination or total appearance, due basically to the competition for different uses of the land. It reaches the depths in southern Oxfordshire, giving (in Lord Esher's words, ten years ago) a 'Landscape in distress'. Pylons and power lines for the Super-grid, other and lesser 'wirescapes', gravel pits, ironstone quarries, motorways, derelict airfields, filling stations, caravan parks—they all mark the crowding culmination of a hundred years of adventitious action. The first telegraph posts appeared along the road from Oxford to Banbury as long ago as 1861, the handiwork of the United Kingdom Electric Telegraph Company. More recently, Oxfordshire has had one of the highest densities of airfields in England, twenty of them during the last war, half a dozen of which are still operational.[1] And when we register the marching lines of Super-grid pylons (at their most obtrusive, for instance, in the 'Polderland' of the upper Thames country between Bampton and Eynsham), we should realise they are there because of cost-evaluation by the Central Electricity Generating Board—a public body, not a private developer—and as such the pylons are adding to our own 'landscape by consent'.

Now some of the worse excesses are over: ironstone excavators are no longer denuding and lowering the Redlands countryside, and its scars are lapsing into the realm of industrial archaeology, like the quarries and calcining kilns of the Brymbo Iron Works at Hook Norton. But the balance sheet of landscape accounting is prone to swing wildly from credit to debit scores. On the one hand, we find the preservation of the Chiltern beechwoods and chalk hills, with designation as an Area of Outstanding Natural Beauty, being made accessible for our leisure: the Chilterns Standing Conference plans a series of recreational zones and amenity sites. Then, six months later in 1972, we are confronted with the surreptitious proposal of the Water Resources Board to submerge 4000 acres of Otmoor to make a reservoir for London—thus undoing a patient reclamation of this fenland since its enclosure (p. 157), and at the very least opening up the general principles on which the idea of conservation should be based. Little wonder the amenity societies look like being a permanent part of living in England, in an age when the innocent field worker cannot walk down a country road, map in hand, without alarming old ladies with the nameless fear of 'development'.

[1] R. N. E. Blake, 'The Impact of Airfields on the British landscape', *Geographical Journal*, Vol. 135 (1969), pp. 508–28.

An awareness of historical origins in the landscape, of the relationship of its inherited parts, of its textures, forms and colours as visual ends in themselves—all should be constantly in the calculations of planners and the thoughts of the man in the street. Many feel with Colin Buchanan that while the worst excesses of urban sprawl are avoided by a planning policy of nudging and edging the developers, the new architecture in town and countryside is too often drab, brash and lacking in imagination. We accept the means to make new lives for ourselves and our families; we seem to forget we also have the power to make new landscapes on a scale not known in the past.

The predicament is spelled out more or less tacitly by many public bodies, for instance by the Council for the Protection of Rural England (which does not exclude the smaller towns from its purview):

> ... decisions (affecting the landscape) are taken piecemeal, without proper consideration being given to their permanent effects; and much unnecessary ugliness, and erosion of town and country alike, results. But it must be pointed out that the local authorities are as much at the mercy of 'economic growth', with all that it implies in extravagant demands on shrinking and irreplaceable resources, as we are in trying to ensure that as little damage as possible is done to the environment. In CPRE Oxon. we are as ever concerned to try to ensure that our county remains beautiful, fertile and prosperous; her towns and villages fit to live in and her countryside not mutilated or torn apart for minerals.[2]

It would be possible to refine and evaluate an exact meaning of some of the terms used in this statement, for instance 'extravagant demands' or the relationship between

[2] Council for the Protection of Rural England, Oxfordshire Branch, *Annual Report, 1971-72*, p. 3.

'economic growth' and a 'prosperous' county. But the
message is clear enough, and it poses an inescapable
challenge for the new and enlarged Oxfordshire that will
be created in 1974. Oxfordshire then will be augmented by
a large piece of what is now Berkshire, including Faringdon,
the Vale of White Horse, Abingdon and Wantage. It will
bring in much the same blend of historical landscapes that
we have encountered between Oxford and the Chilterns
save, perhaps, for the bare chalkland of the Berkshire
Downs. As a result of this addition, the new Oxfordshire
will be more regular and compact in outline and shape
than the old county, whose bizarre form was once compared
to a cloud drifting in the sky. There will be five new districts
within Oxfordshire, Oxford itself being in the central
place and the four others grouped or quartered around
it.

In its division of responsibilities we see that transport
planning, together with the design and maintenance of
highways, will be in the hands of the county, whereas
planning in general ('development control, local plans'),
as well as housing, will rest with the districts. But it is
good to see that parish councils, under the Local Government Act of 1972, will have the right to be consulted about
planning applications affecting land within their boundaries.
This is good because it increases the chances of individual
men and women being able to express their opinions
on the changing appearance of the piece of landscape
best known to them. If they realise our inheritance from
centuries of landscape-making, so much the better.

SELECT BIBLIOGRAPHY

Baird, W. W. and Tarrant, J. R., 'Vanishing Hedgerows', *Geo-
graphical Magazine* (May, 1972), pp. 545–51.
Best, Robin H. and Rogers, Alan W., *The Urban Countryside. The
Land-Use Structure of Small Towns and Villages in England and*

Wales (1973). This book has several references to Oxfordshire, for instance Plate 2 shows Juniper Hill and Plate 6 is of Burford; in the discussion of New Woodstock (p. 160), 'tigher' is a misprint for 'higher'.

Bonham-Carter, Victor, *The Survival of the English Countryside* (1971).

Christian, Garth, *Tomorrow's Countryside* (1966).

Council for the Protection of Rural England, Oxfordshire Branch, *Annual Report, 1971–72*.

C.P.R.E., *Roads and the Landscape* (1971); *Loss of Cover through removal of Hedgerows and Trees* (1971).

Esher, Lord, *Landscape in Distress* (1965).

Fairbrother, Nan, *New Lives, New Landscapes* (Pelican, 1972).

Gresswell, Peter, *Environment* (1971).

Hedges and Local History, published by the National Council for Social Service (1971).

Morris, M. C., *Britain's Changing Countryside* (1971), 'Change in the Villages', pp. 34–43.

Conclusion

As a survey of the historical landscapes of Oxfordshire, this book might seem on the surface to be of concern only to those readers who know Oxford and its surroundings. But instead of regarding it as an exercise of purely local interest, we can now try to single out a few issues of general currency, of principle or of method, posed by writing a survey aimed at understanding the historical landscape—whether it be of Oxfordshire or of elsewhere.

At the outset it seems that the landscape is becoming progressively, directly and completely a reflection of man's actions. As his technological powers have grown, so does the landscape in which he lives become more responsive and vulnerable to them—"a medal struck in the likeness of its people", to adopt the words of a French geographer at the beginning of this century. But whereas all this is familiar and acceptable, we should not use it to justify a belief in the omnipotence of man to determine how his environment should appear and be organised. He is not always able to do so, even in Oxfordshire as one element of 'an advanced Western society' in the 1970s. In fact, the most dramatic threat to the Oxfordshire landscape at the moment is not the self-mutilation inflicted by, say, the M40 motorway, or the projected covering with new houses of forty-five acres of public land at Eynsham.

Instead the danger lies in *Ceratocystis ulmi*, commonly known as Dutch elm disease, caused by an entirely natural insect-borne fungus that chokes the elm tree to death. Epidemic disease may no longer threaten to decimate whole populations of humans as the Black Death did for the peasants of medieval Oxfordshire, but plants are still entirely at risk. In the last few years Dutch elm disease has flared up to become extremely virulent, killing thousands of mature trees in counties close at hand. To see its ravages revealed by gaunt and yellowed trees we need travel no farther than below the Cotswold scarp, where the Vales of Gloucester and Evesham were cruelly hit. So far the number of casualties in Oxfordshire is only moderate. Even here, of course, the hand of man shows itself indirectly: the virulent strain of the fungus seems to have come into this country with imported American timber, and in any case the elms that die are chiefly hedge-timber planted by the Georgian and Victorian enclosers of common fields. No other tree has made such a visual impact on so much of our landscape, and its loss would be in proportion.

A lesson soon learned is the incompleteness of our knowledge of the historical landscape. This is a common experience, no matter which approach or method we follow: the examination of relic features in the modern landscape, or the reconstruction of whole landscapes for past times, or the analysis of themes that had a tangible expression in the landscape. In each direction the first aim has to be to establish as fully as possible just what the patterns are, before going on to explore their genesis and evolution.

The initial step, then, is to make an *investigation* of the facts. See the almost frightening ease with which brand new knowledge came to light when the field archaeologists began to investigate the line of the M40 (p. 34). They found trace after trace of early settlement in a part of Oxfordshire that had always been in the background. Their special *coup* was the finding of a medieval farmstead that was entirely unknown from the historical records. All these were the fruits of a deliberate search, but, as the discovery of a deserted medieval settlement at Nethercote reminds us (p. 104), chance finds are also there for the investigator of landscape changes.

Environmental change with time then becomes a matter of *interpretation*, given the facts that recent investigation of the landscape and modern methods will provide on an increasing scale. We have had to wait until 1972, for example, for virtually the first reconstruction of what the post-Roman landscape looked like in Oxfordshire. As it was the work of a plant ecologist using the evidence of pollen analysis from the excavation of the villa, it was aimed particularly at the succession of vegetation at Shakenoak (p. 49). Here, on the borders of what was to become Wychwood Forest, the Romano-British villa and its fields of crops for the market gave way to a more sub-sistence type of farming from the sixth century; as the Anglo-Saxon settlers gradually established themselves less and less of the land was being cultivated. Free-ranging sheep and cattle fed over the grasslands; beyond these grazings lay a belt of scrubland, then giving way to an open woodland of oak, ash, birch and beech that was recolonising the countryside, regenerating itself actively with the help of herds of swine feeding in these woods. Generally speaking, by the eighth century the Wychwood landscape near Shakenoak would have looked like a some-what neglected and overrun parkland in our time, but with more stands of trees in it. Through this kind of country went the boundaries of the Bishop of Winchester's estate at Witney, set out in its tenth-century charter (p. 60, Fig. 5), while within it Saxon and Norman kings strenuously hunted the boar, stag and wolf.

Fresh interpretations such as these go one stage farther when allied to associative aspects of the same landscape: they then grow into matters of *integration*. When we look at the Old English people who had come into this land-scape, to graze their flocks and herds over it, we also have to face the question or theory of continuity of settlement. Was there a continuation or was there a sharp break, with the replacement of an old order by something different, something new? Here again the Shakenoak villa has its revelations. It is now possible to envisage by the mid-fifth century a racially mixed but culturally sub-Roman community at Shakenoak. Such a population would clearly have a far better chance of survival and adjustment when the time of uncontrolled English settlement began, than would a purely British (Celtic) population.

But even if these links and continuities were manifest in the landscape through a persistent use of old settlements by a newly mixed rural society, as at Shakenoak itself, then their different kind of agrarian economy was bound to produce a fresh change in the landscape—witness the vegetational sequences just outlined. What we need is the excavation of another villa somewhere in Oxfordshire, whose lands did not necessarily go over to scrub and woodland, but possibly remained in cultivation and ran into old English villages with common fields—for instance, the pair of villa sites at Adderbury in the Redlands.

Another kind of continuity comes to light when we regard the Oxfordshire landscape as a structural document. Instead of insisting on continuous or persistent occupation through time of, say, a set of settlement sites, we can also find a contrasting situation between X and Y carried forward from one historical landscape to another, where the contrast between them rests on different functions or relationships. Some of Oxfordshire's villages show this very well. Let us take (as a model) two villages: in the context of what we discussed in Chapters 2 and 3, we find village X recorded as a prosperous place in the Domesday landscape, with a good-sized population of villeins and serfs, plenty of land and plough-teams, meadow and pasture. This estate is owned by a magnate and has a tenant-in-chief living there. Village Y, on the other hand, is smaller, not recorded in Domesday but was created during the medieval expansion of land settlement, and is found by the time of the Hundred Rolls of 1279 as a new place colonised by a fair number of freeholders and tenants; unlike X it does not have the status of a village with church, manor house, manor farm.

Then in the changed circumstances of the Victorian countryside (Chapter 6) we find village X as a closed settlement, where the two or three big landholders are pulling down old cottages and not building new ones. Their motive is to minimise the threat of heavy rating for poor relief on their lands, by keeping to the bare minimum their population of farm labourers, whose ill fortune might make them paupers and so a charge on their parish. Village Y, by contrast, is an open village with a growing population of day labourers and many paupers, crammed into cottages and tenements, some of them ancient dwellings but many others newly built as speculations by local men on their own small parcels of land. They were able to cash in as the closed villages drove the house-seekers in their direction. So X is an orderly, well-designed village, but Y sprawls along with its small, assorted houses, many of them cottages placed with their gable ends to the road.

They maintain their differences in another special way in the contemporary scene (Chapter 8). The planning authorities in 1974 find it much more difficult to approve of new development, especially new housing, in villages like X because their appearance is so coherent, traditional and therefore worthy of protection from modern designs and materials. But in places like Y the planners still find plenty of odd corners for infilling and rounding off, while it does not amount to an intrusion if new housing estates are tacked on to these 'specified villages'. So does the genesis of particular forms of village in Oxfordshire find its own subsequent and continuing expression at the various hands of a medieval landowner, a Victorian squire, and a modern county council.

Another kind of continuity is set in motion by a sharp and total change of land use. When a piece of ground is taken out of agricultural use and put to other purposes, the probability is that it will go on to some other non-agricultural use rather than return to farming. So on that site we have the replacement, in changed circumstances, of one new function by another. A common enough version of this may be found in Oxfordshire in the sphere of rural industry. For instance, not far from Thame, just before Rycote Lane joins the A418, we nowadays see a group of industrial buildings. One of them is the central storage depot for a firm that sells and distributes washing machines, fridges and TV sets by road through a market area reaching from Oxford to Beaconsfield and Buckingham.

But originally this site was abstracted from farming in about 1880 because on the spot there was clay of the right quality for making bricks and tiles. The claypits and brick-works, like so many in the Oxford region, were developed beside a railway line, in this case the now-disused line from Oxford to Princes Risborough, whence the products could be sent by rail and by intersecting roads. The digging of clay and the making of materials for new Victorian build-ings has been replaced by a service business, distributing and repairing the necessities of life in a consumer society. Another instance of this 'alternative continuity', on a far bigger scale, was the creation of a private airfield near Witney in the 1930s, which was taken as an industrial site during the 1939–45 war, and now comprises the huge workshops of Smiths Industries Ltd. If we look ahead to the future, the long-term consequences of present actions are becoming less predictable.

Neither should we forget that there could be, now and in the future, as many different landscapes as there are people looking at them. We can see the same features differently because of variations in our personal experience, prejudices, preferences. In this sense the Oxfordshire landscape is multiple not only because the Redlands are visually and historically distinct from the Chilterns, but also due to the many perceptions of it that people may have had. For this reason it is useful to measure and express numerically the responses made by groups of people to the same piece of countryside, important because it could help broaden the thinking behind the planners' policies for development in the future. Too sharp a break has been allowed to persist between the processes ('economic factors', 'social forces') that now create landscapes, and the visual forms appearing in those new landscapes. Closing that gap can only serve the purpose of lessening the risk of designed and accidental atrocity.

In touching briefly on the whole range of Oxfordshire's landscapes, we have obeyed the logic of a chronological treatment of formative phases. This does nothing more than to provide a basis, one hopes a basis free from distortion, beyond which the landscape can be analysed in other ways. There is the search, for example, after 'relict agricultural margins' caused by the innovations in agrarian life that have diffused themselves through time. 'Detectable landscape margins' would be another way of expressing this idea. Or again we could look for a range or scale of values in the type of community that made a given landscape: this might start with an ideal type such as the single-village township that had a simple history with standard elements, for example at Hanwell in the Redlands. At the other end of the scale might be the obscure, complex situations that have to be unravelled in the Wychwood country. Whatever the mode of study, it should not ignore the essential pleasure to be had through personal exploration of how a piece of countryside was made. We can all have our own pictures to match Flora Thompson's setting for Juniper Hill in the 1880s:

All around, from every quarter, the stiff, clayey soil of the arable fields crept up; bare, brown and wind-swept for eight months out of the twelve. Spring brought a flush of green wheat and there were violets under the hedges . . . but only for a few weeks in later summer had the landscape real beauty. Then the ripened cornfields rippled up to the doorsteps of the cottages and the hamlet became an island in a sea of dark gold.[1]

[1] *Lark Rise to Candleford* (Everyman edn., 1945), p. 15.

Index